T0178996

Algorithms and Ordering Heuristics for Distributed
Constraint Satisfaction Problems

In memory of a great man,

Mouhamed Moumane

FOCUS SERIES

Series Editor Narendra Jussien

Algorithms and Ordering Heuristics for Distributed Constraint Satisfaction Problems

Mohamed Wahbi

WILEY

First published 2013 in Great Britain and the United States by ISTE Ltd and John Wiley & Sons, Inc.

ISTE Ltd
27-37 St George's Road
London SW19 4EU
UK

www.iste.co.uk

John Wiley & Sons, Inc.
111 River Street
Hoboken, NJ 07030
USA

www.wiley.com

Library of Congress Control Number: 2013937865

British Library Cataloguing-in-Publication Data
A CIP record for this book is available from the British Library
ISSN: 2051-2481 (Print)
ISSN: 2051-249X (Online)
ISBN: 978-1-84821-594-8

Printed and bound in Great Britain by CPI Group (UK) Ltd., Croydon, Surrey CR0 4YY

Contents

Preface

Constraint programming is an area in computer science that has gained increasing interest in recent years. Constraint programming is based on its powerful framework called *constraint satisfaction problem* (CSP). CSP is a general framework that can formalize many real-world combinatorial problems such as resource allocation, car sequencing, natural language understanding and machine vision. A CSP consists of looking for solutions to a constraint network, i.e. a set of assignments of values to variables that satisfy the constraints of the problem. These constraints represent restrictions on value combinations allowed for constrained variables.

Various applications that are of a distributed nature exist. In this kind of application, the knowledge about the problem, i.e. variables and constraints, is distributed among physically distributed agents. This distribution is mainly due to privacy and/or security requirements: constraints or possible values may be strategic information that should not be revealed to other agents that can be seen as competitors. Several applications in multi-agent coordination are of such kind. Examples of applications are sensor networks [JUN 01, BÉJ 05], military unmanned aerial vehicle teams [JUN 01], distributed scheduling problems [WAL 02, MAH 04], distributed resource allocation problems [PET 04], log-based reconciliation [CHO 06], distributed vehicle routing problems [LÉA 11], etc. Therefore, the distributed framework *distributed constraint satisfaction problem* (DisCSP) is used to model and solve this kind of problem.

A DisCSP is composed of a group of autonomous agents, where each agent has control of some elements of information about the whole problem, i.e. variables and constraints. Each agent owns its local constraint network. Variables in different agents are connected by constraints. Agents must assign, in a distributed manner, values to their variables so that all constraints are satisfied. Hence, agents assign values to their variables, attempting to generate locally consistent assignments that are also consistent with constraints between agents [YOK 98, YOK 00a]. To achieve this goal, agents check the values assigned to their variables for local consistency and exchange messages to check the consistency of their proposed assignments against constraints that contain variables that belong to other agents.

Many distributed algorithms for solving DisCSPs have been designed in the last two decades. They can be divided into two main groups: synchronous and asynchronous algorithms. The first category includes algorithms in which agents assign values to their variables in a synchronous and sequential way. The second category includes algorithms in which the process of proposing values to the variables and exchanging these proposals is performed asynchronously between the agents. In the former category, agents do not have to wait for decisions of others, whereas, in general, only one agent has the privilege of making a decision in the synchronous algorithms.

This book tries to extend the state of the art by proposing several algorithms and heuristics for solving the DisCSPs. The book starts with a brief introduction to the state of the art in the area of centralized constraint programming. The (CSP) formalism is defined and some academic and real examples of problems that can be modeled and solved by CSP are presented. Then, typical methods for solving centralized CSPs are briefly reported. Next, preliminary definitions on the DisCSP formalism are given. Afterward, the main algorithms that have been developed in the literature to solve DisCSPs are described.

The second part of this book provides three algorithms for solving DisCSPs. These algorithms are classified under the category of synchronous algorithms. The first algorithm is the nogood-based asynchronous forward checking (AFC-ng). AFC-ng is a nogood-based version of the asynchronous forward checking (AFC) [MEI 07] algorithm. Besides its use of nogoods as justification of value removals, AFC-ng allows simultaneous backtracks to go from different agents to different destinations. AFC-ng only needs polynomial space. Proofs of the correctness of the AFC-ng are also given. A comparison of its performance with other well-known distributed algorithms for solving DisCSP is presented. The results are reported for random DisCSPs and instances from real benchmarks: sensor networks and distributed meeting scheduling.

The second algorithm, called asynchronous forward-checking tree (AFC-tree), extends the AFC-ng algorithm using a pseudo-tree arrangement of the constraint graph. To achieve this goal, agents are ordered *a priori* in a pseudo-tree such that agents in different branches of the tree do not share any constraint. AFC-tree does not address the process of ordering the agents in a pseudo-tree arrangement. The construction of the pseudo-tree is done in a preprocessing step. Using this priority ordering, AFC-tree performs multiple AFC-ng processes on the paths from the root to the leaves of the pseudo-tree. The good properties of the AFC-tree are demonstrated. AFC-tree is compared to AFC-ng on random DisCSPs and instances from real benchmarks: sensor networks and distributed meeting scheduling.

In the third synchronous algorithm, maintaining the arc consistency in a synchronous search algorithm is proposed. Instead of using forward checking as a filtering property like the AFC-ng algorithm does, it is suggested maintaining arc consistency asynchronously (MACA). Thus, two new algorithms based on the same mechanism as AFC-ng that enforce arc consistency asynchronously are presented. The first, called MACA-del, enforces arc consistency due to an additional type of message: deletion message. The second, called MACA-not, achieves arc consistency without any new type of message. A theoretical analysis and an experimental evaluation of the proposed approaches are provided.

The third part of the book presents two contributions in the asynchronous algorithms category. Under this category, Zivan *et al.* presented the asynchronous backtracking algorithm with dynamic ordering using retroactive heuristics (ABT_DO-Retro) [ZIV 09]. ABT_DO-Retro allows changing the order of agents during distributed asynchronous complete search. Unfortunately, the description of the time-stamping protocol used to compare orders in ABT_DO-Retro may lead to an implementation in which ABT_DO-Retro may not terminate. The first contribution under the asynchronous category provides a corrigendum of the protocol designed for establishing the priority between orders in ABT_DO-Retro. An example that shows, if ABT_DO-Retro uses that protocol, how it can fall into an infinite loop is presented. The correct method for comparing time stamps and the proof of its correctness are given.

Afterwards, the agile asynchronous backtracking algorithm (Agile-ABT), the second contribution under the asynchronous category, is presented. Agile-ABT is a distributed asynchronous search procedure that is able to change the ordering of agents more than previous asynchronous approaches. In Agile-ABT, the order of agents appearing before the agent receiving a backtrack message can be changed with great freedom, while ensuring polynomial space complexity. This is done via the original notion of termination value, a vector of stamps labeling the new orders exchanged by agents during the search. First, the concepts needed to select new orders that decrease the termination value are described. Next, the details of Agile-ABT algorithm are given. A description of how agents can reorder themselves as much as they want, as long as the termination value decreases as the search progresses, is shown.

The book ends by describing the new version of the DisChoco open-source platform for solving distributed constraint reasoning problems. The new version, DisChoco 2.0, provides an implementation of all algorithms mentioned so far and, obviously, many others. DisChoco 2.0 is a complete redesign of the DisChoco platform. DisChoco 2.0 is a Java library, which aims at implementing distributed constraint reasoning algorithms. DisChoco 2.0 then offers a complete tool to the research community for evaluating algorithms performance or being used for real applications.

This book is the result of 3 years of intense research with the supervisors of my PhD thesis: Christian Bessiere and El-Houssine Bouyakhf. It is with immense gratitude that I acknowledge their support, advice and guidance during my PhD studies at the University of Montpellier, France, and Mohammed V University–Agdal, Morocco. Much of the work presented in this book has been done in collaboration with such highly motivated, smart, enthusiastic and passionate co-authors. I want to thank them for their teamwork and devotion. My special gratitude goes to Redouane Ezzahir and Younes Mechqrane.

Introduction

Constraint satisfaction problems (CSPs) can formalize many real-world combinatorial problems such as resource allocation, car sequencing and machine vision. A CSP consists of looking for solutions to a constraint network, i.e. finding a set of assignments of values to variables that satisfy the constraints of the problem. These constraints specify admissible value combinations. Numerous powerful algorithms have been designed for solving CSPs. Typical systematic search algorithms try to construct a solution to a CSP by incrementally instantiating the variables of the problem. However, proving the existence of solutions or finding a solution in a CSP are NP[1]-complete tasks. Thus, many heuristics have been developed to improve the efficiency of search algorithms.

Sensor networks [JUN 01, BÉJ 05], military unmanned aerial vehicle teams [JUN 01], distributed scheduling problems [WAL 02, MAH 04], distributed resource allocation problems [PET 04], log-based reconciliation [CHO 06], distributed vehicle routing problems [LÉA 11], etc., are real applications of a distributed nature, i.e., the knowledge about the problem is distributed among several entities/agents that are physically distributed. These applications can be naturally modeled and solved by a CSP process once the knowledge about the whole problem is delivered to a centralized solver. However, in such applications, gathering the whole knowledge into a centralized solver is undesirable. In general, this restriction is mainly due to privacy and/or security requirements: constraints or possible values may be strategic information that should not be revealed to other agents that can be seen as competitors. The cost or the inability of translating all information into a single format may be another reason. In addition, a distributed system provides fault tolerance, which means that if some agents disconnect, a solution might be available for the connected part. Thereby, a distributed model allowing a decentralized solving process is more adequate. The *distributed constraint satisfaction problem* (DisCSP) has such properties.

---

1 NP = nondeterministic polynomial time.

A DisCSP is composed of a group of autonomous agents, where each agent has control of some elements of information about the whole problem, i.e. variables and constraints. Each agent owns its local constraint network. Variables in different agents are connected by constraints. To solve a DisCSP, agents must assign values to their variables so that all constraints are satisfied. Hence, agents assign values to their variables, attempting to generate a locally consistent assignment that is also consistent with constraints between agents [YOK 98, YOK 00a]. To achieve this goal, agents check the values assigned to their variables for local consistency and exchange messages among them to check the consistency of their proposed assignments against constraints that contain variables that belong to others agents.

In solving DisCSPs, agents exchange messages about the variable assignments and conflicts of constraints. Several distributed algorithms for solving DisCSPs have been designed in the last two decades. They can be divided into two main groups: synchronous and asynchronous algorithms. The first category are algorithms in which the agents assign values to their variables in a synchronous, sequential way. The second category are algorithms in which the process of proposing values to the variables and exchanging these proposals is performed asynchronously between the agents. In the former category, agents do not have to wait for decisions of others whereas, in general, only one agent has the privilege of making a decision in the synchronous algorithms.

The first complete asynchronous search algorithm for solving DisCSPs is asynchronous backtracking (ABT) [YOK 92, YOK 00a, BES 05]. ABT is an asynchronous algorithm executed autonomously by each agent in the distributed problem. Synchronous backtrack (SBT) is the simplest DisCSP search algorithm [YOK 00a]. SBT performs assignments sequentially and synchronously. SBT agents assign their variables one by one, recording their assignments on a data structure called the current partial assignment (CPA). In SBT, only the agent holding a CPA performs an assignment or backtrack [ZIV 03]. Meisels and Zivan extended SBT to asynchronous forward checking (AFC), an algorithm in which the FC algorithm [HAR 80] is performed asynchronously [MEI 07]. In AFC, whenever an agent succeeds to extend the CPA, it sends the CPA to its successor and sends copies of this CPA to the other unassigned agents in order to perform FC asynchronously.

A major motivation for research on DisCSP is that it is an elegant model for many everyday combinatorial problems that are distributed by nature. Incidentally, DisCSP is a general framework for solving various problems arising in distributed artificial intelligence. Improving the efficiency of existing algorithms for solving DisCSP is an important key for research in the distributed artificial intelligence field. In this book, we extend the state of the art in solving the DisCSPs by proposing several algorithms. We believe that these algorithms are significant as they improve the current state of the art in terms of run-time and number of exchanged messages experimentally.

Nogood-based asynchronous forward checking (AFC-ng):   AFC-ng is a synchronous algorithm based on asynchronous forward checking (AFC) for solving DisCSPs. Instead of using the shortest inconsistent partial assignments, AFC-ng uses nogoods as justifications of value removals. Unlike AFC, AFC-ng allows concurrent backtracks to be performed at the same time, coming from different agents having an empty domain to different destinations. Because of the time stamps integrated into the CPAs, the strongest CPA coming from the highest level in the agent ordering will eventually dominate all others. Interestingly, the search process with the strongest CPA will benefit from the computational effort done by the (killed) lower-level processes. This is done by taking advantage of the computational effort of nogoods recorded when processing these lower-level processes.

Asynchronous forward-checking tree (AFC-tree):   the main feature of the AFC-tree algorithm is using different agents to search non-intersecting parts of the search space concurrently. In AFC-tree, agents are prioritized according to a pseudo-tree arrangement of the constraint graph. The pseudo-tree ordering is built in a preprocessing step. Using this priority ordering, AFC-tree performs multiple AFC-ng processes on the paths from the root to the leaves of the pseudo-tree. The agents that are brothers are committed to concurrently finding the partial solutions of their variables. Therefore, AFC-tree exploits the potential speedup of a parallel exploration in the processing of distributed problems.

Maintaining arc consistency asynchronously (MACA): instead of maintaining forward checking asynchronously on agents not yet instantiated, as is done in AFC-ng, we propose to maintain arc consistency asynchronously on these future agents. We propose two new synchronous search algorithms that *maintain arc consistency asynchronously* (MACA). The first algorithm we propose, MACA-del, enforces arc consistency due to additional type of messages, deletion messages (*del*). Hence, whenever values are removed during a constraint propagation step, MACA-del agents notify other agents that may be affected by these removals, sending them a *del* message. The second algorithm, MACA-not, achieves arc consistency without any new type of message. We have achieved this by storing all deletions performed by an agent on domains of its neighboring agents, and sending this information to these neighbors within the CPA message.

Corrigendum to "min-domain retroactive ordering for asynchronous backtracking": a corrigendum of the protocol designed for establishing the priority between orders in the asynchronous backtracking algorithm with dynamic ordering using retroactive heuristics (ABT_DO-Retro) is proposed. We present an example that shows how ABT_DO-Retro can enter an infinite loop following the natural understanding of the description given by the authors of ABT_DO-Retro. We describe the correct way for comparing time stamps of orders. We give the proof that our method for comparing orders is correct.

Agile asynchronous backtracking (Agile-ABT): Agile-ABT is an asynchronous dynamic ordering algorithm that does not follow the standard restrictions in ABT algorithms. The order of agents appearing before the agent receiving a backtrack message can be changed with a great freedom while ensuring polynomial space complexity. Furthermore, the agent receiving the backtrack message, called the backtracking target, is not necessarily the agent with the lowest priority among the conflicting agents in the current order. The principle of Agile-ABT is built on termination values exchanged by agents during search. A termination value is a tuple of positive integers attached to an order. Each positive integer in the tuple represents the expected current domain size of the agent in that position in the order. Orders are changed by agents without any global control so that the termination value decreases lexicographically as the search progresses. Because a domain size can never be negative, termination values cannot decrease indefinitely. An agent informs the others of a new order by sending them its new order and its new termination value. When an agent compares two contradictory orders, it keeps the order associated with the smallest termination value.

DisChoco 2.0: DisChoco 2.0[2] is an open-source platform for solving distributed constraint reasoning problems. The new version 2.0 is a complete redesign of the DisChoco platform. DisChoco 2.0 is not a distributed version of the centralized solver Choco[3], but it implements a model to solve distributed constraint networks with local complex problems (i.e. several variables per agent) by using Choco as the local solver to each agent. The novel version we propose has several interesting features: it is reliable and modular, it is easy to personalize and extend, its kernel is independent from the communication system and it allows for a deployment in a real distributed system as well as a simulation on a single Java virtual machine. DisChoco 2.0 is an open-source Java library, which aims at implementing distributed constraint reasoning algorithms from an abstract model of agent (already implemented in DisChoco). A single implementation of a distributed constraint reasoning algorithm can run as simulation on a single machine, or on a network of machines that are connected via the Internet or via a wireless *ad hoc* network or even on mobile phones compatible with J2ME.

---

2 http://www2.lirmm.fr/coconut/dischoco/.
3 http://choco.emn.fr/.

PART 1

Background on Centralized and Distributed Constraint Reasoning

1

Constraint Satisfaction Problems

This chapter provides the state of the art in the area of centralized constraint programming. In section 1.1, we define the constraint satisfaction problem (CSP) formalism and present some academic and real examples of problems modeled and solved by centralized CSP. Typical methods for solving centralized CSP are described in section 1.2.

1.1. Centralized constraint satisfaction problems

Many real-world combinatorial problems in artificial intelligence arising from areas related to resource allocation, scheduling, logistics and planning are solved using constraint programming. Constraint programming is based on its powerful framework called CSP. A CSP is a general framework that involves a set of variables and constraints. Each variable can assign a value from a domain of finite possible values. Constraints specify the allowed values for a set of variables. Hence, a large variety of applications can be naturally formulated as CSPs. Examples of applications that have been successfully solved by constraint programming are picture processing [MON 74], planning [STE 81], job-shop scheduling [FOX 82], computational vision [MAC 83], machine design and manufacturing [FRA 87, NAD 90], circuit analysis [DEK 80], diagnosis [GEF 87], belief maintenance [DEC 88], automobile transmission design [NAD 91], etc.

Solving a CSP consists of looking for solutions to a constraint network, that is a set of assignments of values to variables that satisfy the constraints of the problem. A constraint represents restrictions on value combinations allowed for constrained variables. Many powerful algorithms have been designed for solving CSPs. Typical systematic search algorithms try to develop a solution to a CSP by incrementally instantiating the variables of the problem.

There are two main classes of algorithms searching solutions for CSPs, namely those of a look-back scheme and those of look-ahead scheme. The first category of search algorithms (look-back scheme) corresponds to search procedures checking the validity of the assignment of the current variable against the already assigned (past) variables. When the assignment of the current variable is inconsistent with assignments of past variables, a new value is tried. When no value remains, a past variable must be reassigned (i.e. change its value). Chronological backtracking (BT) [GOL 65], backjumping (BJ) [GAS 78], graph-based backjumping (GBJ) [DEC 90], conflict-directed backjumping (CBJ) [PRO 93] and dynamic backtracking (DBT) [GIN 93] are algorithms performing a look-back scheme.

The second category of search algorithms (look-ahead scheme) corresponds to search procedures that check forward the assignment of the current variable. In a look-ahead scheme, the not yet assigned (future) variables are made consistent, to some degree, with the assignment of the current variable. Forward checking (FC) [HAR 80] and maintaining arc consistency (MAC) [SAB 94] are algorithms that perform a look-ahead scheme.

Proving the existence of solutions or finding them in CSP are nondeterministic polynomial time (NP)-complete tasks. Thereby, numerous *heuristics* were developed to improve the efficiency of solution methods. Although being numerous, these heuristics can be categorized into two kinds: variable ordering and value ordering heuristics. Variable ordering heuristics address the order in which the algorithm assigns the variables, whereas the value ordering heuristics establish an order on which values will be assigned to a selected variable. Many studies have shown that the ordering of selecting variables and values dramatically affects the performance of search algorithms.

We present in the following an overview of typical methods for solving centralized CSPs after formally defining a CSP and give some examples of problems that can be encoded in CSPs.

1.1.1. *Preliminaries*

A CSP (or a constraint network) [MON 74] involves a finite set of variables, a finite set of domains determining the set of possible values for a given variable and a finite set of constraints. Each constraint restricts the combination of values that a set of variables it involves can assign. A solution is an assignment of values to all variables satisfying all constraints.

DEFINITION 1.1.– *A constraint satisfaction problem or a* constraint network *was formally defined by a triple* $(\mathcal{X}, \mathcal{D}, \mathcal{C})$, *where:*

– $\mathcal{X}$ *is a set of* n *variables* $\{x_1, \ldots, x_n\}$;

– $\mathcal{D} = \{D(x_1), \ldots, D(x_n)\}$ *is a set of* n *current* domains, *where* $D(x_i)$ *is a finite set of possible values to which variable* x_i *may be assigned;*

$-\mathcal{C} = \{c_1, \ldots, c_e\}$ *is a set of e* constraints *that specify the combinations of values (or* tuples*) allowed for the variables they involve. The variables involved in a constraint* $c_k \in \mathcal{C}$ *form its* scope *(*scope$(c_k) \subseteq \mathcal{X}$*).*

During a search procedure, values may be pruned from the domain of a variable. At any node, the set of possible values for variable x_i is its *current domain*, $D(x_i)$. We introduce the particular notation of *initial domains* (or definition domains) $\mathcal{D}^0 = \{D^0(x_1), \ldots, D^0(x_n)\}$, which represents the set of domains before pruning any value (i.e. $\mathcal{D} \subseteq \mathcal{D}^0$).

The number of variables on the scope of a constraint $c_k \in \mathcal{C}$ is called a the arity of the constraint c_k. Therefore, a constraint involving one variable (respectively, two or n variables) is called a unary (respectively, *binary* or n-ary) constraint. In this book, we are concerned with binary constraint networks where we assume that all constraints are binary constraints (they involve two variables). A constraint in $\mathcal{C}$ between two variables x_i and x_j is then denoted by c_{ij}. c_{ij} is a subset of the Cartesian product of their domains (i.e. $c_{ij} \subseteq D^0(x_i) \times D^0(x_j)$). A direct result of this assumption is that the connectivity between the variables can be represented with a constraint graph G [DEC 92].

DEFINITION 1.2.– *A binary constraint network can be represented by a* constraint graph $G = \{X_G, E_G\}$, *where vertices represent the variables of the problem (*$X_G = \mathcal{X}$*) and edges (*E_G*) represent the constraints (i.e.* $\{x_i, x_j\} \in E_G$ *iff* $c_{ij} \in \mathcal{C}$*).*

DEFINITION 1.3.– *Two variables are* adjacent *iff they share a constraint. Formally,* x_i *and* x_j *are adjacent iff* $c_{ij} \in \mathcal{C}$. *If* x_i *and* x_j *are adjacent, we also say that* x_i *and* x_j *are* neighbors. *The set of neighbors of a variable* x_i *is denoted by* $\Gamma(x_i)$.

DEFINITION 1.4.– *Given a constraint graph* G, *an ordering* $\mathcal{O}$ *is a mapping from the variables (vertices of* G*) to the set* $\{1, \ldots, n\}$. $\mathcal{O}(i)$ *is the ith variable in* $\mathcal{O}$.

Solving a CSP is equivalent to finding a combination of assignments of values to all variables in a way that all the constraints of the problem are satisfied.

In the following, we present some typical examples of problems that can be intuitively modeled as CSPs. These examples range from academic problems to real-world applications.

1.1.2. *Examples of CSPs*

Various problems in artificial intelligence can be naturally modeled as a CSP. We present here some examples of problems that can be modeled and solved by the CSP framework. First, we describe the classical n-queens problem. Next, we present the graph coloring problem. Finally, we introduce the problem of meeting scheduling.

1.1.2.1. *The n-queens problem*

The n-queens problem is a classical combinatorial problem that can be formalized and solved by a CSP. In the n-queens problem, the goal is to put n queens on an $n \times n$ chessboard so that none of them are able to attack (capture) any other. Two queens attack each other if they are located on the same row, column or diagonal on the chessboard. This problem is called a CSP because the goal is to find a configuration that satisfies the given conditions (constraints).

In the case of 4-queens ($n = 4$, Figure 1.1), the problem can be encoded as a CSP as follows[1]:

– $\mathcal{X} = \{q_1, q_2, q_3, q_4\}$, each variable q_i corresponds to the queen placed in the ith column;

– $\mathcal{D} = \{D(q_1), D(q_2), D(q_3), D(q_4)\}$, where $D(q_i)=\{1, 2, 3, 4\}$ $\forall i \in 1.4$. The value $v \in D(q_i)$ corresponds to the row where the queen representing the ith column can be placed;

– $\mathcal{C} = \{c_{ij} : (q_i \neq q_j) \wedge (\mid q_i - q_j \mid \neq \mid i - j \mid) \; \forall \; i, j \in \{1, 2, 3, 4\}$ and $i \neq j\}$ is the set of constraints. A constraint between each pair of queens exists that forbids the involved queens to be placed in the same row or diagonal line.

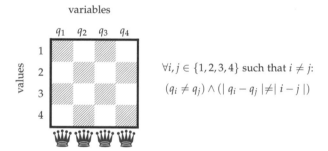

Figure 1.1. *The 4-queens problem*

The n-queen problem permits, in the case of $n = 4$ (4-queens), two configurations as solutions. We present the two possible solution in Figure 1.2. The first solution, Figure 1.2(a), is ($q_1 = 2, q_2 = 4, q_3 = 1, q_4 = 3$), where we put q_1 in the second row, q_2 in the fourth row q_3 in the first row and q_4 is placed in the third row. The second solution, Figure 1.2(b), is ($q_1 = 3, q_2 = 1, q_3 = 4, q_4 = 2$).

1.1.2.2. *The graph coloring problem*

Another typical problem is the graph coloring problem. Graph coloring is one of the most combinatorial problem studied in artificial intelligence because many real

---

[1] This is not the only possible encoding of the n-queens problem as a CSP.

applications such as time-tabling and frequency allocation can be easily formulated as a graph coloring problem. The goal in this problem is to color all nodes of a graph so that any two adjacent vertices should get different colors where each node has a finite number of possible colors. The graph coloring problem is simply formalized as a CSP. Hence, the nodes of the graph are the variables to color and the possible colors of each node/variable form its domain. A constraint between each pair of adjacent variables/nodes exists that prohibits these variables from having the same color.

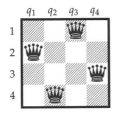   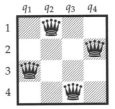

a) $(q_1 = 2, q_2 = 4, q_3 = 1, q_4 = 3)$ b) $(q_1 = 3, q_2 = 1, q_3 = 4, q_4 = 2)$

Figure 1.2. *The solutions for the 4-queens problem*

A practical application of the graph coloring problem is the problem of coloring a map (Figure 1.3). The objective in this case is to assign a color to each region so that no neighboring regions have the same color. An instance of the map coloring problem is illustrated in Figure 1.3(a), where we present the map of Morocco with its 16 provinces. We present this map-coloring instance as a constraint graph in Figure 1.3(b). This problem can be modeled as a CSP by representing each node of the graph as a variable. The domain of each variable is defined by the possible colors. A constraint exists between each pair neighboring regions. Therefore we get the following CSP:

- $\mathcal{X} = \{x_1, x_2, \ldots, x_{16}\}$;

- $\mathcal{D} = \{D(x_1), D(x_2), \ldots, D(x_{16})\}$, where $D(x_i) = \{red, blue, green\}$;

- $\mathcal{C} = \{c_{ij} : x_i \neq x_j \mid x_i \text{ and } x_j \text{ are neighbors}\}$.

1.1.2.3. *The meeting scheduling problem*

The *meeting scheduling problem* (MSP) [SEN 95, GAR 96, MEI 04] is a decision-making process that consists of scheduling several meetings among various people with respect to their personal calendars. The MSP has been defined in many versions with different parameters (e.g. duration of meetings [WAL 02] and preferences of agents [SEN 95]). In MSP, we have a set of attendees, each with his/her own calendar (divided into time-slots), and a set of n meetings to coordinate. In general, people/participants may have several slots already filled in their calendars.

Each meeting m_i takes place in a specified location denoted by $location(m_i)$. The proposed solution must enable the participating people to travel among locations where their meetings will be held. Thus, an *arrival-time* constraint is required between two meetings m_i and m_j when at least one attendee participates in both the meetings. The arrival-time constraint between two meetings m_i and m_j is defined in equation [1.1]:

$$| \, time(m_i) - time(m_j) \, | - duration > TravelingTime(location(m_i),$$
$$location(m_j)). \qquad\qquad [1.1]$$

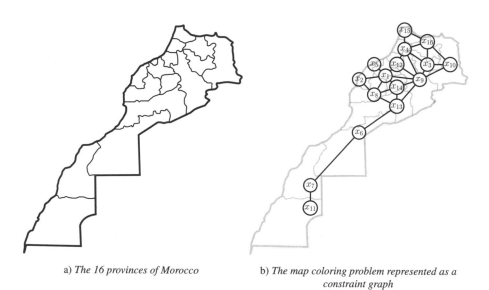

a) *The 16 provinces of Morocco*   b) *The map coloring problem represented as a constraint graph*

Figure 1.3. *An example of the graph coloring problem*

The MSP [MEI 04] can be encoded in a centralized CSP as follows:

− $\mathcal{X} = \{m_1, \ldots, m_n\}$ is the set of variables where each variable represents a meeting;

− $\mathcal{D} = \{D(m_1), \ldots, D(m_n)\}$ is a set of domains, where $D(m_i)$ is the domain of variable/meeting m_i. $D(m_i)$ is the intersection of time-slots from the personal calendar of all agents attending m_i, that is $D(m_i) = \bigcap\limits_{A_j \in \text{ attendees of } m_i} calendar(A_j)$;

− $\mathcal{C}$ is a set of arrival-time constraints. An arrival-time constraint for every pair of meetings (m_i, m_j) exists if there is an agent that participates in both meetings.

A simple instance of a MSP is illustrated in Table 1.1. There are four attendees: *Adam*, *Alice*, *Fred* and *Med*, each having a personal calendar. There are four meetings to be scheduled. The first meeting (m_1) will be attended by *Alice* and *Med*. *Alice* and *Fred* will participate in the second meeting (m_2). The agents attending the third meeting (m_3) are *Fred* and *Med*, while the last meeting (m_4) will be attended by *Adam*, *Fred* and *Med*.

Meeting	Attendees	Location
m_1	Alice, Med	Paris
m_2	Alice, Fred	Rabat
m_3	Fred, Med	Montpellier
m_4	Adam, Fred, Med	Agadir

Table 1.1. *A simple instance of the meeting scheduling problem*

The instance presented in Table 1.1 is encoded as a centralized CSP in Figure 1.4. The nodes are the meetings/variables (m_1, m_2, m_3, m_4). The edges represent binary arrival-time constraints. Each edge is labeled by the person, attending both meetings. Thus,

– $\mathcal{X} = \{m_1, m_2, m_3, m_4\}$;

– $\mathcal{D} = \{D(m_1), D(m_2), D(m_3), D(m_4)\}$;

  – $D(m_1) = \{s \mid s$ is a slot in $calendar(Alice) \cap calendar(Med)\}$,

  – $D(m_2) = \{s \mid s$ is a slot in $calendar(Alice) \cap calendar(Fred)\}$,

  – $D(m_3) = \{s \mid s$ is a slot in $calendar(Fred) \cap calendar(Med)\}$,

  – $D(m_4) = \{s \mid s$ is a slot in $calendar(Adam) \cap calendar(Fred) \cap calendar(Med)\}$;

– $\mathcal{C} - \{c_{12}, c_{13}, c_{14}, c_{23}, c_{24}, c_{34}\}$, where c_{ij} is an arrival-time constraint between m_i and m_j.

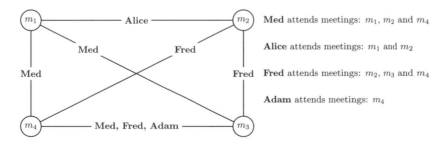

Figure 1.4. *The constraint graph of the meeting scheduling problem*

The previous examples show the power of the CSP framework to easily model various combinatorial problems arising from different issues. In the following section, we describe the well-known generic methods for solving a CSP.

1.2. Algorithms and techniques for solving centralized CSPs

In this section, we describe the basic methods for solving CSPs. These methods can be considered under two broad approaches: constraint propagation and search. Here, we also describe a combination of those two approaches. In general, the search algorithms explore all possible combinations of values for the variables in order to find a solution of the problem, that is a combination of values for the variables that satisfies the constraints. However, the constraint propagation techniques are used to reduce the space of combinations that will be explored by the search process. Afterward, we present the main heuristics used to boost the search in the centralized CSPs. We particularly summarize the main variable ordering heuristics, while we briefly describe the main value ordering heuristics used in the CSPs.

1.2.1. Algorithms for solving centralized CSPs

Usually, algorithms for solving centralized CSPs search systematically through the possible assignments of values to variables in order to find a combination of these assignments that satisfies the constraints of the problem.

DEFINITION 1.5.– *An* assignment *of value v_i to a variable x_i is a pair (x_i, v_i) where v_i is a value from the domain of x_i, that is $v_i \in D(x_i)$. We often denote this assignment by $x_i = v_i$.*

Henceforth, when a variable is assigned a value from its domain, we say that the variable is assigned or instantiated.

DEFINITION 1.6.– *An* instantiation $\mathcal{I}$ *of a subset of variables $\{x_i, \ldots, x_k\} \subseteq \mathcal{X}$ is an ordered set of assignments $\mathcal{I} = \{[(x_i = v_i), \ldots, (x_k = v_k)] \mid v_j \in D(x_j)\}$. The variables assigned on instantiation $\mathcal{I} = [(x_i = v_i), \ldots, (x_k = v_k)]$ are denoted by* vars$(\mathcal{I}) = \{x_i, \ldots, x_k\}$.

DEFINITION 1.7.– *A* full instantiation *is an instantiation $\mathcal{I}$ that instantiates all the variables of the problem (i.e.* vars$(\mathcal{I}) = \mathcal{X}$*), and conversely we say that an instantiation is* a partial instantiation *if it instantiates in only a part.*

DEFINITION 1.8.– *An instantiation $\mathcal{I}$* satisfies *a constraint $c_{ij} \in \mathcal{C}$ if and only if the variables involved in c_{ij} (i.e. x_i and x_j) are assigned in $\mathcal{I}$ (i.e. $(x_i = v_i), (x_j = v_j) \in \mathcal{I}$) and the pair (v_i, v_j) is allowed by c_{ij}. Formally, $\mathcal{I}$ satisfies c_{ij} iff $[(x_i = v_i) \in \mathcal{I}] \wedge [(x_j = v_j) \in \mathcal{I}] \wedge [(v_i, v_j) \in c_{ij}]$.*

DEFINITION 1.9.– *An instantiation* $\mathcal{I}$ *is* locally consistent *iff it satisfies all of the constraints whose scopes have no uninstantiated variables in* $\mathcal{I}$. $\mathcal{I}$ *is also called a partial solution. Formally,* $\mathcal{I}$ *is locally consistent iff* $\forall c_{ij} \in \mathcal{C} \mid$ scope$(c_{ij}) \subseteq$ vars$(\mathcal{I})$ *and* $\mathcal{I}$ *satisfies* c_{ij}.

DEFINITION 1.10.– *A* solution *to a constraint network is a full instantiation* $\mathcal{I}$*, which is locally consistent.*

The intuitive way to search a solution for a CSP is to *generate and test* all possible full instantiations and check their validity (i.e. if they satisfy all constraints of the problem). The full instantiations satisfying all constraints are then solutions. This is the principle of the *generate & test* algorithm. In other words, a full instantiation is generated and then tested if it is locally consistent. In the generate & test algorithm, the consistency of an instantiation is not checked until it is full. This method drastically increases the number of combinations that will be generated. The number of full instantiations considered by this algorithm is the size of the Cartesian product of all the variable domains. Intuitively, one can check the local consistency of instantiation as soon as its respective variables are instantiated. In fact, this is the systematic search strategy of the chronological BT algorithm. We present the chronological BT in the following.

1.2.1.1. *Chronological backtracking*

The chronological BT [DAV 62, GOL 65, BIT 75] is the basic systematic search algorithm for solving CSPs. The BT is a recursive search procedure that incrementally attempts to extend a current partial solution (a locally consistent instantiation) by assigning values to variables not yet assigned, toward a full instantiation. However, when all values of a variable are inconsistent with previously assigned variables (a *dead-end* occurs), BT backtracks to the variable immediately instantiated in order to try another alternative value for it.

DEFINITION 1.11.– *When no value is possible for a variable, a* dead-end *state occurs. We usually say that the domain of the variable is* wiped out (DWO).

The pseudo-code of the BT algorithm is illustrated in algorithm 1.1. The BT assigns a value to each variable in turn. When assigning a value v_i to a variable x_i, the consistency of the new assignment with values assigned thus far is checked (line 6, algorithm 1.1). If the new assignment is consistent with previous assignments, BT attempts to extend these assignments by selecting another unassigned variable (line 7). Otherwise (the new assignment violates any of the constraints), another alternative value is tested for x_i if it is possible. If all values of a variable are inconsistent with previously assigned variables (a dead-end occurs), BT to the variable immediately preceding the dead-end variable takes place in order to check alternative values for this variable. In this way, either a solution is found when the last variable has been successfully assigned or BT can conclude that no solution exists if all values of the first variable are removed.

Algorithm 1.1. *The chronological backtracking algorithm.*

procedure Backtracking($\mathcal{I}$)
01.   **if** (isFull($\mathcal{I}$)) **then report** $\mathcal{I}$ as solution;   /* all variables are assigned in $\mathcal{I}$ */
02.   **else**
03.   select x_i in $\mathcal{X} \setminus$ vars($\mathcal{I}$) ;   /* let x_i be an unassigned variable */
04.   **foreach** ($v_i \in D(x_i)$) **do**
05. $x_i \leftarrow v_i$;
06.   **if** (isLocallyConsistent($\mathcal{I} \cup \{(x_i = v_i)\}$)) **then**
07.   Backtracking($\mathcal{I} \cup \{(x_i = v_i)\}$);

Figure 1.5 illustrates an example of running the BT algorithm on the 4-queens problem (Figure 1.1). First, variable q_1 is assigned to 1 (the first queen representing the queen to place in the first column, is placed in the first row of the 4×4 chessboard) and added to the partial solution $\mathcal{I}$. Next, BT attempts to extend $\mathcal{I}$ by assigning the next variable q_2. Because we cannot assign values 1 or 2 for q_2 as these values violate the constraint c_{12} between q_1 and q_2, we select value 3 to be assigned to q_2 ($q_2 = 3$). Then, BT attempts to extend $\mathcal{I} = [(q_1 = 1), (q_2 = 3)]$ by assigning the next variable q_3. No value from $D(q_3)$ exists that satisfies all of the constraints with ($q_1 = 1$) and ($q_2 = 3$) (i.e. c_{13} and c_{23}). Therefore, a BT is performed to the most recently instantiated variable (i.e. q_2) in order to change its current value (i.e. 3). Hence, variable q_2 is assigned to 4. Afterward, the value 2 is assigned to next variable q_3 because value 1 violates the constraint c_{13}. Then, the algorithm backtracks to variable q_3 after attempting to assign variable q_4 because no possible assignment for q_4 exists that is consistent with previous assignments $\mathcal{I} = [(q_1 = 1), (q_2 = 4), (q_3 = 2)]$. Thus, $q_3 = 2$ must be changed. However, no value consistent with ($q_1 = 1$) and ($q_2 = 4$) is available for q_3. Hence, another backtrack is performed to q_2. In the same way BT backtracks again to q_1 as no value for q_2 is consistent with ($q_1 = 1$). Then, $q_1 = 2$ is selected for the first variable q_1. After that, q_2 is assigned to 4 because other values (1, 2 and 3) violate the constraint c_{12}. Next, $\mathcal{I}$ is extended by adding a new assignment ($q_3 = 1$) of the next variable q_3 consistent with $\mathcal{I}$. Finally, an assignment, consistent with the extended partial solution $\mathcal{I}$, is sought for q_4. The first and the second values (row number 1 and 2) from $D(q_4)$ are not consistent with $\mathcal{I} = [(q_1 = 2), (q_2 = 4), (q_3 = 1)]$. Then, BT chooses 3 that is consistent with $\mathcal{I}$ to be instantiated to q_4. Hence, a solution is found because all variables are instantiated in $\mathcal{I}$, where $\mathcal{I} = [(q_1 = 2), (q_2 = 4), (q_3 = 1), (q_4 = 3)]$.

On the one hand, it is clear that we need only linear space to perform the BT. However, it requires time exponential in the number of variables for most nontrivial problems. On the other hand, the BT is clearly better than "generate & test" because a subtree from the search space is pruned whenever a partial instantiation violates a constraint. Thus, BT can detect early unfruitful instantiation compared to "generate & test".

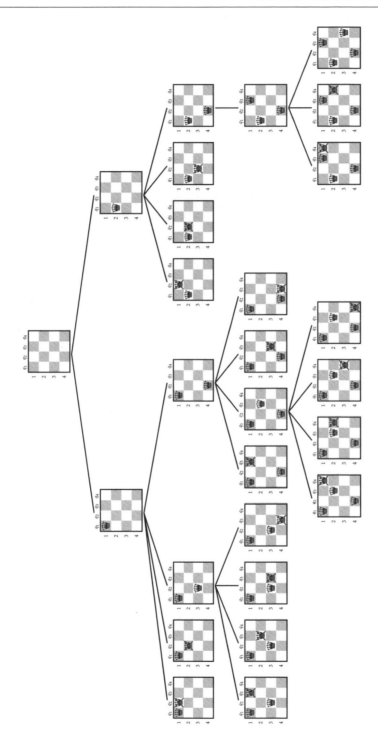

Figure 1.5. *The chronological backtracking algorithm running on the 4-queens problem*

Although the BT improves the "generate & test", it still suffers from many drawbacks. The main drawback is the *thrashing* problem. Thrashing is the fact that the same failure due to the same reason can be rediscovered an exponential number of times when solving the problem. Therefore, a variety of refinements of BT have been developed in order to improve it. These improvements can be classified under two main schemes: look-back methods such as CBJ or look-ahead methods such as FC.

1.2.1.2. *Conflict-directed backjumping*

From the earliest work in the area of constraint programming, researchers were concerned by the trashing problem of the BT algorithm and then they proposed a number of techniques to avoid it. The BJ concept was one of the pioneer techniques used for this reason. Thus, several non-chronological BT (intelligent BT) search algorithms have been designed to solve centralized CSPs. In the standard form of BT, each time a dead-end occurs, the algorithm attempts to change the value of the most recently instantiated variable. However, BT chronologically to the most recently instantiated variable may not address the reason of the failure. This is no longer the case in the BJ algorithms that identify and then *jump* directly to the responsible dead-end (*culprit*). Hence, the culprit variable is reassigned if it is possible or another jump is performed. Incidentally, the subtree of the search space where the thrashing may occur is pruned.

DEFINITION 1.12.– *Given a total ordering on variables $\mathcal{O}$, a constraint c_{ij} is earlier than c_{kl} if the latest variable in* scope(c_{ij}) *precedes the latest one in* scope(c_{kl}) *on $\mathcal{O}$.*

EXAMPLE 1.1.– Given the lexicographic ordering on variables $([x_1, \ldots, x_n])$, the constraint c_{25} is earlier than constraint c_{35} because x_2 precedes x_3 since x_5 belongs to both scopes (i.e. scope(c_{25}) and scope(c_{35})).

Gaschnig designed the first explicit non-chronological (BJ) algorithm in [GAS 78]. For each variable x_i BJ records the *deepest* variable with which it checks its consistency with the assignment of x_i. When a dead-end occurs on a domain of a variable x_i, BJ jumps back to the deepest variable, say x_j, against which the consistency of x_i is checked. However, if there are no more values remaining for x_j, BJ perform a simple backtrack to the last assigned variable before assigning x_j.[2] Dechter [DEC 90, DEC 02] presented the GBJ algorithm, a generalization of the BJ algorithm. Basically, GBJ attempts to jump back directly to the source of the failure by using only information extracted from the constraint graph. Whenever a dead-end occurs on a domain of the current variable x_i, GBJ jumps back to the most recent assigned variable (x_j) adjacent to x_i in the constraint graph. Unlike BJ, if a dead-end occurs again on a domain of x_j, GBJ jumps back to the most recent variable x_k

---

2 BJ cannot execute two "jumps" in a row, only performing steps back after a jump.

connected to x_i or x_j. Prosser [PRO 93] proposed the CBJ that rectifies the bad behavior of Gaschnig's algorithm.

The pseudo-code of CBJ is illustrated in algorithm 1.2. Instead of recording only the *deepest* variable, for each variable x_i CBJ records the set of variables that were in conflict with some assignment of x_i. Thus, CBJ maintains an *earliest minimal conflict set* for each variable x_i (i.e. $EMCS[i]$) where it stores the variables involved in the earliest violated constraints with an assignment of x_i. Whenever a variable x_i is chosen to be instantiated (line 3), CBJ initializes $EMCS[i]$ to the empty set. Next, CBJ initializes the current domain of x_i to its initial domain (line 5). Afterward, a consistent value v_i with the current search state is looked for the selected variable x_i. If v_i is inconsistent with the current partial solution, then v_i is removed from the current domain $D(x_i)$ (line 13), and x_j such that c_{ij} is the earliest violated constraint by the new assignment of x_i (i.e. $x_i = v_i$) is then added to the earliest minimal conflict set of x_i, that is $EMCS[i]$ (line 15). $EMCS[i]$ can be seen as the subset of the past variables in conflict with x_i. When a dead-end occurs on the domain of a variable x_i, CBJ jumps back to the last variable, say x_j, in $EMCS[i]$ (lines 16, 9 and 10). The information in $EMCS[i]$ is earned upwards to $EMCS[j]$ (line 11). Hence, CBJ performs a form of "intelligent backtracking" to the source of the conflict allowing the search procedure to avoid rediscovering the same failure due to the same reason.

Algorithm 1.2. *The conflict-directed backjumping algorithm.*

---

procedure CBJ$(\mathcal{I})$
01.	**if** (isFull$(\mathcal{I})$) **then** **report** $\mathcal{I}$ as solution;	/* all variables are assigned in $\mathcal{I}$ */
02.	**else**	
03.	choose x_i in $\mathcal{X} \setminus$ vars$(\mathcal{I})$;	/* let x_i be an unassigned variable */
04.	$EMCS[i] \leftarrow \emptyset$;	
05.	$D(x_i) \leftarrow D^0(x_i)$;	
06.	**foreach** ($v_i \in D(x_i)$) **do**	
07.	$x_i \leftarrow v_i$;	
08.	**if** (isConsistent$(\mathcal{I} \cup (x_i = v_i))$) **then**	
09.	$CS \leftarrow$ CBJ$(\mathcal{I} \cup \{(x_i = v_i)\})$;	
10.	**if** ($x_i \notin CS$) **then** **return** CS ;	
11.	**else** $EMCS[i] \leftarrow EMCS[i] \cup CS \setminus \{x_i\}$;	
12.	**else**	
13.	remove v_i from $D(x_i)$;	
14.	let c_{ij} be the earliest violated constraint by $(x_i = v_i)$;	
15.	$EMCS[i] \leftarrow EMCS[i] \cup x_j$;	
16.	**return** $EMCS[i]$;	

When a dead-end occurs, the CBJ algorithm jumps back to address the culprit variable. During the BJ process, CBJ erases all assignments that were obtained since and then wastes a meaningful effort made to achieve these assignments. To overcome this drawback, Ginsberg have proposed DBT [GIN 93].

1.2.1.3. *Dynamic backtracking*

In the naive chronological of BT, each time a dead-end occurs the algorithm attempts to change the value of the most recently instantiated variable. Intelligent BT algorithms were developed to avoid the trashing problem caused by the BT. Although these algorithms identify and then jump directly to the responsible dead-end (*culprit*), they erase a great deal of the work performed thus far on the variables that are backjumped over. When backjumping, all variables between the culprit variable responsible for the dead-end and the variable where the dead-end occurs will be re-assigned.

Ginsberg proposed the DBT algorithm in order to keep the progress performed before BJ [GIN 93]. In DBT, the assignments of non-conflicting variables are preserved during the BJ process. Thus, the assignments of all variables following the culprit are kept and the culprit variable is moved so as to be the last among the assigned variables.

To detect the culprit of the dead-end, CBJ associates a conflict set ($EMCS[i]$) with each variable (x_i). $EMCS[i]$ contains the set of the assigned variables whose assignments are in conflict with a value from the domain of x_i. In a similar way, DBT uses nogoods to justify the value elimination [GIN 93]. Based on the constraints of the problem, a search procedure can infer inconsistent sets of assignments called nogoods.

DEFINITION 1.13.– *A nogood is a conjunction of individual assignments, which has been found inconsistent either because of the initial constraints or because of searching for all possible combinations.*

EXAMPLE 1.2.– The following nogood $\neg[(x_i = v_i) \wedge (x_j = v_j) \wedge \ldots \wedge (x_k = v_k)]$ means that assignments it contains are not simultaneously allowed because they cause an inconsistency.

DEFINITION 1.14.– *A directed nogood ruling out value v_k from the initial domain of variable x_k is a clause of the form $x_i = v_i \wedge x_j = v_j \wedge \ldots \rightarrow x_k \neq v_k$, meaning that the assignment $x_k = v_k$ is inconsistent with the assignments $x_i = v_i, x_j = v_j, \ldots$. When a nogood ($ng$) is represented as an implication (directed nogood), the* left-hand side, lhs(ng), and the right-hand side, rhs(ng), are defined from the position of $\rightarrow$.

In DBT, when a value is found to be inconsistent with previously assigned values, a directed nogood is stored as a justification of its removal. Hence, the current domain $D(x_i)$ of a variable x_i contains all values from its initial domain that are not ruled out by a stored nogood. When all values of a variable x_i are ruled out by some nogoods (i.e. a dead-end occurs), DBT resolves these nogoods producing a new nogood ($newNogood$). Let x_j be the last variable in the left-hand side of all these nogoods and $x_j = v_j$. In CBJ algorithm, x_j is the culprit variable. The lhs($newNogood$) is the conjunction of the left-hand sides of all nogoods except

$x_j = v_j$ and rhs $(newNogood)$ is $x_j \neq v_j$. Unlike the CBJ, DBT only removes the current assignment of x_j and keeps assignments of all variables between it and x_i because they are consistent with former assignments. Therefore, the work done when assigning these variables is preserved. The culprit variable x_j is then placed after x_i and a new assignment for it is searched for because the generated nogood $(newNogood)$ eliminates its current value (v_j).

Because the number of nogoods that can be generated increases monotonically, recording all of the nogoods, as is done in dependency-directed backtracking algorithm [STA 77], requires an exponential space complexity. To keep a polynomial space complexity, DBT stores only nogoods compatible with the current state of the search. Thus, when BT to x_j, DBT destroys all nogoods containing $x_j = v_j$. As a result, with this approach, a variable assignment can be ruled out by at most one nogood. Because each nogood requires $O(n)$ space and there are at most nd nogoods, where n is the number of variables and d is the maximum domain size, the overall space complexity of DBT is in $O(n^2 d)$.

1.2.1.4. *Partial order dynamic backtracking*

Instead of BT to the most recently assigned variable in the nogood, Ginsberg and McAllester [GIN 94] proposed the *partial order dynamic backtracking* (PODB), an algorithm that offers more freedom than DBT in the selection of the variable to put on the right-hand side of the generated nogood. PODB is a polynomial space algorithm that attempted to address the rigidity of DBT.

When resolving the nogoods that led to a dead-end, DBT always selects the most recently assigned variable among the set of inconsistent assignments to be the right-hand side of the generated directed nogood. However, there are clearly many different ways of representing a given nogood as an implication (directed nogood). For example, $\neg[(x_i = v_i) \wedge (x_j = v_j) \wedge \cdots \wedge (x_k = v_k)]$ is logically equivalent to $[(x_j = v_j) \wedge \cdots \wedge (x_k = v_k)] \rightarrow (x_i \neq v_i)$ meaning that the assignment $x_i = v_i$ is inconsistent with the assignments $x_j = v_j, \ldots, x_k = v_k$. Each directed nogood imposes ordering constraints called the set of *safety conditions* for completeness [GIN 94]. Since all variables on the left-hand side of a directed nogood participate in eliminating the value on its right-hand side, these variables must precede the variable on the right-hand side.

DEFINITION 1.15.– *The* safety conditions *imposed by a directed nogood ng, that is $S(ng)$, ruling out a value from the domain of x_j are the set of assertions of the form $x_k \prec x_j$, where x_k is a variable in the left-hand side of ng, that is $x_k \in$ lhs (ng).*

The PODB attempts to offer more freedom in the selection of the variable to put on the right-hand side of the generated directed nogood. In PODB, the only restriction to respect is that the partial order induced by the resulting directed nogood must safeguard the existing partial order required by the set of safety conditions, say S. In a later study, Bliek [BLI 98] shows that PODB is not a generalization of DBT and then proposes the *generalized partial order dynamic backtracking* (GPODB), a new algorithm that generalizes both PODB and DBT. To achieve this, GPODB follows the same mechanism of PODB. The difference between the two (PODB and GPODB) resides in the obtained set of safety conditions S' after generating a new directed nogood ($newNogood$). The new order has to respect the safety conditions existing in S'. While S and S' are similar for PODB, when computing S', GPODB relaxes all safety conditions from S of the form: rhs ($newNogood$) $\prec x_k$. However, both algorithms generate only directed nogoods that satisfy the already existing safety conditions in S. To the best of our knowledge, no systematic evaluation of either PODB or GPODB has been reported.

All algorithms presented so far incorporate a form of look-back scheme. Avoiding possible future conflicts may be more attractive than recovering from them. In the BT, BJ and DBT, we cannot detect that an instantiation is unfruitful until all variables of the conflicting constraint are assigned. Intuitively, each time a new assignment is added to the current partial solution (instantiation), one can look ahead by performing a forward check of consistency of the current partial solution .

1.2.1.5. *Forward checking*

The FC algorithm [HAR 79, HAR 80] is the simplest procedure of checking every new instantiation against the future (as yet uninstantiated) variables. The purpose of the FC is to propagate information from assigned to unassigned variables. Then, it is classified among those procedures performing a look-ahead.

The pseudo-code of FC procedure is presented in algorithm 1.3. FC is a recursive procedure that attempts to foresee the effects of choosing an assignment on the not-yet- assigned variables. Each time a variable is assigned, FC checks forward the effects of this assignment on the domains of future variables (Check-Forward call, line 6). So, all values from the domains of future variables, which are inconsistent with the assigned value (v_i) of the current variable (x_i), are removed (line 11). Future variables concerned by this filtering process are only those sharing a constraint with x_i, the current variable being instantiated (line 10). Incidentally, each domain of a future variable is filtered in order to keep only consistent values with past variables (variables already instantiated). Hence, FC does not need to check consistency of new assignments against already instantiated ones as opposed to chronological BT. The FC is then the easiest way to prevent assignments that guarantee later failure.

We illustrate the FC algorithm on the 4-queens problem (Figure 1.6). In the first iteration, the FC algorithm selects the first value of the domain (1), (i.e. ($q_1 = 1$)). Once, value 1 is assigned to q_1, FC checks forward this assignment. Thus, all values from domain of variables not yet instantiated sharing a constraint with q_1 (i.e. q_2, q_3 and q_4) will be removed if they are inconsistent with the assignment of q_1. Thus, the check-forward results in the following domains: $D(q_2) = \{3, 4\}$, $D(q_3) = \{2, 4\}$ and $D(q_4) = \{2, 3\}$. In the second iteration, the algorithm selects the first available value on the domain of q_2 (i.e. 3), then FC checks forward this new assignment (i.e. $q_2 = 3$). When checking forward ($q_2 = 3$), the assignment is rejected because a dead-end occurs on the $D(q_3)$ as values 2 and 4 for q_3 are not consistent with $q_2 = 3$. Thus, the FC algorithm then chooses $q_2 = 4$, which generates the following domains $D(q_3) = \{2\}$ and $D(q_4) = \{3\}$. Afterward, FC assigns the only possible value (2) for q_3 and checks forward the assignment $q_3 = 2$. The domain of q_4 (i.e. $D(q_4) = \{3\}$) is then filtered. Hence, value 3 is removed from $D(q_4)$ because it is not consistent with $q_3 = 2$. This removal generates a dead-end on $D(q_4)$, requiring another value for q_3. A backtrack to q_2 takes place because there is no possible value on $D(q_2)$. In a similar way, FC backtracks to q_1 requiring a new value.

Algorithm 1.3. *The forward checking algorithm.*

---

procedure ForwardChecking($\mathcal{I}$)
01.   **if** (isFull($\mathcal{I}$)) **then report** $\mathcal{I}$ as solution;   /* all variables are assigned in $\mathcal{I}$ */
02.   **else**
03.   select x_i in $\mathcal{X} \setminus$ vars($\mathcal{I}$) ;   /* let x_i be an unassigned variable */
04.   **foreach** ($v_i \in D(x_i)$) **do**
05. $x_i \leftarrow v_i$;
06.   **if** (Check-Forward($\mathcal{I}$, $(x_i = v_i)$),) **then**
07.   ForwardChecking($\mathcal{I} \cup \{(x_i = v_i)\}$);
08.   **else**
09.   **foreach** ($x_j \notin$ vars($\mathcal{I}$) such that $\exists\, c_{ij} \in \mathcal{C}$) **do** restore $D(x_j)$;

function Check-Forward($\mathcal{I}$, $x_i = v_i$)
10.   **foreach** ($x_j \notin$ vars($\mathcal{I}$) such that $\exists\, c_{ij} \in \mathcal{C}$) **do**
11.   **foreach** ($v_j \in D(x_j)$ such that $(v_i, v_j) \notin c_{ij}$) **do** remove v_j from $D(x_j)$;
12.   **if** ($D(x_j) = \emptyset$) **then return** *false* ;
13.   **return** *true*;

A new assignment is generated for q_1 assigning it the next value 2. Next, $q_1 = 2$ is checked forward producing removals on the domains of q_2, q_3 and q_4. The obtained domains are as follows: $D(q_2) = \{4\}$, $D(q_3) - \{1, 3\}$ and $D(q_4) = \{1, 3, 4\}$. Afterward, the next variable is assigned (i.e. $q_2 = 4$) and checked forward producing the following domains: $D(q_3) = \{1\}$ and $D(q_4) = \{1, 4\}$. Next, variables are assigned sequentially without any value removal ($q_3 = 1$ and $q_4 = 3$). Thus, FC has generated a full, consistent instantiation and the solution is $\mathcal{I} = [(q_1 = 2), (q_2 = 4), (q_3 = 1), (q_4 = 3)]$.

The example (Figure 1.6) shows how the FC algorithm improves the BT and FC detects the inconsistency earlier compared to the chronological BT. Thus, FC prunes branches of the search tree that will lead to failure earlier than BT. This purpose allows us to reduce the search tree and (hopefully) the overall amount of time. This can be seen when comparing the size of the search tree of both algorithms on the example of the 4-queens (Figures 1.5 and 1.6). However, we have highlighted that when generating a new assignment, FC requires greater efforts compared to the BT.

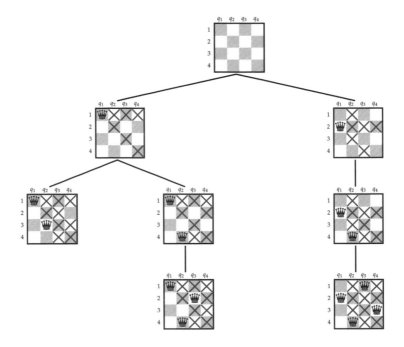

Figure 1.6. *The forward checking algorithm running on the 4-queens problem*

Unlike BT, FC algorithm enables us to prevent assignments that guarantee later failure. This improves the performance of BT. However, FC reduces the domains of future variables, checking only the constraints relating them to variables already instantiated. In addition to these constraints, we can also check the constraints relating future variables to each other. Incidentally, domains of future variables may be reduced and further possible conflicts will be avoided. This is the principle of the *full* look-ahead scheme or constraint propagation. This approach is called MAC.

1.2.1.6. *Arc consistency*

In CSPs, checking the existence of solutions is NP-complete. Therefore, the research community has devoted great interest to studying the *constraint propagation* techniques. Constraint propagation techniques are filtering mechanisms that aim to improve the performance of the search process by attempting to reduce the search space. They have been widely used to simplify the search space before or during the search. Thus, constraint propagation became a central process of solving CSPs [BES 06]. Historically, different kinds of constraint propagation techniques have been proposed: node consistency [MAC 77], AC [MAC 77] and path consistency [MON 74] . The oldest and most commonly used technique for propagating constraints in literature is the AC.

DEFINITION 1.16.– *A value $v_i \in D(x_i)$ is consistent with c_{ij} in $D(x_j)$ iff there exists a value $v_j \in D(x_j)$ such that (v_i, v_j) is allowed by c_{ij}. Value v_j is called a* support *for v_i in $D(x_j)$.*

Let us assume the constraint graph $G = \{X_G, E_G\}$ (see definition 1.2) associated with our CSP.

DEFINITION 1.17.– *An arc $\{x_i, x_j\} \in E_G$ (constraint c_{ij}) is arc consistent iff $\forall v_i \in D(x_i), \exists v_j \in D(x_j)$ such that (v_i, v_j) is allowed by c_{ij} and $\forall v_j \in D(x_j), \exists v_i \in D(x_i)$ such that (v_i, v_j) is allowed by c_{ij}. A constraint network is arc consistent iff all its arcs (constraints) are arc consistent.*

A constraint network is arc consistent if and only if for any value v_i in the domain, $D(x_i)$, of a variable x_i there exist in the domain $D(x_j)$ of any adjacent variable x_j a value v_j that is compatible with v_i. Clearly, if an arc $\{x_i, x_j\}$ (i.e. a constraint c_{ij}) is not arc consistent, it can be made arc consistent by simply deleting all values from the domains of the variables in its scope for which there is not a support in the other domain. It is obvious that these deletions maintain the problem solutions since the deleted values are in no solution. The process of removing values from the domain of a variable x_i, when making an arc $\{x_i, x_j\}$ arc consistent is called *revising* $D(x_i)$ with respect to constraint c_{ij}. A wide variety of algorithms establishing AC on CSPs have been developed: AC-3 [MAC 77], AC-4 [MOH 86], AC-5 [VAN 92], AC-6 [BES 93, BES 94], AC-7 [BES 99], AC-2001 [BES 01c], etc. The basic and the most well-known algorithm is Mackworth's AC-3.

We illustrate the pseudo-code of AC-3 in algorithm 1.4. The AC-3 algorithm maintains a queue Q [3] of arcs to render arc consistent. AC-3 algorithm will return true once the problem is made arc consistent or false if an empty domain was generated (a domain is *wiped out*) meaning that the problem is not satisfiable. Initially, Q is filled with all ordered pair of variables that participates in a constraint. Thus, for each constraint c_{ij} ($\{x_i, x_j\}$) we add to Q the ordered pair (x_i, x_j) to revise the domain of x_i and the ordered pair (x_j, x_i) the revise the domain of x_j (line 8). Next, the algorithm loops until it is guaranteed that all arcs have been made arc consistent (i.e. while Q is not empty). The ordered pair of variables are selected and removed one by one from Q to revise the domain of the first variable. Each time an ordered pair of variables (x_i, x_j) is selected and removed from Q (line 10), AC-3 calls function Revise(x_i, x_j) to revise the domain of x_i. When revising $D(x_i)$ with respect to an arc $\{x_i, x_j\}$ (Revise call, line 11), all values that are not consistent with c_{ij} are removed from $D(x_i)$ (lines 2–4). Thus, only values having a support on $D(x_j)$ are kept in $D(x_i)$. The function Revise returns true if the domain of variable x_i has been reduced, false otherwise (line 6). If Revise results in the removal of values from $D(x_i)$, it can be the case that a value for another variable x_k has lost its support on $D(x_i)$. Thus, all ordered pairs (x_k, x_i) such that $k \neq j$ are added onto Q

---

3 Other data structures as queue or stack can perfectly serve the purpose.

so long as they are not already on Q in order to revise the domain of x_k. Obviously, the AC-3 algorithm will not terminate as long as there is any pair in Q. When Q is empty, we are guaranteed that all arcs have been made arc consistent. Hence, the constraint network is arc consistent. The while loop of AC-3 can be intuitively understood as constraint propagation process (i.e. propagation the effect of value removals on other domains potentially affected by these removals).

Algorithm 1.4. *The AC-3 algorithm.*

---

function Revise(x_i, x_j)
01. $change \leftarrow$ **false**;
02.   **foreach** ($v_i \in D(x_i)$) **do**
03.   **if** ($\nexists\, v_j \in D(x_j)$ such that $(v_i, v_j) \in c_{ij}$) **then**
04.   remove v_i from $D(x_i)$;
05. $change \leftarrow$ **true**;
06.   **return** $change$;

function AC-3()
07.   **foreach** ($\{x_i, x_j\} \in E_G$) **do**   /* $\{x_i, x_j\} \in E_G$ iff $\exists\, c_{ij} \in \mathcal{C}$ */
08. $Q \leftarrow Q \cup \{(x_i, x_j); (x_j, x_i)\}$;
09.   **while** ($Q \neq \emptyset$) **do**
10. $(x_i, x_j) \leftarrow Q.pop()$;   /* Select and remove (x_i, x_j) from Q */
11.   **if** (Revise(x_i, x_j)) **then**
12.   **if** ($D(x_i) = \emptyset$) **then return** *false* ;   /* The problem is unsatisfiable */
13.   **else** $Q \leftarrow Q \cup \{ (x_k, x_i) \mid \{x_k, x_i\} \in E_G,\ k \neq i,\ k \neq j \}$;
14.   **return** *true* ;   /* The problem is arc consistent */

1.2.1.7. *Maintaining arc consistency*

Historically, constraint propagation techniques are used in a preprocessing step to prune values before a search. Thus, the search space that will be explored by the search algorithm is reduced because domains of all variables are refined. Incidentally, subsequent search efforts by the solution method will be reduced. Afterward, the search method can be called for searching a solution. Constraint propagation techniques are also used during search. This strategy is that used by the FC algorithm. FC combines backtrack search with a limited form of AC maintenance on the domains of future variables. Instead of performing a limited form of AC, Sabin and Freuder proposed [SAB 94] the MAC algorithm that establishes and maintains a *full AC* on the domains of future variables.

The MAC algorithm is a modern version of CS2 algorithm [GAS 74]. MAC alternates the search process and constraint propagation steps as is done in FC [HAR 80]. Nevertheless, before starting the search method, MAC makes the constraint network arc consistent. In addition, when instantiating a variable x_i to a value v_i, all the other values in $D(x_i)$ are removed and the effects of these removals are propagated through the constraint network [SAB 94]. MAC algorithm enforces AC in the search process as follows. At each step of the search, a variable assignment is followed by a filtering process that corresponds to enforcing AC. Therefore, MAC maintains the AC each time an instantiation is added to the partial solution. In other words, whenever a value v_i is instantiated to a variable x_i, $D(x_i)$ is reduced momentarily to a single value v_i (i.e. $D(x_i) \leftarrow \{v_i\}$) and the resulting constraint network is then made arc consistent.

Figure 1.7 shows the search process performed by the MAC procedure on the 4-queens problem. Obviously, MAC is able to prune the search space earlier than the FC. This statement can be seen in our example. For instance, when the first queen q_1 is selected to be placed in the first row (i.e. $q_1 = 1$), $D(q_1)$ is restricted to $\{1\}$. Afterward, the conflicts between the current assignment of q_1 and the future variables are removed (i.e. values $\{1, 2\}$, $\{1, 3\}$ and $\{1, 4\}$ are removed respectively from $D(q_2)$, $D(q_3)$ and $D(q_4)$). After that, MAC checks the conflicts among the future variables starting with the first available value (3) for next variable q_2. This, value is removed from $D(q_2)$ since it does not have a support in $D(q_3)$, its only support in $D(q_3)$ was value 1 that is already removed. The MAC algorithm follows with the last value 4 from $D(q_2)$, which has a support in c_{23} (i.e. 2). However, when MAC revises the next variable q_3 this only support (i.e. $2 \in D(q_3)$) for value $4 \in D(q_2)$ will be removed since it does not have a support in $D(q_4)$. Its only support in $D(q_4)$ was 4 that has already been removed from $D(q_4)$. This removal will lead to revisiting $D(q_2)$ and thus removing 4 from $D(q_2)$. A dead-end then occurs and we backtrack to q_1. Hence, value 2 is assigned to q_1. The same process follows until the result is reached on the right subtree.

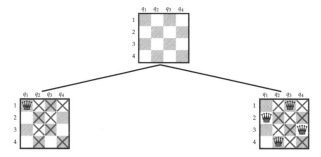

Figure 1.7. *The Maintaing arc consistency algorithm running on the 4-queens problem*

1.2.2. *Variable ordering heuristics for centralized CSPs*

Numerous efficient search algorithms for solving CSPs have been developed. The performance of these algorithms were evaluated in different studies and then shown to be powerful tools for solving CSPs. Nevertheless, because CSPs are in general NP-complete, these algorithms are still exponential. Therefore, a large variety of *heuristics* were developed to improve their efficiency, i.e. search algorithms solving CSPs are commonly combined with heuristics for boosting the search. The literature is rich in heuristics designed for this task. The order in which variables are assigned by a search algorithm was one of the early concerns for these heuristics. The order on variables can be either static or dynamic.

1.2.2.1. *Static variable ordering heuristics*

The first kind of heuristics addressing the ordering of variables was based on the initial structure of the constraint graph. Thus, the order of the variables can be determined prior to the search of solution. These heuristics are called static variable ordering (SVO) heuristics. When presenting the main search procedures (section 1.2), we always assumed, without specifying it each time, an SVO. Therefore, in the previous examples we have always used the lexicographic ordering of variables. That lexicographic ordering can be simply replaced by another ordering more appropriate to the structure of the network before starting the search.

SVO heuristics are heuristics that keep the same ordering on variables all along the search. This ordering is computed in a preprocessing step. Hence, this ordering only exploits (structural) information about the initial state of the search. Examples of such SVO heuristics are:

min-width: the *minimum width* heuristic [FRE 82] chooses an ordering that minimizes the width of the constraint graph. The *width* of a constraint graph is the minimum width over all orderings of variables of that graph. The *width* of an ordering $\mathcal{O}$ is the maximum number of neighbors of any variable x_i that occur earlier than x_i under $\mathcal{O}$. Because minimizing the width of the constraint graph G is NP-complete, it can be accomplished by a greedy algorithm. Hence, variables are ordered from last to first by choosing, at each step, a variable having the minimum number of neighbors (min degree) in the remaining constraint graph after deleting from the constraint graph all variables, which have been already ordered.

max-degree: the *maximum degree* heuristic [DEC 89] orders the variables in a decreasing order of their degrees in the constraint graph (i.e. the size of their neighborhood). This heuristic also aims at, without any guarantee, finding a minimum-width ordering.

max-cardinality: the *maximum cardinality* heuristic [DEC 89] orders the variables according to the initial size of their neighborhood. *max-cardinality* puts in the first position of the resulting ordering an arbitrarily variable. Afterward, other variables are ordered from second to last by choosing, at each step, the most connected variable with previously ordered variables. In a particular case, *max-cardinality* may choose as the first variable the one that has the largest number of neighbors.

min-bandwidth: the *minimum bandwidth* heuristic [ZAB 90] minimizes the bandwidth of the constraint graph. The *bandwidth* of a constraint graph is the minimum bandwidth over all orderings on variables of that graph. The *bandwidth* of an ordering is the maximum distance between any two adjacent variables in the ordering. Zabih claims that an ordering with a small bandwidth will reduce the need for BJ because the culprit variable will be close to the variable where a dead-end occurs. Many heuristic procedures for finding minimum bandwidth orderings have been developed and a survey of these procedures is given in [CHI 82]. However, there is currently little empirical evidence that *min-bandwidth* is an effective heuristic. Moreover, bandwidth minimization is NP-complete.

Another SVO heuristic that tries to exploit the structural information residing in the constraint graph is presented in [FRE 85]. Freuder and Quinn have introduced the use of pseudo-tree arrangement of a constraint graph in order to enhance the research complexity in centralized CSPs.

DEFINITION 1.18.– *A* pseudo-tree *arrangement* $T = (X_T, E_T)$ *of a constraint graph* $G = (X_G, E_G)$ *is a rooted tree with the same set of vertices as G (i.e.* $X_G = X_T$*) such that vertices in different branches of T do not share any edge in G.*

The concept of *pseudo-tree* arrangement of a constraint graph has been introduced to perform searches in parallel on independent branches of the pseudo-tree in order to improve the search in centralized CSPs. A recursive procedure for heuristically building pseudo-trees have been presented by Freuder and Quinn in [FRE 85]. The heuristic aims to select from G_X the minimal subset of vertices named *cutset* whose removal divides G into disconnected sub-graphs. The selected *cutset* will form the first levels of the pseudo-tree, while next levels are built by recursively applying the procedure to the disconnected sub-graphs obtained previously. Incidentally, the connected vertices in the constraint graph G belongs to the same branch of the obtained tree. Thus, the tree obtained is a pseudo-tree arrangement of the constraint graph. Once the pseudo-tree arrangement of the constraint graph is built, several search procedures can be performed in parallel on each branch of the pseudo-tree.

Although SVO heuristics are undoubtedly cheaper because they are computed once and for all, using this kind of variable ordering heuristics does not change the worst-case complexity of the classical search algorithms. On the other hand, researchers have expected that dynamic variable ordering (DVO) heuristics can be more efficient. DVO heuristics were expected to be potentially more powerful because they can take advantage of the information about the current search state.

1.2.2.2. *Dynamic variable ordering heuristics*

Instead of fixing an ordering as is done is SVO heuristics, DVO heuristics determine the order of the variables as search progresses. The order of the variables may then differ from one branch of the search tree to another. It has been shown empirically for many practical problems that DVO heuristics are more effective than choosing a good static ordering [HAR 80, PUR 83, DEC 89, BAC 95, GEN 96]. Hence, researchers in the field of constraint programming had so far mainly focused on such kind of heuristics. Therefore, many DVO heuristics for solving constraint networks have been proposed and evaluated over the years. These heuristics are usually combined with search procedures performing some form of look ahead (see sections 1.2.1.5 and 1.2.1.7) in order to take into account changes on not-yet-instantiated (future) variables.

The guiding idea of the most DVO heuristic is to select the future variable with the smallest domain size. Henceforth, this heuristic is named *dom*. Historically, Golomb and Baumert [GOL 65] were the first to propose the *dom* heuristic. However, it was popularized when it was combined with the FC procedure by Haralick and Elliott [HAR 80]. *dom* investigates the future variables (remaining sub-problem) and provides choosing as next variable the one with the smallest remaining domain. Haralick and Elliott proposed *dom* under the rubric of an intuition called the fail first principle: *"to succeed, try first where you are likely to fail"*. Moreover, they assume that *"the best search order is the one which minimizes the expected length or depth of each branch"* [HAR 80]. Thus, they estimate that minimizing branch length in a search procedure should also minimize search effort.

Many studies have been carried out to understand the *dom* heuristic, a simple but effective heuristic. Following the same principle of Haralick and Elliott saying that search efficiency is due to earlier failure, Smith and Grant [SMI 98] have derived from *dom* new heuristics that detect failures earlier than *dom*. Their study is based on an intuitive hypothesis saying that earlier detection of failure should lead the heuristic to lower search effort. Surprisingly, Smith and Grant's experiments refuted this hypothesis contrary to their expectations. They concluded that increasing the ability to fail early in the search did not always lead to increase its efficiency. In another work, Beck *et al.* (2005) showed that in FC (see section 1.2.1.5) minimizing branch depth is associated with an increase in the branching factor. This can lead FC to perform badly. Nevertheless, their experiments show that minimizing branch depth in MAC (see section 1.2.1.7) reduces the search effort. Therefore, Beck *et al.* do not overlook the principle of trying to fail earlier in the search. They propose to redefine failing early in a such way to combine both the branching factor and the branch depth as was suggested by Nadel [NAD 83] (for instance, minimizing the number of nodes in the failed subtrees).

In addition to the studies that have been carried out to understand the *dom*, considerable research effort has been spent on improving it by suggesting numerous variants. These variants express the intuitive idea that a variable that is constrained with many future variables can also lead to a failure (a dead-end). Thus, these variants attempt to take into account the neighborhood of the variables as well as their domain size. We present in the following a set of well-known variable ordering heuristics derived from *dom*:

dom+deg: a variant of *dom*, *dom+deg*, has been designed in [FRO 94] to break ties when all variables have the same initial domain size. *dom+deg* heuristic breaks ties by giving priority to the variable with the highest *degree* (i.e. the one with the largest number of neighbors).

dom+futdeg: another variant breaking ties of *dom* is the *dom+futdeg* heuristic [BRÉ 79, SMI 99]. Originally, *dom+futdeg* was developed by Brélaz for the graph coloring problem and then applied later to CSPs. *dom+futdeg* chooses a variable with smallest remaining domain (*dom*), but in case of a tie, it chooses from these the variable with the largest future degree, that is the one having the largest number of neighbors in the remaining sub-problem (i.e. among future variables).

dom/deg: both *dom+deg* and *dom+futdeg* use the domain size as the main criterion. The degree of the variables is considered only in case of ties. Alternatively, Bessiere and Régin [BES 96] combined *dom* with *deg* in a new heuristic called *dom/deg*. The *dom/deg* does not give priority to the domain size or degree of variables but uses them equally. This heuristic selects the variable that minimizes the ratio of current domain size to static degree. Bessiere and Régin have been shown that *dom/deg* gives good results in comparison with *dom* when the constraint graphs are sparse but performs badly on dense constraint graphs. They considered a variant of this heuristic which minimizes the ratio of current domain size to future degree *dom/futdeg*. However, they found that the performance of *dom/futdeg* is roughly similar to that of *dom/deg*.

Multi-level-DVO: a general formulation of DVO heuristics that approximates the constrainedness of variables and constraints, denoted *Multi-level-DVO*, have been proposed in [BES 01a]. *Multi-level-DVO* heuristics are considered as neighborhood generalizations of *dom* and *dom/deg* and the selection function for variable x_i they suggested is as follows:

$$H_\alpha^\odot(x_i) = \frac{\sum\limits_{x_j \in \Gamma(x_i)} (\alpha(x_i) \odot \alpha(x_j))}{\mid \Gamma(x_i) \mid^2}$$

where $\Gamma(x_i)$ is the set of x_i neighbors, $\alpha(x_i)$ can be any syntactical property of the variable such as *dom* or *dom/deg* and $\odot \in \{+, \times\}$. Therefore, *Multi-level-DVO* take into account the neighborhood of variables which have shown to be quite promising. Moreover, they allow using functions to measure the weight of a given constraint.

dom/wdeg: conflict-driven variable ordering heuristics have been introduced in [BOU 04]. These heuristics learn from previous failures to manage the choice of future variables. A *weight* is associated with each constraint. When a constraint leads to a dead-end, its weight is incremented by one. Each variable has a weighted degree, which is the sum of the weights over all constraints involving this variable. This heuristic can simply select the variable with the largest weighted degree (*wdeg*) or incorporating the domain size of variables to give the domain-over-weighted-degree heuristic (*dom/wdeg*). *dom/wdeg* selects among future variables the variable with minimum ratio between current domain size and weighted degree. *wdeg* and *dom/wdeg* (especially *dom/wdeg*) have been shown to perform well on a variety of problems.

In addition to the variable ordering heuristics we presented here, other elegant dynamic heuristics have been developed for centralized CSPs in many studies [GEN 96, HOR 00]. However, these heuristics require extra computation and have only been tested on random problems. On other hand, it has been shown empirically that MAC combined with the *dom/deg* or the *dom/wdeg* can reduce or remove the need for BJ on some problems [BES 96, LEC 04]. Although the variable ordering heuristics proposed are numerous, we have yet to see any of these heuristics to be efficient in every instance of the problems.

Besides different variable ordering heuristics designed to improve the efficiency of search procedure, researchers developed many look-ahead value ordering (LVO) heuristics. This is because value ordering heuristics are a powerful way of reducing the efforts of search algorithms [HAR 80]. Therefore, the constraint programming community developed various LVO heuristics that choose which value to instantiate to the selected variable. Many designed value ordering heuristics attempt to choose the *least constraining* values next, that is the values that are most likely to succeed. Incidentally, values that are expected to participate in many solutions are privileged. Minton *et al.* [MIN 92] designed a value ordering heuristic, the *min-conflicts*, that attempts to minimize the number of constraint violations after each step. Selecting *min-conflicts* values first maximizes the number of values available for future variables. Therefore, partial solutions that cannot be extended will be avoided. Other heuristics try to select values maximizing the product first [GIN 90, GEE 92] or the sum of support in future domain after propagation [FRO 95]. Nevertheless, all these heuristics are costly. Literature is rich on other LVOs, to mention a few [DEC 88, FRO 95, MEI 97, VER 99, KAS 04].

1.3. Summary

We have described in this chapter the basic issues of centralized CSPs. After defining the CSP formalism and presenting some examples of academic and real combinatorial problems that can be modeled as CSPs, we reported the main existing algorithms and heuristics used for solving centralized CSPs.

Distributed Constraint Satisfaction Problems

This chapter provides the state of the art in the area of distributed constraint reasoning. We give preliminary definitions of the distributed constraint satisfaction problem (DisCSP) framework in section 2.1. The state-of-the-art algorithms and heuristics for solving DisCSPs are provided in section 2.2.

2.1. Distributed constraint satisfaction problems

A wide variety of problems in artificial intelligence are solved using the constraint satisfaction problem (CSP) framework. However, applications that are of a distributed nature exist. In this kind of application, the knowledge about the problem, i.e. variables and constraints, may be logically or geographically distributed among physical distributed agents. This distribution is mainly due to privacy and/or security requirements: constraints or possible values may be strategic information that should not be revealed to other agents that can be seen as competitors. In addition, a distributed system provides fault tolerance, which means that if some agents disconnect, a solution might be available for the connected part. Several applications in multi-agent coordination are of such kind. Examples of such applications are sensor networks [JUN 01, BÉJ 05], military unmanned aerial vehicle teams [JUN 01], distributed scheduling problems [WAL 02, MAH 04], distributed resource allocation problems [PET 04], log-based reconciliation [CHO 06], distributed vehicle routing problems [LÉA 11], etc. Therefore, a distributed model allowing a decentralized solving process is more adequate to model and solve such kind of problem. The DisCSP has such properties.

A DisCSP is composed of a group of autonomous agents, where each agent has control of some elements of information about the whole problem, i.e. variables and constraints. Each agent owns its local constraint network. Variables in different agents are connected by constraints. Agents must assign values to their variables so that all constraints are satisfied. Hence, agents assign values to their variables, attempting to generate locally consistent assignments that are also consistent with constraints between agents [YOK 98, YOK 00a]. To achieve this goal, agents check the value assignments of their variables for local consistency and exchange messages among them to check consistency of their proposed assignments against constraints that contain variables that belong to other agents.

2.1.1. *Preliminaries*

The DisCSP is a constraint network where variables and constraints are distributed among multiple automated agents [YOK 98].

DEFINITION 2.1.– *A* DisCSP *(or a* distributed constraint network*) has been formalized as a tuple* $(\mathcal{A}, \mathcal{X}, \mathcal{D}, \mathcal{C})$*, where:*

– $\mathcal{A} = \{A_1, \ldots, A_p\}$ *is a set of* p agents*;*

– $\mathcal{X} = \{x_1, \ldots, x_n\}$ *is a set of* n variables *such that each variable* x_i *is controlled by one agent in* $\mathcal{A}$*;*

– $\mathcal{D} = \{D(x_1), \ldots, D(x_n)\}$ *is a set of current* domains*, where* $D(x_i)$ *is a finite set of possible values for variable* x_i*;*

– $\mathcal{C} = \{C_1, \ldots, C_e\}$ *is a set of* e constraints *that specify the combinations of values allowed for the variables they involve.*

Values may be pruned from the domain of a variable. At any node, the set of possible values for variable x_i is its current domain, $D(x_i)$. In the same manner, for centralized CSPs, we introduce the particular notation of initial domains (or definition domains), $\mathcal{D}^0 = \{D^0(x_1), \ldots, D^0(x_n)\}$, that represents the set of domains before pruning any value (i.e. $\mathcal{D} \subseteq \mathcal{D}^0$).

In the following, we provide some material assumptions in the context of DisCSPs. First, we assume a binary distributed constraint network where all constraints are binary constraints (they involve two variables). A constraint $c_{ij} \in \mathcal{C}$ between two variables x_i and x_j is a subset of the Cartesian product of their domains, that is $c_{ij} \subseteq D^0(x_i) \times D^0(x_j)$. For simplicity purposes, we consider a restricted version of DisCSPs where each agent controls exactly one variable ($p = n$). Thus, we use the terms agent and variable interchangeably, and we identify the agent ID with its variable index. We also assume that each agent (A_i) knows all the constraints involving its variable and its *neighbors*, that is $\Gamma(x_i)$, with whom it shares these constraints. We also assume that only the agent who is assigned a variable has control on its value and knowledge of its domain. In this book, we adopt the model of communication between agents presented in [YOK 00b] where it is assumed that:

– agents communicate by exchanging messages;

– the delay in delivering a message is random but finite;

– an agent can communicate with other agents if it knows their addresses.

Initially, each agent knows the addresses of all its neighbors without excluding the possibility of getting the addresses of other agents if it is necessary. Unlike the majority of work in the field of DisCSP, we discard the first in, first out (FIFO) assumption on communication channels between agents. Hence, we assume that communication between two agents is not necessarily generalized FIFO (aka causal order) channels [SIL 06].

Almost all distributed algorithms designed for solving DisCSPs require a total priority ordering on agents. The total order on agents is denoted by $\mathcal{O}$ (see definition 1.4). In this book, we present two classes of distributed algorithms with regard to agents' ordering. The first category of distributed algorithms for solving DisCSPs corresponds to those using a static ordering on agents. The second category of distributed algorithms for solving DisCSPs corresponds to those performing a dynamic reordering of agents during a search. For the first category of algorithms and without loss any generality, we will assume that the total order on agents is the lexicographic ordering, that is $[A_1, A_2, \ldots, A_n]$.

For each agent $A_i \in \mathcal{A}$, an agent A_j has a *higher priority* than A_i if it appears before A_i in the total ordering $\mathcal{O}$. We say that x_j precede x_i in the ordering and we denote this by $x_j \prec x_i$. Conversely, A_j has a *lower priority* than A_i if it appears after A_i in the total ordering on agents (i.e. $x_j \succ x_i$). Hence, the higher priority agents are those appearing before A_i in $\mathcal{O}$. Conversely, the lower priority agents are those appearing after A_i. As a result, $\mathcal{O}$ divides the neighbors of A_i, $\Gamma(x_i)$, into *higher priority neighbors*, $\Gamma^-(x_i)$, and *lower priority neighbors*, $\Gamma^+(x_i)$.

Because we assumed that communication between agents is not necessarily FIFO, we adopt a model where each agent (A_i) maintains a counter that is incremented whenever A_i changes its value. The current value of the counter *tags* each generated assignment.

DEFINITION 2.2.– *An assignment for an agent $A_i \in \mathcal{A}$ is a tuple (x_i, v_i, t_i), where v_i is a value from the domain of x_i and t_i is the tag value. When comparing two assignments, the* most up to date *is the one with the greatest tag t_i. Two sets of assignments* $\{(x_{i_1}, v_{i_1}, t_{i_1}), \ldots, (x_{i_k}, v_{i_k}, t_{i_k})\}$ *and* $\{(x_{j_1}, v_{j_1}, t_{j_1}), \ldots, (x_{j_q}, v_{j_q}, t_{j_q})\}$ are compatible *if every common variable is assigned the same value in both sets.*

To solve DisCSPs, agents try to generate locally consistent assignments and exchange their proposals with other agents to achieve a global consistency. An agent stores assignments received from other agents in its AgentView.

DEFINITION 2.3.– *The* AgentView *of an agent* $A_i \in \mathcal{A}$ *is an array containing the most up to date assignments received from other agents.*

2.1.2. *Examples of DisCSPs*

A major motivation for research on DisCSPs is that it is an elegant model for many everyday combinatorial problems arising in distributed artificial intelligence. Thus, DisCSPs have a wide range of applications in multi-agent coordination. Sensor networks [JUN 01, BÉJ 05], distributed resource allocation [PRO 92, PET 04], distributed meeting scheduling [WAL 02, MAH 04], log-based reconciliation [CHO 06] and military unmanned aerial vehicles teams [JUN 01] are non-exhaustive examples of real applications that are successfully modeled and solved by the DisCSP framework. We present in the following some instances of these applications.

2.1.3. *Distributed meeting scheduling problem (DisMSP)*

In section 1.1.2.3, we presented the meeting scheduling problem as a centralized CSP. Nonetheless, it is a problem of a distributed nature. The *distributed meeting scheduling problem* (DisMSP) is a truly distributed problem where agents may not desire to deliver their personal information to a centralized agent to solve the whole problem [WAL 02, MEI 04]. The DisMSP involves a set of n agents each having a personal private calendar and a set of m meetings each taking place in a specified location. Each agent, $A_i \in \mathcal{A}$, knows the set of the k_i among m meetings he/she must attend. It is assumed that each agent knows the traveling time between the locations where his/her meetings will be held. The traveling time between locations where two meetings m_i and m_j will be held is denoted by $TravellingTime(m_i, m_j)$. Solving the problem consists of satisfying the following constraints: (1) all agents attending a meeting must agree on when it will occur, (2) an agent cannot attend two meetings at the same time and (3) an agent must have enough time to travel from the location where he/she is to the location where the next meeting will be held.

DisMSP is encoded in DisCSP as follows. Each DisCSP agent represents a real agent and contains k variables representing the k meetings in which the agent participates. The domain of each variable contains the $d \times h$ slots where a meeting can be scheduled such that there are h slots per day and d days. There is an equality constraint for each pair of variables corresponding to the same meeting in different agents. This equality constraint means that all agents attending a meeting must schedule it at the same slot (constraint (1)). There is an *arrival-time* constraint between all variables/meetings belonging to the same agent. The arrival-time constraint between two variables m_i and m_j is defined as follows (equation [2.1]):

$$|m_i - m_j| - duration > TravellingTime(m_i, m_j), \qquad [2.1]$$

where $duration$ is the duration of every meeting. This arrival-time constraint allows us to express both constraints (2) and (3).

Figure 2.1 shows the instance of the meeting scheduling problem presented in Table 1.1 in its distributed form. This figure shows four agents where each agent has a personal private calendar and four meetings to be scheduled, each taking place in a specified location. The first meeting (m_1) will be attended by Alice and Med. Alice and Fred will participate on the second meeting (m_2). The agents who are going to attend the third meeting (m_3) are Fred and Med while the last meeting (m_4) will be attended by Adam, Fred and Med.

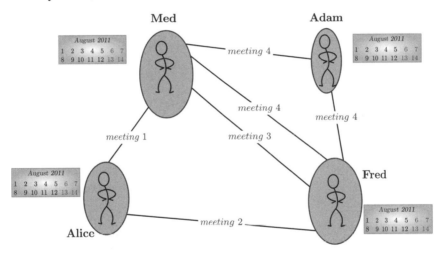

Figure 2.1. *A simple instance of the meeting scheduling problem*

We illustrate in Figure 2.2 the encoding of the instance of the meeting scheduling problem shown in Figure 2.1 in the DisCSP formalism. Thus, we get the following DisCSP:

– $\mathcal{A} = \{A_1,\ A_2,\ A_3,\ A_4\}$, each agent A_i corresponds to a real agent;

– For each agent $A_i \in \mathcal{A}$, there is a variable m_{ik} for every meeting m_k that A_i attends, $\mathcal{X} = \{m_{11},\ m_{13},\ m_{14},\ m_{21},\ m_{22},\ m_{32},\ m_{33},\ m_{34},\ m_{44}\}$;

– $\mathcal{D} = \{D(m_{ik}) \mid m_{ik} \in \mathcal{X}\}$, where:

- $D(m_{11}) = D(m_{13}) = D(m_{14}) = \{s \mid s \text{ is a slot in } calendar(A_1)\}$,

- $D(m_{21}) = D(m_{22}) = \{s \mid s \text{ is a slot in } calendar(A_2)\}$,

- $D(m_{32}) = D(m_{33}) = D(m_{34}) = \{s \mid s \text{ is a slot in } calendar(A_3)\}$,

- $D(m_{44}) = \{s \mid s \text{ is a slot in } calendar(A_4)\}$.

– For each agent A_i, there is a *private* arrival-time constraint (c^i_{kl}) between every pair of its local variables (m_{ik}, m_{il}). For each two agents A_i, A_j that attend the same meeting m_k there is an equality interagent constraint (c^{ij}_k) between the variables m_{ik} and m_{jk} corresponding to the meeting m_k on agent A_i and A_j. Then, $\mathcal{C} = \{c^i_{kl}, c^{ij}_k\}$.

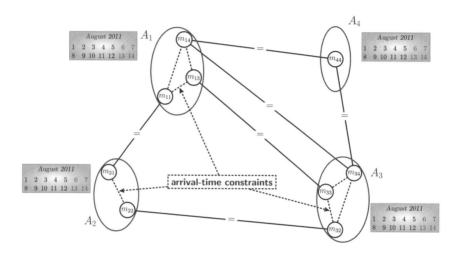

Figure 2.2. *The distributed meeting scheduling problem modeled as DisCSP*

2.1.4. *Distributed sensor network problem (SensorDCSP)*

The *distributed sensor network problem* (SensorDCSP) is a real distributed resource allocation problem [JUN 01, BÉJ 05]. This problem consists of a set of n stationary sensors, $\{s_1, \ldots, s_n\}$, and a set of m targets, $\{t_1, \ldots, t_m\}$, moving through their sensing range. The objective is to track each target by sensors. Thus, sensors have to cooperate for tracking all targets. In order for a target to be tracked accurately, at least three sensors must concurrently turn on overlapping sectors. This allows the target's position to be triangulated. However, each sensor can track at most one target. Hence, a solution is an assignment of three distinct sensors to each target. A solution must satisfy visibility and compatibility constraints. The visibility constraint defines the set of sensors to which a target is visible. The compatibility constraint defines the compatibility among sensors (sensors within the sensing range of each other).

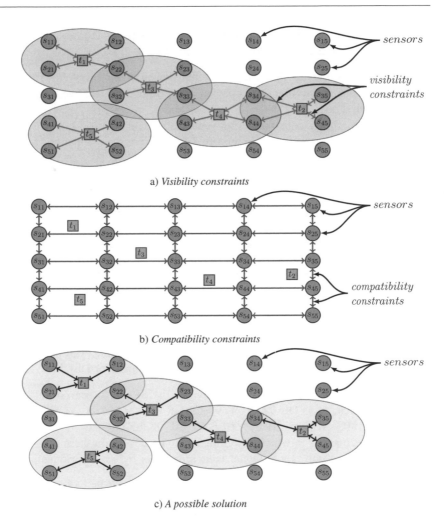

a) *Visibility constraints*

b) *Compatibility constraints*

c) *A possible solution*

Figure 2.3. *An instance of the distributed sensor network problem*

The SensorDCSP was formalized in [BÉJ 05] as follows:

- $S = \{s_1, \ldots, s_n\}$ is a set of n sensors;

- $T = \{t_1, \ldots, t_m\}$ is a set of m targets.

Each agent represents one target (i.e. $\mathcal{A} = T$). There are three variables per agent, one for each sensor that we need to allocate to the corresponding target. The domain of each variable is the set of sensors that can detect the corresponding target (the visibility constraint defines such sensors). The interagent constraints between the variables of one agent (target) specify that the three sensors assigned to the target must be distinct and pairwise compatible. The interagent constraints between the variables of different agents specify that a given sensor can be selected by at most one agent.

Figure 2.3 illustrates an instance of the SensorDCSP problem. This example includes 25 sensors (circular disks) placed on a grid of 5×5 and five targets (squares) to be tracked. Thus, $S = \{s_{11}, \ldots, s_{55}\}$ and $T = \{t_1, \ldots, t_5\}$. Figure 2.3(a) specifies the visibility constraints (between mobiles and sensors), that is, the set of sensors to which a target is visible. Figure 2.3(b) defines the compatibility constraints between sensors. Two sensors are compatible if and only if they are in sensing range of each other. A possible solution of this instance is shown in Figure 2.3(c).

2.2. Methods for solving DisCSPs

A trivial method for solving DisCSPs is to gather all information about the problem (i.e. the variables, their domains and the constraints) into a *leader* agent (i.e. system agent). Afterward, the leader agent can solve the problem alone by a centralized solver. Such a leader agent can be elected using a leader election algorithm. An example of a leader election algorithm was presented in [ABU 88]. However, the cost of gathering all information about a problem can be a major obstacle of such an approach. Moreover, for security/privacy reasons, gathering the whole knowledge into a centralized agent may be undesirable or impossible in some applications. Thus, a decentralized solver is more adequate for DisCSPs.

Several distributed algorithms for solving DisCSPs have been developed in the last two decades, to [YOK 92, YOK 95a, YOK 95b, HAM 98, YOK 98, BES 01b, MEI 02a, BRI 03, MEI 03, BRI 04, BES 05, SIL 05, EZZ 09], to mention only a few. Regarding the manner in which assignments are processed on these algorithms, they can be categorized into synchronous, asynchronous or hybrid algorithms.

In synchronous search algorithms for solving DisCSPs, agents assign their variables sequentially. Synchronous algorithms are based on notion of token, that is the privilege of assigning the variable. The token is passed among agents in synchronous algorithms, and then only the agent holding the token is activated while the rest of the agents are waiting. Thus, an agent can assign its variable only when it holds the token. Although synchronous algorithms do not exploit the parallelism inherent from the distributed system, their agents receive consistent information from each other.

In the asynchronous search algorithms, agents act concurrently and asynchronously without any global control. Hence, all agents are activated and then have the privilege of assigning their variables asynchronously. Asynchronous algorithms are executed autonomously by each agent in the distributed problem where agents do not need to wait for decisions of other agents. Thus, agents take advantage of the distributed formalism to enhance the degree of concurrency. However, in asynchronous algorithms, the global assignment state at any particular agent is, in general, inconsistent.

2.2.1. *Synchronous search algorithms on DisCSPs*

Synchronous backtracking (SBT) is the simplest search algorithm for solving DisCSPs [YOK 00b]. SBT is a straightforward extension of the chronological backtracking algorithm for centralized CSPs (section 1.2.1.1). SBT requires a total order in which agents will be instantiated. Following this ordering, agents perform assignments sequentially and synchronously. Thus, SBT agents assign their variables one by one, recording their assignments on a data structure called the current partial assignment (CPA) (see definition 2.4). When an agent receives a CPA from its predecessor (i.e. the agent it succeeds in the agents ordering), it assigns its variable a value satisfying all the constraints it knows. If it succeeds in finding such a value, it extends the CPA by adding its assignment to it and passes it on to its successor (i.e. the agent it precedes in the agents ordering). When no value is possible for its variable, then it *backtracks* to its predecessor. In SBT, only the agent holding the CPA performs an assignment or a backtrack.

Zivan and Meisels [ZIV 03] proposed the *synchronous conflict-based backjumping* (SCBJ), a distributed version of the centralized (CBJ) algorithm [PRO 93] (see section 1.2.1.2). While SBT performs chronological backtracking, SCBJ performs backjumping. Each agent A_i keeps the conflict set (CS_i). When a wipeout occurs on its domain, a jump is performed to the closest variable in CS_i. The *backjumping* message will contain CS_i. When an agent receives a backjumping message, it discards its current value and updates its conflict set to be the union of its old conflict set and the one received from A_i.

Extending SBT, Meisels and Zivan [MEI 07] proposed the asynchronous forward checking (AFC) algorithm. Besides assigning variables sequentially as is done in SBT, agents in AFC perform forward checking (FC [HAR 80], see section 1.2.1.5) asynchronously. The key here is that each time an agent succeeds in extending the CPA (by assigning its variable), it sends the CPA to its successor and sends copies of this CPA to all agents connected to itself whose assignments are not yet on the CPA. When an agent receives a copy of the CPA, it performs the FC phase. In the FC phase, all inconsistent values with assignments on the received CPA are removed. The FC operation is performed asynchronously – where the name of the algorithm comes from. When an agent generates an empty domain as a result of a FC, it informs all agents with unassigned variables on the (inconsistent) CPA. Afterwards, only the agent that receives the CPA from its predecessor and is holding the inconsistent CPA will eventually backtrack. Hence, in AFC, backtracking is done sequentially, and at any given time there is only either one CPA or one backtrack message being sent in the network.

2.2.1.1. *Asynchronous forward checking*

The AFC is the standard synchronous search algorithm [MEI 07]. AFC processes only consistent partial assignments. These assignments are processed synchronously. In AFC, the state of the search process is represented by a data structure called CPA.

DEFINITION 2.4.– *A CPA is an ordered set of assignments* $\{[(x_1, v_1, t_1), \ldots, (x_i, v_i, t_i)] \mid x_1 \prec \cdots \prec x_i\}$. *Two CPAs are* compatible *if every common variable is assigned the same value in both CPAs.*

Each CPA is associated with a counter that is updated by each agent when it succeeds in assigning its variable onto the CPA. This counter, called *step counter* (SC), acts as a time stamp for the CPA. In the AFC algorithm, each agent stores the current assignments state of its higher priority agents on the AgentView. The AgentView of an agent $A_i \in \mathcal{A}$ has a form similar to a CPA. The AgentView contains a consistency flag, $AgentView.Consistent$, that represents whether the partial assignment it holds is consistent. The pseudo-code of AFC algorithm executed by a generic agent A_i is shown in algorithm 2.1.

Agent A_i starts the search by calling procedure AFC() in which it initializes counters to 0. Next, if A_i is the initializing agent IA (the first agent in the agent ordering $\mathcal{O}$), it initiates the search by calling procedure Assign() (line 2). Then, a loop considers the reception and the processing of the possible message types. Thus, agents wait for messages and then call the procedures dealing with the relevant type of message received.

When calling procedure Assign(), A_i tries to find an assignment consistent with its AgentView. If A_i fails to find a consistent assignment, it calls procedure Backtrack() (line 13). If A_i succeeds, it generates a CPA from its AgentView augmented by its assignment, increments the SC (lines 10-11) and then calls procedure SendCPA(CPA) (line 12). If the CPA includes all agents' assignments (A_i is the last agent in the ordering, line 14), A_i reports the CPA as a solution of the problem and marks the *end* flag *true* to stop the main loop (line 14). Otherwise, A_i sends forward the CPA to every agent whose assignments are not yet on the CPA (line 16). The next agent on the ordering (i.e. A_{i+1}) will receive the CPA in a *cpa* message and then will try to extend this CPA by assigning its variable on it (line 16). Other unassigned agents will receive the CPA, generated by A_i, in *fc_cpa* messages (line 17). Therefore, these agents will perform the FC phase asynchronously to check the consistency of the CPA within the *fc_cpa* messages.

Agent A_i calls procedure Backtrack() when it is holding the CPA in one of two cases. Either A_i cannot find a consistent assignment for its variable (line 13) or its AgentView is inconsistent and is found to be compatible with the received CPA (line 29). If A_i is the initializing agent IA, the problem is unsolvable. A_i then ends the search by marking the *end* flag *true* to stop the main loop and sending a *stp* message to all agents informing them that search has ended unsuccessfully (line 18). Other agents performing a backtrack operation, copy to their AgentView the shortest inconsistent partial assignment (line 20) and set its flag to *false*. Next, they send the AgentView back to the agent, which is the owner of the last variable in the inconsistent partial assignment (line 22).

Algorithm 2.1. *The AFC algorithm running by agent A_i*

---

procedure AFC()
01. $v_i \leftarrow empty$; $t_i \leftarrow 0$; $SC \leftarrow 0$; $end \leftarrow$ **false**; $AgentView.Consistent \leftarrow$ **true**;
02. **if** ($A_i = IA$) **then** Assign() ;
03. **while** ($\neg end$) **do**
04. $msg \leftarrow$ getMsg();
05.   **switch** ($msg.type$) **do**
06. cpa : ProcessCPA(msg); fc_cpa : ProcessFCCPA($msg.CPA$);
07. $back\_cpa$: ProcessCPA(msg); not_ok : ProcessNotOk($msg.CPA$);
08. stp : $end \leftarrow$ **true**;

procedure Assign()
09. **if** ($D(x_i) \neq \emptyset$) **then**
10. $v_i \leftarrow$ ChooseValue(); $t_i \leftarrow t_i + 1$;
11. $CPA \leftarrow \{AgentView \cup myAssig\}$; $CPA.SC \leftarrow AgentView.SC + 1$;
12.   SendCPA(CPA) ;
13. **else** Backtrack() ;

procedure SendCPA(CPA)
14. **if** (A_i is the last agent in $\mathcal{O}$) **then** $end \leftarrow$ **true**;   broadcastMsg: $stp(CPA)$;
15. **else**
16.   sendMsg: $cpa(CPA)$ **to** A_{i+1} ;   /* A_{i+1} is the agent next A_i */
17.   **foreach** ($A_k \succ A_{i+1}$) **do** sendMsg: $fc\_cpa(CPA)$ **to** A_k ;

procedure Backtrack()
18. **if** ($A_i = IA$) **then** $end \leftarrow$ **true**;   broadcastMsg: $stp()$;
19. **else**
20. $AgentView \leftarrow$ shortest inconsistent partial assignment ;
21. $AgentView.Consistent \leftarrow$ **false**;
22.   sendMsg: $back\_cpa(AgentView)$ **to** A_j ;   /* A_j denotes the last agent on AgentView */

procedure ProcessCPA(msg)
23. CheckConsistencyOfAgentView($msg.CPA$) ;
24. **if** ($AgentView.Consistent$) **then**
25.   **if** ($msg.Sender \succ x_i$) **then** store $msg.CPA$ as justification of v_i removal ;
26.   **else** UpdateAgentView($msg.CPA$) ;
27.   Assign() ;

procedure CheckConsistencyOfAgentView(CPA)
28. **if** ($\neg AgentView.Consistent$) **then**
29.   **if** ($AgentView \subseteq CPA$) **then** Backtrack() ;
30.   **else** $AgentView.Consistent \leftarrow$ **true** ;

procedure UpdateAgentView(CPA)
31. $AgentView \leftarrow CPA$; $AgentView.SC \leftarrow CPA.SC$;
32. **foreach** ($v \in D(x_i)$ such that $\neg$isConsistent(v, CPA)) **do**
33.   store the shortest inconsistent partial assignment as justification of v removal;

procedure ProcessFCCPA(CPA)
34. **if** ($CPA.SC > AgentView.SC$) **then**
35.   **if** ($\neg AgentView.Consistent$) **then**
36.   **if** ($\neg AgentView \subseteq CPA$) **then** $AgentView.Consistent \leftarrow$ **true** ;
37.   **if** ($AgentView.Consistent$) **then**
38.   UpdateAgentView(CPA) ;
39.   **if** ($D(x_i) = \emptyset$) **then** sendMsg: $not\_ok(CPA)$ **to** *unassigned agents on AgentView* ;

procedure ProcessNotOk(CPA)
40. **if** ($CPA \subseteq AgentView \vee (AgentView \not\subseteq CPA \wedge CPA.SC > AgentView.SC)$) **then**
41. $AgentView \leftarrow msg.CPA$;
42. $AgentView.Consistent \leftarrow$ **false** ;

Whenever it receives a *cpa* or a *back_cpa* messages, A_i calls procedure `ProcessCPA()`. A_i then checks the consistency of its AgentView (`CheckConsistencyOfAgentView` call, line 23). If the AgentView is not consistent and it is a subset of the received CPA, this means that A_i has to backtrack (line 29). If the AgentView is not consistent and not a subset of the received CPA, A_i marks its AgentView consistent by setting *AgentView.Consistent* flag to *true* (line 30). Afterward, A_i checks the consistency of its AgentView. If it is consistent, A_i calls procedure `Assign()` to assign its variable (line 27) once it removes its current value v_i storing the received CPA as a justification of its removal if the received message is a *back_cpa* message (line 25) or it updates its AgentView if the received message is a *cpa* message (line 26). When calling procedure `UpdateAgentView`, A_i sets its AgentView to the received CPA and the step counter of its AgentView to that associated with the received CPA (line 31). Then, A_i performs the FC to remove all values inconsistent with the received CPA from its domain (lines 32–33).

Whenever a *fc_cpa* message is received, A_i calls procedure `ProcessFCCPA`(*msg*) to process it. If the SC associated to the received CPA is less than or equal that of the AgentView, this message is ignored because it is obsolete. Otherwise, A_i sets its AgentView to be consistent, if it was not consistent, and it is not included in the received CPA (line 36). Afterward, A_i checks the consistency of its AgentView. If it is the case, it calls procedure `UpdateAgentView` to perform the FC (line 38). When an empty domain is generated as a result of the FC phase, A_i initiates a backtrack process by sending *not_ok* messages to all agents with unassigned variables on the (inconsistent) CPA (line 39). *not_ok* messages carry the shortest inconsistent partial assignment that caused the empty domain.

When an agent A_i receives the *not_ok* message (procedure `ProcessNotOk`(*msg*)), it checks the relevance of the CPA carried in the received message with its AgentView. If the received CPA is relevant, A_i replaces its AgentView with the content of the *not_ok* message and sets it to be inconsistent (lines 41–42)

In AFC, only the agent that receives the CPA from its predecessor can perform an assignment or a backtrack. Hence, at any given time there is only either one CPA or one backtrack message being sent in the network. Thus, due to the manner in which the backtrack operation is performed, AFC does not draw all the benefit it could from the asynchronism of the FC phase.

2.2.2. Asynchronous search algorithms on DisCSPs

Unlike synchronous search algorithms, in asynchronous search algorithms all agents are activated and then have the privilege of assigning their variable. Thus, these algorithms process assignments of agents asynchronously and concurrently. Several distributed asynchronous search algorithms for solving DisCSPs have been developed, among which asynchronous backtracking (ABT) is the important one.

2.2.2.1. *Asynchronous backtracking*

The first complete asynchronous search algorithm for solving DisCSPs is the ABT [YOK 92, YOK 00a, BES 05]. ABT is an asynchronous algorithm executed autonomously by each agent in the distributed problem. Agents do not have to wait for decisions of others but they are subject to a total (priority) order. Each agent tries to find an assignment satisfying the constraints with what is currently known from higher priority neighbors. When an agent assigns a value to its variable, the selected value is sent to lower priority neighbors. When no value is possible for a variable, the inconsistency is reported to higher agents in the form of a nogood (see definition 1.13). ABT computes a solution (or detects that no solution exists) in a finite time. To be complete, ABT requires a total ordering on agents. The total ordering on agents is static.

The required total ordering on agents in ABT provides a directed acyclic graph. Constraints are then directed according to the total order among agents. Hence, a direct link between each two constrained agents is established. ABT uses this structure between agents to perform the asynchronous search. Thus, the agent from which a link departs is the value-sending agent, and the agent to which the link arrives is the constraint-evaluating agent. The pseudo-code executed by a generic agent $A_i \in \mathcal{A}$ is presented in algorithm 2.2.

In ABT, each agent keeps some amount of local information about the global search, namely an AgentView and a NogoodStore. A generic agent, say A_i, stores in its AgentView the most up to date values that it believes are assigned to its higher priority neighbors. A_i stores in its NogoodStore nogoods justifying values' removal. Agents exchange the following types of messages (where A_i is the sender):

ok?: A_i informs a lower priority neighbor about its assignment.

ngd: A_i informs a higher priority neighbor of a new nogood.

adl: A_i requests a higher priority agent to set up a link.

stp: the problem is unsolvable because an empty nogood has been generated.

In the main procedure ABT(), each agent assigns a value to its variable and informs its lower neighbors agents (CheckAgentView call, line 2). Then, it loops for processing the received messages. (line 3–7). Procedure CheckAgentView checks if the current value (v_i) is consistent with AgentView. If v_i is inconsistent with assignments of higher priority neighbors, A_i tries to select a consistent value (ChooseValue call, line 9). During this process, some values from $D(x_i)$ may appear as inconsistent. Thus, nogoods justifying their removal are added to the NogoodStore of A_i (line 39). When two nogoods are possible for the same value, A_i selects the best nogood using the *highest possible lowest variable* heuristic [HIR 00, BES 05]. If a consistent value exists, it is returned and then assigned to x_i.

Next, A_i notifies all agents in $\Gamma^+(x_i)$ about its new assignment through *ok?* messages (line 11). Otherwise, A_i has to backtrack (procedure Backtrack() call, line 12).

Whenever A_i receives an *ok?* message, it processes it by calling procedure ProcessInfo(*msg*). The AgentView of A_i is updated (UpdateAgentView call, line 13) only if the received message contains an assignment more up to date than that already stored for the sender (line 16), and all nogoods become non-compatible when the AgentView of A_i is removed (line 18). Then, a consistent value for A_i is searched after the change in the AgentView (CheckAgentView call, line 14).

When every value of A_i is forbidden by its NogoodStore, procedure Backtrack() is called. In procedure Backtrack(), A_i resolves its nogoods, deriving a new nogood, *newNogood* (line 19). If *newNogood* is empty, the problem has no solution. A_i broadcasts the *stp* messages to all agents and terminates the execution (line 20). Otherwise, the new nogood is sent in an *ngd* message to the agent, say A_j, owning the variable appearing in its rhs (line 22). Then, the assignment of x_j is deleted from the AgentView (UpdateAgentView call, line 23). Finally, a new consistent value is selected (CheckAgentView call, line 24).

Whenever A_i receives an *ngd* message, procedure ResolveConflict is called. The nogood included in the *ngd* message is accepted only if its *lhs* is compatible with assignments on the AgentView of A_i. Next, A_i calls procedure CheckAddLink (line 26). In procedure CheckAddLink(), the assignments in the received nogood for variables not directly linked with A_i are taken to update the AgentView (line 32) and a request for a new link is sent to agents owning these variables (line 34). Next, the nogood is stored, acting as justification for removing the value on its *rhs* (line 27). A new consistent value for A_i is then searched for (CheckAgentView call, line 28) if the current value was removed by the received nogood. If the nogood is not compatible with the AgentView, it is discarded because it is obsolete. However, if the value of x_i was correct in the received nogood, A_i resends its assignment to the nogood sender by an *ok?* message (lines 29–30).

When a link request is received, A_i calls procedure AddLink(*msg*). Then, the sender is included in $\Gamma^+(x_i)$ (line 35). Afterward, A_i sends its assignment through an *ok?* message to the sender of the request if its value is different than that included in the received *msg* (line 36).

To be complete, ABT in its original version may request adding links between initially unrelated agents. Given the manner in which these links are set, Bessiere *et al.* [BES 05] proposed four versions of ABT that have all been proven to be complete. In this way, they rediscover already existing algorithms such as ABT [YOK 98] or distributed backtracking (DIBT) [HAM 98].

Algorithm 2.2. *The ABT algorithm running by agent A_i.*

procedure ABT()
01. $v_i \leftarrow empty$; $t_i \leftarrow 0$; $end \leftarrow$ **false**;
02. CheckAgentView();
03. **while** ($\neg end$) **do**
04. $msg \leftarrow$ getMsg();
05.   **switch** ($msg.type$) **do**
06. $ok?$: ProcessInfo(msg); ngd : ResolveConflict(msg);
07. adl : AddLink(msg); stp : $end \leftarrow$ **true**;

procedure CheckAgentView()
08. **if** ($\neg$isConsistent(v_i, $AgentView$)) **then**
09. $v_i \leftarrow$ ChooseValue();
10.   **if** ($v_i \neq$ empty) **then**
11.   **foreach** ($x_k \in \Gamma^+(x_i)$) **do** sendMsg: $ok?$($myAssig\langle x_i, v_i, t_i \rangle$) **to** A_k ;
12.   **else** Backtrack() ;

procedure ProcessInfo(msg)
13. UpdateAgentView($msg.Assig$) ;
14. CheckAgentView() ;

procedure UpdateAgentView($newAssig$)
15. **if** ($newAssig.tag > AgentView[j].tag$) **then**   /* $x_j \in newAssig$ */
16. $AgentView[j] \leftarrow newAssig$;
17. **foreach** ($ng \in myNogoodStore$) **do**
18.   **if** ($\neg$Compatible(lhs(ng), $AgentView$)) **then** remove($ng,myNogoodStore$) ;

procedure Backtrack()
19. $newNogood \leftarrow$ solve($myNogoodStore$) ;
20. **if** ($newNogood =$ empty) **then** $end \leftarrow$ **true**; sendMsg: $stp(system)$;
21. **else**
22.   sendMsg: $ngd(newNogood)$ **to** A_j ;   /* Let x_j denote the variable on rhs($newNogood$) */
23.   UpdateAgentView($x_j \leftarrow$ empty) ;
24.   CheckAgentView() ;

procedure ResolveConflict(msg)
25. **if** ($\neg$Compatible(lhs($msg.Nogood$), $AgentView$)) **then**
26.   CheckAddLink($msg.Nogood$);
27.   add($msg.Nogood, myNogoodStore$) ;
28.   CheckAgentView();
29. **else if** (rhs($msg.Nogood$).$Value = v_i$) **then**
30.   sendMsg: $ok?(myAssig)$ **to** $msg.Sender$;

procedure CheckAddLink($nogood$)
31. **foreach** ($x_j \in$ lhs($nogood$) $\setminus \Gamma^-(x_i)$) **do**
32.   add($x_j = v_j$, $AgentView$) ;
33. $\Gamma^-(x_i) \leftarrow \Gamma^-(x_i) \cup \{x_j\}$;
34.   sendMsg: $adl(x_j = v_j)$ **to** A_j ;

procedure AddLink(msg)
35. add($msg.Sender, \Gamma^+(x_i)$) ;
36. **if** ($v_i \neq msg.Assig.Value$) **then** sendMsg: $ok?(myAssig)$ **to** $msg.Sender$;

function ChooseValue()
37. **foreach** ($v \in D(x_i)$) **do**
38.   **if** (isConsistent($v, AgentView$)) **then return** v ;
39.   **else** store the best nogood for v ;
40. **return** empty;

ABT (*adding links during search*): in ABT, presented above, new links between unrelated agents may be added during the search. A link is requested by an agent when it receives an *ngd* message containing unrelated agents in the ordering. New links are permanent. These links are used to remove obsolete information stored by a given agent.

ABT_{all} (*adding links as preprocessing*): in ABT_{all}, all the potentially useful links are added during a preprocessing step. New links are permanent.

$ABT_{temp(k)}$ (*adding temporary links*): in $ABT_{temp(k)}$, unrelated agents may be requested to add a link between them. However, the added links are temporary. This idea was first introduced in [SIL 01d]. New links are kept only for a fixed number of messages (k). Hence, each added link is removed after exchanging k messages through it.

ABT_{not} (*no links*): in ABT_{not}, no more needs links to be complete. To achieve its completeness, it has only to remove obsolete information in finite time. Thus, all nogoods that could hypothetically become obsolete are forgotten after each backtrack.

Figure 2.4 illustrates an example of ABT algorithm's execution in a simple instance (Figure 2.4(a)). This instance includes three agents, each holding one variable (x_1, x_2 and x_3). Their domains are, respectively, $\{1,2\}$, $\{2\}$ and $\{1,2\}$. This instance includes two constraints $x_1 \neq x_3$ and $x_2 \neq x_3$. In Figure 2.4(b), by receiving *ok?* messages from x_1 and x_2, the AgentView of x_3 will be $[x_1 = 1, x_2 = 2]$. These assignments remove values 1 and 2 from $D(x_3)$ storing two nogoods as justification of their removal (i.e. $x_1=1 \rightarrow x_3 \neq 1$, respectively, $x_2=2 \rightarrow x_3 \neq 2$). Since there is no possible value consistent with its AgentView, agent x_3 resolves its nogoods producing a new nogood ($x_1=1 \rightarrow x_2 \neq 2$) (Figure 2.4(c)). This nogood is then sent to x_2 in *ngd* message. By receiving this *ngd* message, agent x_2 records this nogood. This nogood contains assignment of agent x_1, which is not connected to x_2 by a link to x_1. Therefore, agent x_2 requests a new link between itself and x_1 by sending an *adl* message (Figure 2.4(d)). Agent x_2 checks whether its value is consistent with its AgentView ($[x_1 = 1]$). Because its only value 2 is removed by the nogood received from x_3, agent x_2 resolves its NogoodStore producing a new nogood, $[] \rightarrow x_1 \neq 1$. This nogood is then sent to agent x_1 (Figure 2.4(e)). This nogood will lead x_1 to change its current value to 1, and henceforth, it will send its assignment on an *ok?* message to both agents x_2 and x_3. Simultaneously, agent x_2 assigns its variable and then sends its assignment to its lower priority neighbor x_3. Hence, we get the situation shown in Figure 2.4(f).

2.2.3. *Dynamic ordering heuristics on DisCSPs*

In algorithms presented above for solving DisCSPs, the total ordering on agents is static. Therefore, a single mistake on the order is very penalizable. Moreover, it is known from centralized CSPs that dynamic reordering of variables during a search drastically fastens the search procedure (see section 1.2.2.2). Many attempts were made to apply this principle for improving distributed constraint satisfaction algorithms.

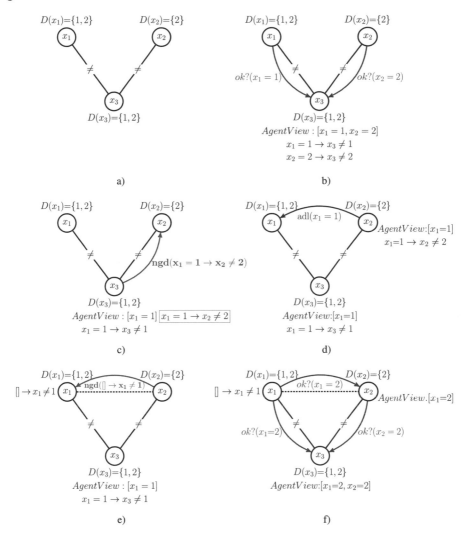

Figure 2.4. *An example of asynchronous backtracking execution*

The first reordering algorithm for DisCSP is the asynchronous weak commitment (AWC) [YOK 95a]. AWC dynamically reorders agents during search by moving the sender of a nogood higher in the order than the other agents in the nogood. Whenever a wipeout occurs on the domain of a variable x_i, the total agent ordering is revised so as to assign the highest priority to the agent x_i. AWC was shown to outperform ABT empirically on small problems. However, contrary to ABT, AWC requires an exponential space for storing all generated nogoods.

Silaghi *et al.* [SIL 01c] later proposed asynchronous backtracking with reordering (ABTR) an attempt to hybridize ABT with AWC. Abstract agents fulfill the reordering operation to guarantee a finite number of asynchronous reordering operations. ABTR is the first asynchronous complete algorithm with polynomial space requirements that enables the largest number of reordering heuristics in an asynchronous search. However, to achieve this, the position of first agent on the ordering must be fixed. A dynamic variable reordering heuristic for ABTR that exactly imitates the heuristic employed in centralized dynamic backtracking [GIN 93] and that requires no exchange of heuristic messages was presented in [SIL 06].

Zivan and Meisels [ZIV 06a] proposed dynamic ordering for asynchronous backtracking (ABT_DO aka ABTR). ABT_DO is a simple dynamic ordering algorithm in ABT search. Agents choose orders dynamically and asynchronously while keeping space complexity polynomial. When an ABT_DO agent changes its assignment, it can reorder all agents with lower priority. Zivan and Meisels proposed three different ordering heuristics in ABT_DO. In the best of those heuristics called *Nogood-triggered heuristic*, inspired by dynamic backtracking [GIN 93], the agent that generates a nogood is placed in front of all other lower priority agents.

A new kind of ordering heuristics for ABT_DO is presented in [ZIV 09]. These heuristics, called retroactive heuristics, enable the generator of the nogood to be moved to a higher position than that of the target of the backtrack. The degree of flexibility of these retroactive heuristics depends on a parameter K. K defines the level of flexibility of the heuristic with respect to the amount of information an agent can store in its memory. Agents that detect a dead-end move themselves to a higher priority position in the order. If the length of the nogood generated is not larger than K, the agent can move to any position it desires (even to the highest priority position) and all agents that are included in the nogood are required to add the nogood to their set of constraints and hold it until the algorithm terminates. Because agents must store nogoods that are smaller than or equal to K, the space complexity of agents is exponential in K. If the size of the generated nogood is larger than K, the agent that generated the nogood can move up to the place that is right after the second to last agent in the nogood.

The best retroactive heuristic introduced in [ZIV 09] is called ABT_DO-Retro-MinDom. This heuristic does not require any additional storage (i.e. $K = 0$). In this heuristic, the agent that generates a nogood is placed in the new order between the last and the second to last agents in the generated nogood. However, the generator of the nogood moves to a higher priority position than the backtracking target (the agent the nogood was sent to) only if its domain is smaller than that of the agents it passes on the way up. Otherwise, the generator of the nogood is placed right after the last agent with a smaller domain between the last and the second to last agents in the nogood.

2.2.4. *Maintaining arc consistency on DisCSPs*

Although its success for solving centralized CSPs was empirically demonstrated, the maintenance of arc consistency (MAC) has not yet been well investigated in DisCSPs. Silaghi *et al.* [SIL 01b] introduced the distributed maintaining asynchronously consistency for ABT (DMAC-ABT); the first algorithm able to maintain arc consistency in DisCSPs. DMAC-ABT considers consistency maintenance as a hierarchical nogood-based inference. However, the improvement obtained on ABT was minor.

Brito and Meseguer [BRI 08] proposed ABT-uac and ABT-dac, two algorithms that connect ABT with arc consistency. The first algorithm they proposed, ABT-uac, propagates unconditionally deleted values (i.e. values removed by a nogood having an empty left-hand side) to enforce an amount of full arc consistency. The intuitive idea behind ABT-uac is that, because unconditionally deleted values are removed once and for all, their propagation may cause new deletions in the domains of other variables. Thus, the search effort required to solve the DisCSP can be reduced. The second algorithm they proposed, ABT-dac, extends the first algorithm in order to propagate conditionally and unconditionally deleted values using directional arc consistency. ABT-uac shows minor improvement in communication load and ABT-dac is harmful in many instances.

2.3. Summary

In this chapter, we have formally defined the DisCSP framework. Some examples of real-world applications have been presented and then encoded in DisCSP. Finally, the state-of-the-art methods for solving DisCSPs have been provided.

PART 2

Synchronous Search Algorithms for DisCSPs

3

Nogood-based Asynchronous Forward Checking (AFC-ng)

This chapter introduces a synchronous algorithm for solving distributed constraint satisfaction problems (DisCSPs). This algorithm is a nogood-based version of asynchronous forward checking (AFC) [WAH 13]. Hence, it is called nogood-based asynchronous forward checking (AFC-ng). Besides its use of nogoods as justification of value removal, AFC-ng allows simultaneous backtracks going from different agents to different destinations. AFC-ng only needs polynomial space. The performance of AFC-ng is demonstrated with respect to other DisCSP algorithms on random DisCSPs and instances from real benchmarks: sensor networks and distributed meeting scheduling.

3.1. Introduction

As seen in section 2.2.1, AFC incorporates the idea of the forward-checking (FC) algorithm for centralized CSPs [HAR 80] into a distributed synchronous search procedure. However, agents perform the FC phase asynchronously [MEI 03, MEI 07]. As in synchronous backtracking, agents assign their variables only when they hold the current partial assignment (*cpa*). The *cpa* is a unique message (token) passed from one agent to another in the ordering. The *cpa* message carries the partial assignment (CPA) that agents try to extend into a complete solution by assigning their variables to it. When an agent succeeds in assigning its variable to the CPA, it sends this CPA to its successor. Furthermore, copies of the CPA are sent to all agents whose assignments are not yet on the CPA. These agents perform the FC asynchronously in order to detect inconsistent partial assignments as early as possible. The FC process is performed as follows. When an agent receives a CPA, it updates the domain of its variable, removing all values that are in conflict with assignments on the received CPA. Furthermore, the shortest CPA producing the inconsistency is stored as justification of the value deletion.

When an agent generates an empty domain as a result of an FC, it initiates a backtrack process by sending *not_ok* messages. *not_ok* messages carry the shortest inconsistent partial assignments which cause the empty domain. *not_ok* messages are sent to all agents with unassigned variables on the (inconsistent) CPA. When an agent receives the *not_ok* message, it checks if the CPA carried in the received message is compatible with its AgentView. If it is the case, the receiver stores the *not_ok*; otherwise, the *not_ok* is discarded. When an agent holding a *not_ok* receives a CPA on a *cpa* message from its predecessor, it sends this CPA back in a *back_cpa* message. When multiple agents reject a given assignment by sending *not_ok* messages, only the first agent that receives a *cpa* message from its predecessor and is holding a relevant *not_ok* message will finally backtrack. After receiving a new *cpa* message, the *not_ok* message becomes obsolete when the CPA it carries is no longer a subset of the received CPA.

The manner in which the backtrack operation is performed is a major drawback of the AFC algorithm. The backtrack operation requires a lot of work on the part of the agents. In addition, the backtrack is performed synchronously, and at any time, there is only either one *cpa* or one *back_cpa* message being sent in the network.

In [NGU 05], Nguyen *et al.* proposed distributed backjumping (DBJ), an improved version of the basic AFC that addresses its backtrack operation. In DBJ, the agent who detects the empty domain can itself perform the backtrack operation by backjumping directly to the culprit agent. It sends a backtrack message to the last agent assigned in the inconsistent CPA. The agent who receives a backtrack message generates a new CPA that will dominate older ones due to a time stamp mechanism. DBJ still sends the inconsistent CPA to unassigned agents on it. DBJ does not use nogoods for justification of value removal. Consequently, DBJ only mimics the simple *Backjumping* (BJ) [GAS 78] although the authors report on performing the graph-based backjumping (GBJ) [DEC 90][1]. Section 3.2.2 illustrates through an example that DBJ does not perform GBJ but only BJ. In the same work, Nguyen *et al.* presented the dynamic distributed backjumping (DDBJ) algorithm. DDBJ is an improvement of the DBJ that integrates heuristics for dynamic variable and value ordering, called the *possible conflict heuristics*. However, DDBJ requires additional messages to compute the dynamic ordering heuristics.

We present in this chapter the AFC-ng, an algorithm for solving DisCSPs based on AFC. Instead of using the shortest inconsistent partial assignments, we use nogoods as justification of value removal. Unlike the AFC, AFC-ng allows concurrent backtracks to be performed at the same time, coming from different agents having an empty domain to different destinations. As a result, several CPAs could be generated simultaneously by the destination agents. Because of the time stamps integrated into the CPAs, the *strongest* CPA coming from the highest level in

---

1 BJ cannot execute two "jumps" in a row, only performing steps back after a jump, whereas GBJ can perform sequences of consecutive jumps.

the agent ordering will finally dominate all others. Interestingly, the search process with the strongest CPA will benefit from the computational effort done by the (killed) lower-level processes. Concretely, a strongest CPA will take advantage from nogoods recorded when processing these killed lower-level processes to avoid the thrashing problem (see section 1.2.1.1).

3.2. Nogood-based asynchronous forward checking

The AFC-ng is based on the AFC. AFC-ng tries to enhance the asynchronism of the FC phase. The two main features of AFC-ng are the following. First, it uses the nogoods as justification of value deletion. Each time an agent performs an FC, it revises its *initial domain* (including values already removed by a stored nogood) in order to store the best nogoods for removed values (one nogood per value). When comparing two nogoods eliminating the same value, the nogood with the *highest possible lowest variable* involved is selected (HPLV heuristic) [HIR 00]. As a result, when an empty domain is found, the resolvent nogood contains variables as high as possible in the ordering so that the backtrack message is sent as high as possible, thus saving unnecessary search effort [BES 05].

Second, each time an agent A_i generates an empty domain, it no longer sends *not_ok* messages. It resolves the nogoods ruling out values from its domain, producing a new nogood $newNogood$. The $newNogood$ is the conjunction of the left-hand sides of all nogoods stored by A_i. Then, A_i sends the resolved nogood $newNogood$ in an ngd (backtrack) message to the lowest agent in $newNogood$. Hence, multiple backtracks may be performed at the same time, coming from different agents having an empty domain. These backtracks are sent concurrently by these different agents to different destinations. The reassignment of the destination agents then happens simultaneously and generates several CPAs. However, the strongest CPA coming from the highest level in the agent ordering will finally dominate all others. Agents use the time stamp (see definition 3.1) to detect the strongest CPA. Interestingly, the search process of higher levels with stronger CPAs can use nogoods reported by the (killed) lower-level processes so that it benefits from their computational effort.

3.2.1. *Description of the algorithm*

In the AFC, only the agent holding the CPA (definition 2.4) can perform an assignment or backtracking. To enhance the asynchronism of the FC phase, unlike the AFC, the AFC-ng algorithm allows simultaneous backtracks going from different agents to different destinations. The reassignments of the destination agents then happen simultaneously and generate several CPAs. For allowing agents to simultaneously propose new CPAs, they must be able to decide which CPA to select. We propose that the priority between the CPAs is based on *time stamp*.

DEFINITION 3.1.– *A time stamp associated with a CPA is an ordered list of counters* $[t_1, t_2, \ldots, t_i]$ *where* t_j *is the tag of the variable* x_j. *When comparing two CPAs, the strongest CPA is the one that is associated with the lexicographically greater time stamp i.e., the CPA with the greatest value on the first counter on which they differ, if any, otherwise the longest one.*

Based on the time stamp associated with each CPA, now agents can detect the strongest CPA. Therefore, the strongest CPA coming from the highest level in the agent ordering will finally dominate all others.

Each agent $A_i \in \mathcal{A}$ executes the pseudo-code as shown in algorithm 3.1. Agent A_i stores a nogood per removed value in the NogoodStore. The other values that are not removed by a nogood form the current domain of x_i ($D(x_i)$). Moreover, A_i keeps an AgentView that stores the most up-to-date assignments received from the higher priority agents. It has a form similar to the CPA (see, definition 2.4) and is initialized to the set of empty assignments $\{(x_j, empty, 0) \mid x_j \prec x_i\}$.

Agent A_i starts the search by calling procedure AFC-ng() in which it initializes its AgentView (line 1) by setting counters to zero (line 8). The AgentView contains a consistency flag that represents whether the partial assignment it holds is consistent. If A_i is the initializing agent IA (the first agent in the agent ordering), it initiates the search by calling procedure Assign() (line 2). Then, a loop considers the reception and the processing of the possible message types (lines 3–7). In AFC-ng, agents exchange the following types of messages (where A_i is the sender):

cpa: A_i passes on the CPA to a lower priority agent. According to its position on the ordering, the receiver will try to extend the CPA (when it is the next agent on the ordering) or perform the FC phase.

ngd: A_i reports the inconsistency to a higher priority agent. The inconsistency is reported by a nogood.

stp: A_i informs agents either if a solution is found or the problem is unsolvable.

When calling Assign(), A_i tries to find an assignment, which is consistent with its AgentView. If A_i fails to find a consistent assignment, it calls procedure Backtrack() (line 13). If A_i succeeds, it increments its counter t_i and generates a CPA from its AgentView augmented by its assignment (line 11). Afterward, A_i calls procedure SendCPA(CPA) (line 12). If the CPA includes all agents assignments (A_i is the lowest agent in the order, line 14), A_i reports the CPA as a solution of the problem and marks the *end* flag true to stop the main loop (line 15). Otherwise, A_i sends forward the CPA to every agent whose assignments are not yet on the CPA (line 17). So, the next agent on the ordering (successor) will try to extend this CPA by assigning its variable to it, while other agents will perform the FC phase asynchronously to check its consistency.

Algorithm 3.1. *AFC-ng algorithm running by agent* A_i

procedure AFC-ng()
01. $end \leftarrow$ **false**; $AgentView.Consistent \leftarrow$ **true**; InitAgentView();
02.   **if** ($A_i = IA$) **then** Assign() ;
03.   **while** ($\neg end$) **do**
04. $msg \leftarrow$ getMsg();
05.   **switch** ($msg.type$) **do**
06.   **cpa** : ProcessCPA(msg);   **ngd** : ProcessNogood(msg);
07.   **stp** : $end \leftarrow$ **true**;

procedure InitAgentView()
08.   **foreach** ($x_j \prec x_i$) **do** $AgentView[j] \leftarrow \{(x_j, empty, 0)\}$;

procedure Assign()
09.   **if** ($D(x_i) \neq \emptyset$) **then**
10. $v_i \leftarrow$ ChooseValue() ; $t_i \leftarrow t_i + 1$;
11. $CPA \leftarrow \{AgentView \cup myAssig\}$;
12.   SendCPA(CPA) ;
13.   **else** Backtrack() ;

procedure SendCPA(CPA)
14.   **if** ($size(CPA) = n$) **then**   /* A_i is the last agent in $\mathcal{O}$ */
15.   broadcastMsg: $stp(CPA)$; $end \leftarrow$ **true**
16.   **else**
17.   **foreach** ($x_k \succ x_i$) **do** sendMsg : $cpa(CPA)$ **to** A_k ;

procedure ProcessCPA(msg)
18.   **if** ($\neg AgentView.Consistent \wedge AgentView \subset msg.CPA$) **then** **return** ;
19.   **if** ($msg.CPA$ is stronger than $AgentView$) **then**
20.   UpdateAgentView($msg.CPA$) ; $AgentView.Consistent \leftarrow$ **true**;
21.   Revise();
22.   **if** ($D(x_i) = \emptyset$) **then** Backtrack() ;
23.   **else** CheckAssign($msg.Sender$) ;

procedure CheckAssign($sender$)
24.   **if** ($A_{i-1} = sender$) **then** Assign() ;   /* the $sender$ is the predecessor of A_i */

procedure Backtrack()
25. $newNogood \leftarrow$ solve($myNogoodStore$) ;
26.   **if** ($newNogood =$ empty) **then** broadcastMsg: $stp(\emptyset)$; $end \leftarrow$ **true**;
27.   **else**
28.   sendMsg : $ngd(newNogood)$ **to** A_j ;   /* x_j denotes the variable on rhs ($newNogood$) */
29.   **foreach** ($x_k \succ x_j$) **do** $AgentView[k].value \leftarrow empty$;
30.   **foreach** ($ng \in NogoodStore$) **do**
31.   **if** ($\neg$Compatible($ng, AgentView$) $\vee$ $x_j \in ng$) **then** remove($ng, myNogoodStore$) ;
32. $AgentView.Consistent \leftarrow$ **false**; $v_i \leftarrow empty$;

procedure ProcessNogood(msg)
33.   **if** (Compatible($msg.Nogood, AgentView$)) **then**
34.   add($msg.nogood, NogoodStore$) ;   /* according to the HPLV */
35.   **if** (rhs($msg.nogood$).$Value = v_i$) **then** $v_i \leftarrow empty$; Assign() ;

procedure Revise()
36.   **foreach** ($v \in D^0(x_i)$) **do**
37.   **if** ($\neg$isConsistent($v, AgentView$)) **then** store the best nogood for v ;

procedure UpdateAgentView(CPA)
38. $AgentView \leftarrow CPA$;   /* update values and tags */
39.   **foreach** (($ng \in myNogoodStore$)) **do**
40.   **if** ($\neg$Compatible($ng, AgentView$)) **then** remove($ng, myNogoodStore$) ;

Whenever A_i receives a *cpa* message, procedure ProcessCPA(*msg*) is called (line 6). A_i checks its AgentView status. If it is not consistent and the AgentView is a subset of the received CPA, meaning that A_i has already backtracked, then A_i does nothing (line 18). Otherwise, if the received CPA is stronger than its AgentView, A_i updates its AgentView and marks it as consistent (lines 19–20). Procedure UpdateAgentView(CPA) (lines 38–40) sets the AgentView and the NogoodStore to be consistent with the received CPA. Each nogood in the NogoodStore containing a value for a variable different from that on the received CPA will be deleted (line 40). Next, A_i calls procedure Revise() (line 21) to store nogoods for values inconsistent with the new AgentView or to try to find a better nogood for values already having one in the NogoodStore (line 37). A nogood is better according to the *HPLV* heuristic if the lowest variable in the body (lhs) of the nogood is higher. If A_i generates an empty domain as a result of calling Revise(), it calls procedure Backtrack() (line 22); otherwise, A_i calls procedure CheckAssign(*sender*) to check if it has to assign its variable (line 23). In CheckAssign(*sender*), A_i calls procedure Assign to try to assign its variable only if sender is the predecessor of A_i (i.e., CPA was received from the predecessor, line 24).

When every value of A_i's variable is ruled out by a nogood (line 22), the procedure Backtrack() is called. These nogoods are resolved by computing a new nogood *newNogood* (line 25). The *newNogood* is the conjunction of the left-hand sides of all nogoods stored by A_i in its NogoodStore. If the new nogood (*newNogood*) is empty, A_i terminates execution after sending an *stp* message to all agents in the system, meaning that the problem is unsolvable (line 26). Otherwise, A_i backtracks by sending one *ngd* message to the agent owner of the variable on the right-hand side (rhs) of *newNogood*, say A_j, (line 28). The *ngd* message carries the generated nogood (*newNogood*). Next, A_i updates its AgentView by removing assignments of every agent that is placed after the agent A_j owner of rhs(*newNogood*) in the total order (line 29). A_i also updates its NogoodStore by removing obsolete nogoods (line 31). Obsolete nogoods are nogoods that are inconsistent with the AgentView or contain the assignment of x_j, that is the variable on the rhs of *newNogood*, (line 31). Finally, A_i marks its AgentView as inconsistent and removes its last assignment (line 32). A_i remains in an inconsistent state until receiving a stronger CPA holding at least one agent assignment with counter higher than that in the AgentView of A_i.

When an *ngd* message is received by an agent A_i, it checks the validity of the received nogood (line 33). If the received nogood is consistent with the AgentView, this nogood is a valid justification for removing the value on its rhs. Then if the value on the rhs of the received nogood is already removed, A_i adds the received nogood to its NogoodStore if it is better (according to the HPLV heuristic [HIR 00]) than the current stored nogood. If the value on the rhs of the received nogood belongs to the current domain of x_i, A_i simply adds it to its NogoodStore. If the value on the rhs of the received nogood equals v_i, the current value of A_i, A_i dis-instantiates its variable and calls the procedure Assign() (line 35).

Whenever an *stp* message is received, A_i marks *end* flag true to stop the main loop (line 7). If the CPA attached to the received message is empty, then there is no solution. Otherwise, the solution of the problem is retrieved from the CPA.

3.2.2. *A simple example of the backtrack operation on AFC-like algorithms*

Figure 3.1 illustrates the backtrack operation on AFC, DBJ and AFC-ng when detecting a dead-end. Figure 3.1a) shows a simple instance of a DisCSP containing 20 agents $\mathcal{X} = \{x_1, \ldots, x_{20}\}$. The domains of x_1, x_2, x_{10}, x_{15} are $D^0(x_1) = \{a, f\}$, $D^0(x_2) = \{a, b\}$, $D^0(x_{10}) = D(x_{15}) = \{a, b, c\}$; the others can be anything. The constraints are $x_1 \neq x_2$, $x_1 \neq x_{10}$, $x_1 \neq x_{15}$, $x_2 \neq x_{10}$, $x_2 \neq x_{15}$. Let us assume that the ordering of agents is the lexicographic ordering $[x_1, \ldots, x_{20}]$. Assume also that when trying to solve this instance, the algorithms, that is AFC, DBJ and AFC-ng, fall into the same situation as shown in Figure 3.1(b). Agent x_1 assigns value a from its domain, and then x_2 removes value a from its domain and assigns value b (i.e. $x_2 = b$) when receiving the *cpa* from x_1. When receiving the CPA from x_2, agent x_{10} (respectively, x_{15}) removes values a and b from $D(x_{10})$ (respectively, $D(x_{15})$) because of constraints connecting x_{10} (respectively, x_{15}) to x_1 and x_2. Assume that agents x_3 to x_9 assign values successfully. When agent x_{10} receives the CPA from x_9, it assigns the last value in $D(x_{10})$, that is $x_{10} = c$. Agent x_{10} sends the CPA to x_{11} and copies to the lower neighbors (including x_{15}). When receiving this copy of the CPA, x_{15} removes the last value from its domain generating a dead-end (Figure 3.1(b)).

Compared with this situation of dead-end, AFC, DBJ and AFC-ng behave differently. In AFC (Figure 3.1(c)), agent x_{15} sends *not_ok* messages to unassigned agents (i.e. $[x_{11}, \ldots, x_{20}]$) informing them that the CPA $[x_1 = a, x_2 = b, \ldots, x_{10} = c]$ is inconsistent. Only the agent who will receive the CPA from its predecessor when holding this *not_ok* (i.e. one among $x_{11}, .., x_{14}$) will send the backtrack to x_{10}. In DBJ (Figure 3.1(d)), agent x_{15} backtracks directly to x_{10} and informs unassigned agents (i.e. $[x_{11}, \ldots, x_{20}]$) that the CPA $[x_1 = a, x_2 = b, \ldots, x_{10} = c]$ is inconsistent. In AFC-ng (Figure 3.1(e)), when agent x_{15} produces an empty domain after receiving the copy of the CPA from x_{10}, it resolves the nogoods from its NogoodStore (i.e. $[x_1 = a \rightarrow x_{15} \neq a]$, $[x_2 = b \rightarrow x_{15} \neq b]$ and $[x_{10} = c \rightarrow x_{15} \neq c]$). The resolved nogood $[x_1 = a \wedge x_2 = b \rightarrow x_{10} \neq c]$ is sent to agent x_{10} in an *ngd* message. In AFC-ng, we do not inform unassigned agents about the inconsistency of the CPA.

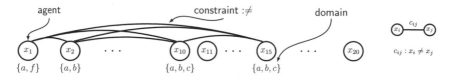

a) *A simple example of a DisCSP containing 20 agents*

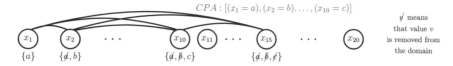

b) *The dead-end occurs on the domain of x_{15} after receiving the cpa $[(x_1 = a), (x_2 = b), \ldots, (x_{10} = c)]$*

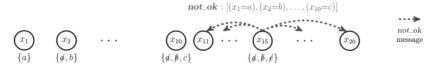

c) *In AFC, agent x_{15} initiates the backtrack operation by sending not_ok to unassigned agents*

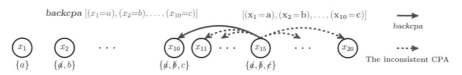

d) *In DBJ, agent x_{15} initiates the backtrack operation by sending the inconsistent CPA to unassigned agents and a back_cpa to agent x_{10}*

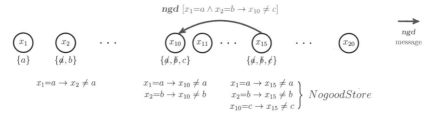

e) *In AFC-ng, agent x_{15} backtracks by sending a ngd to agent x_{10}*

Figure 3.1. *The backtrack operation on AFC, DBJ and AFC-ng using a simple example*

We are now in a situation where in all three algorithms AFC, DBJ and AFC-ng, x_{10} has received a backtrack message. After receiving the backtrack, x_{10} removes the last value, that is c, from $D(x_{10})$ and needs to backtrack. In AFC and DBJ, x_{10} backtracks to x_9. We see that the backjump to x_{10} is followed by a backtrack step, as done by BJ in the centralized case, because BJ does not remember who the other culprits of the initial backjump were [GAS 78]. In AFC-ng, when x_{10} receives the backtrack from x_{15}, it removes value c and stores the received nogood as justification of its removal (i.e. $[x_1=a \land x_2=b \rightarrow x_{10} \neq c]$). After removing this last value, x_{10} resolves its nogoods, generating a new nogood $[x_1=a \rightarrow x_2 \neq b]$. Thus, x_{10} backtracks to x_2. We see that a new backjump follows the one to x_{10}. AFC-ng mimics the conflict-directed backjumping (CBJ) technique of the centralized case [PRO 93], which always jumps to the causes of the conflicts.

3.3. Correctness proofs

THEOREM 3.1.– The spatial complexity of AFC-ng is polynomially bounded by $O(nd)$ per agent.

PROOF.– In AFC-ng, the size of nogoods is bounded by n, the total number of variables. Now, on each agent, AFC-ng only stores one nogood per removed value. Thus, the space complexity of AFC-ng is in $O(nd)$ on each agent.

LEMMA 3.1.– AFC-ng is guaranteed to terminate.

PROOF.– We prove by induction on the agent ordering that there will be a finite number of new generated CPAs (at most d^n, where d is the size of the initial domain and n is the number of variables), and that agents can never fall into an infinite loop for a given CPA. The base case for induction ($i = 1$) is obvious. The only messages that x_1 can receive are ngd messages. All nogoods contained in these ngd messages have an empty left-hand side (lhs). Hence, values on their rhs are removed once and for all from the domain of x_1. Now, x_1 only generates a new CPA when it receives a nogood ruling out its current value. Thus, the maximal number of CPAs that x_1 can generate equals the size of its initial domain (d). Suppose that the number of CPAs that agents $x_1, \ldots, x_{i-1}$ can generate is finite (and bounded by d^{i-1}). Given such a CPA on $[x_1, \ldots, x_{i-1}]$, x_i generates new CPAs (line 11, algorithm 3.1) only when it changes its assignment after receiving a nogood ruling out its current value v_i. Given that any received nogood can include, in its lhs, only the assignments of higher priority agents ($[x_1, \ldots, x_{i-1}]$), this nogood will remain valid as long as the CPA on $[x_1, \ldots, x_{i-1}]$ does not change. Thus, x_i cannot regenerate a new CPA containing v_i without changing an assignment of a higher priority agent on ($[x_1, \ldots, x_{i-1}]$). Because there are a finite number of values on the domain of variable x_i, there will be a finite number of new CPAs generated by x_i (d^i). Therefore, by induction we have that there will be a finite number of new CPAs (d^n) generated by the AFC-ng.

Let cpa be the strongest CPA generated in the network and A_i be the agent that generated cpa. After a finite amount of time, all unassigned agents on cpa ($[x_{i+1}, \ldots, x_n]$) will receive cpa and thus will discard all other CPAs. Two cases occur. In the first case, at least one agent detects a dead-end and thus backtracks to an agent A_j included in cpa (i.e. $j \leq i$) forcing it to change its current value on cpa and to generate a new stronger CPA. In the second case (no agent detects a dead-end), if $i < n$, A_{i+1} generates a new stronger CPA by adding its assignment to cpa, else ($i = n$), a solution is reported. As a result, agents can never fall into an infinite loop for a given CPA and AFC-ng is thus guaranteed to terminate.

LEMMA 3.2.– AFC-ng cannot infer inconsistency if a solution exists.

PROOF.– Whenever a stronger CPA or an ngd message is received, AFC-ng agents update their NogoodStore. Hence, for every CPA that may potentially lead to a solution, agents only store valid nogoods. In addition, every nogood resulting from a CPA is redundant with regard to the DisCSP to solve. Because all additional nogoods are generated by logical inference when a domain wipeout occurs, the empty nogood cannot be inferred if the network is solvable. This means that AFC-ng is able to produce all solutions.

THEOREM 3.2.– AFC-ng is correct.

PROOF.– The argument for soundness is close to the one given in [MEI 07, NGU 04]. The fact that agents only forward consistent partial solutions in the CPA messages at only one place in procedure Assign() (line 11, algorithm 3.1) implies that the agents receive only consistent assignments. A solution is reported by the last agent only in procedure SendCPA(CPA) in line 15. At this point, all agents have assigned their variables, and their assignments are consistent. Thus, the AFC-ng algorithm is sound. Completeness comes from the fact that AFC-ng is able to terminate and does not report inconsistency if a solution exists (lemmas 3.1 and 3.2).

3.4. Experimental evaluation

In this section, we experimentally compare AFC-ng with two other algorithms: AFC [MEI 07] and asynchronous backtracking (ABT) [YOK 98, BES 05]. Algorithms are evaluated on three benchmarks: uniform binary random DisCSPs, distributed sensor-target networks and distributed meeting scheduling problems. All experiments were performed on the DisChoco 2.0 platform[2] [WAH 11] in which agents are simulated by Java threads that communicate only through message passing (see Chapter 8). All algorithms were tested on the same static agents ordering using the *dom/deg* heuristic [BES 96] and the same nogood selection heuristic (*HPLV*) [HIR 00]. For ABT, we implemented an improved version of Silaghi's solution detection [SIL 06] and counters for tagging assignments.

---

2 http://dischoco.sourceforge.net/.

We evaluate the performance of the algorithms by communication load [LYN 97] and computation effort. Communication load is measured by the total number of exchanged messages among agents during algorithm execution ($\#msg$), including those of termination detection (system messages). Computation effort is measured by the number of non-concurrent constraint checks ($\#ncccs$) [ZIV 06b]. The metric $\#ncccs$ is used in distributed constraint solving to simulate the computation time.

3.4.1. *Uniform binary random DisCSPs*

The algorithms are tested on uniform binary random DisCSPs which are characterized by $\langle n, d, p_1, p_2 \rangle$, where n is the number of agents/variables, d is the number of values in each of the domains, p_1 is the network connectivity defined as the ratio of existing binary constraints and p_2 is the constraint tightness defined as the ratio of forbidden value pairs. We solved instances for two classes of constraint graphs: sparse graphs $\langle 20, 10, 0.2, p_2 \rangle$ and dense graphs $\langle 20, 10, 0.7, p_2 \rangle$. We varied the tightness from 0.1 to 0.9 by steps of 0.05. For each pair of fixed density and tightness (p_1, p_2), we generated 25 instances, solved four times each. Thereafter, we averaged over the 100 runs.

Figure 3.2 presents computational effort of AFC-ng, AFC and ABT running on the sparse instances ($p_1 = 0.2$). We observe that at the complexity peak, AFC is the less efficient algorithm. It is better than ABT (the second worst) only in the instances to the right of the complexity peak (overconstrained region). In the most difficult instances, the AFC-ng improves the performance of standard AFC by a factor of 3.5 and outperforms ABT by a factor of 2.

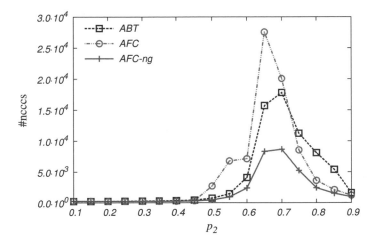

Figure 3.2. *The number of non-concurrent constraint checks ($\#nccccs$) performed on sparse problems ($p_1 = 0.2$)*

The total number of exchanged messages by algorithms compared on sparse problems (p_1 =0.2) is illustrated in Figure 3.3. When comparing the communication load, the AFC significantly deteriorates compared to other algorithms. AFC-ng improves AFC by a factor of 7. The AFC-ng exchanges slightly fewer messages than the ABT in the over-constrained area. In the complexity peak, both algorithms (ABT and AFC-ng) require almost the same number of messages.

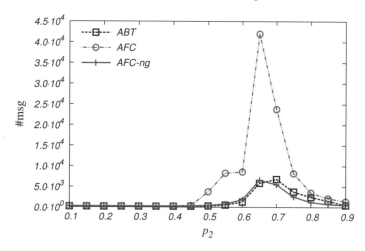

Figure 3.3. *The total number of messages sent on sparse problems ($p_1 = 0.2$)*

Figure 3.4 presents the number of non-concurrent constraint checks (#nccs) performed by algorithms compared on dense instances (p_1 =0.7). The results obtained show that ABT significantly deteriorates compared to synchronous algorithms. This is consistent with results presented in [MEI 07]. Among all the algorithms compared, AFC-ng is the fastest on these dense problems.

Regarding the number of exchanged messages (Figure 3.5), ABT is again significantly the worst. AFC requires fever messages than ABT. AFC-ng algorithm outperforms AFC by a factor 3. Hence, our experiments on uniform random DisCSPs show that AFC-ng improves on AFC and ABT algorithms.

3.4.2. *Distributed sensor-target problems*

The *distributed sensor-target problem* (SensorDisCSP) [BÉJ 05] is a benchmark based on a real distributed problem (see section 2.1.4). It consists of n sensors that track m targets. Each target must be tracked by three sensors. Each sensor can track at most one target. A solution must satisfy visibility and compatibility constraints. The visibility constraint defines the set of sensors to which a target is visible. The compatibility constraint defines the compatibility among sensors. In our implementation of the DisCSP algorithms, the encoding of the SensorDisCSP presented in section 2.1.4 is translated into an equivalent formulation where we have three virtual agents for every real agent, each virtual agent handling a single variable.

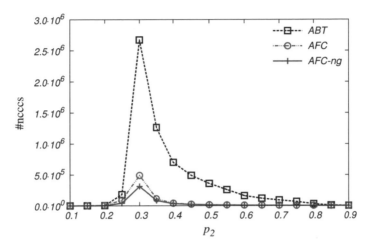

Figure 3.4. *The number of non-concurrent constraint checks (#ncccs) performed on dense problems ($p_1 = 0.7$)*

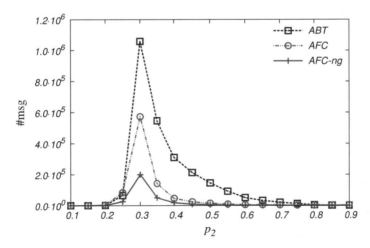

Figure 3.5. *The total number of messages sent on the dense problems ($p_1 = 0.7$)*

Problems are characterized by $\langle n, m, p_c, p_v \rangle$, where n is the number of sensors, m is the number of targets, each sensor can communicate with a fraction p_c of the sensors that are in its sensing range and each target can be tracked by a fraction p_v

of the sensors having the target in their sensing range. We present results for the class $\langle$ 25, 5, 0.4, $p_v \rangle$, where we vary p_v from 0.1 to 0.9 by steps of 0.05. For each pair (p_c, p_v), we generated 25 instances, solved four times each and averaged over the 100 runs.

Figure 3.6 presents the computational effort performed by AFC-ng, AFC and ABT on sensor-target problems where $\langle n = 25, m = 5, p_c = 0.4 \rangle$. Our results show that ABT outperforms the AFC, whereas AFC-ng outperforms both ABT and AFC. We observe that in the exceptionally hard instances (where $0.1 < p_v < 0.25$), the improvement on the ABT is minor.

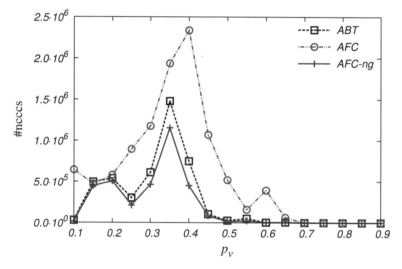

Figure 3.6. *The number of non-concurrent constraint checks performed on sensor-target instances where $p_c = 0.4$*

Concerning the communication load (Figure 3.7), the ranking of algorithms is similar to that on computational effort, although differences tend to be smaller between ABT and AFC-ng. AFC-ng remains the best on all problems.

3.4.3. *Distributed meeting scheduling problems*

The *distributed meeting scheduling problem* (DisMSP) is a truly distributed benchmark where agents may not desire to deliver their personal information to a centralized agent to solve the whole problem [WAL 02, MEI 04] (see section 2.1.3). The DisMSP consists of a set of n agents having a personal private calendar and a set of m meetings each taking place in a specified location.

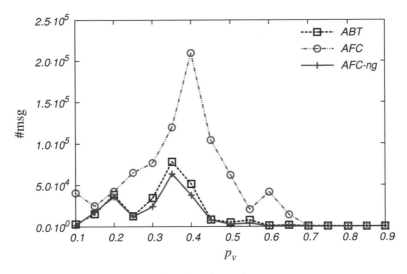

Figure 3.7. *The total number of exchanged messages on sensor-target instances where* $p_c = 0.4$

We encode the DisMSP in DisCSP as follows. Each DisCSP agent represents a real agent and contains k variables representing the k meetings in which the agent participates. These k meetings are selected randomly among the m meetings. The domain of each variable contains the $d \times h$ slots where a meeting can be scheduled. A slot is 1 h long, and there are h slots per day and d days. There is an equality constraint for each pair of variables corresponding to the same meeting in different agents. There is an *arrival-time* constraint between all variables/meetings belonging to the same agent. We place meetings randomly on the nodes of a uniform grid of size $g \times g$ and the traveling time between two adjacent nodes is 1 h. Thus, the traveling time between two meetings equals the Euclidean distance between nodes representing the locations where they will be held. For varying the tightness of the arrival-time constraint, we vary the size of the grid on which meetings are placed.

Problems are characterized by $\langle n, m, k, d, h, g \rangle$, where n is the number of agents, m is the number of meetings, k is the number of meetings/variables per agent, d is the number of days and h is the number of hours per day, and g is the grid size. The duration of each meeting is 1 h. In our implementation of the DisCSP algorithms, this encoding is translated into an equivalent formulation where we have k (number of meetings per agent) virtual agents for every real agent, each virtual agent handling a single variable. We present results for the class $\langle 20, 9, 3, 2, 10, g \rangle$ where we vary g from 2 to 22 by steps of 2. Again, for each g, we generated 25 instances, solved four times each and averaged over the 100 runs.

On this class of meeting scheduling benchmarks, AFC-ng continues to perform well. AFC-ng is significantly better than ABT and AFC, both for computational effort (Figure 3.8) and communication load (Figure 3.9). Concerning the computational effort, ABT is the slowest algorithm to solve such problems. AFC outperforms ABT by a factor of 2 at the peak (i.e. where the $GridSize$ equals 8). However, ABT requires less messages than AFC.

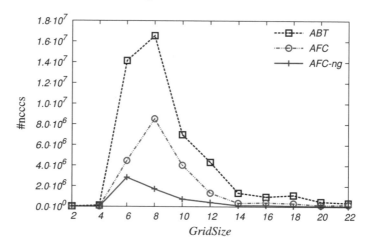

Figure 3.8. *The number of non-concurrent constraint checks performed on meeting scheduling benchmarks where the number of meetings per agent is 3*

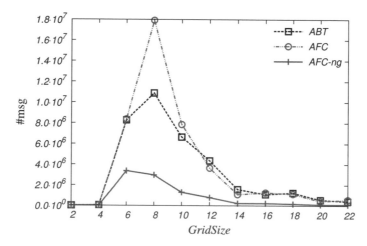

Figure 3.9. *The total number of exchanged messages on meeting scheduling benchmarks where the number of meetings per agent is 3*

3.4.4. *Discussion*

We present in Tables 3.1, 3.2, 3.4 and 3.3 the percentage of messages per type exchanged by the AFC algorithm to solve instances around the complexity peak of, respectively, sparse random DisCSPs, dense random DisCSPs, distributed sensor-target problems where p_c=0.4 and DisMSP where $k = 3$. These tables allow us to better understand the behavior of the AFC algorithm and to explain the good performance of AFC-ng compared to AFC.

The first observation of our experiments is that AFC-ng is always better than AFC, both in terms of exchanged messages and computational effort ($\#ncccs$). A closer look at the type of exchanged messages shows that the backtrack operation in AFC requires exchanging a lot of *not_ok* messages (approximately 50% of the total number of messages sent by agents). This confirms the significance of using nogoods as justification of value removal and allowing several concurrent backtracks in AFC-ng. The second observation of these experiments is that ABT performs badly in dense graphs compared to synchronous algorithms.

p_2	$\#msg$	cpa %	back_cpa %	**fc_cpa %**	not_ok %
0.55	8,297	5.93	3.76	50.99	38.58
0.60	8,610	4.49	2.75	52.46	39.57
0.65	41,979	3.37	1.77	42.20	52.60
0.70	23,797	3.00	1.75	43.48	51.68
0.75	8,230	2.61	1.53	40.66	54.97

Table 3.1. *The percentage of messages per type exchanged by AFC to solve instances of uniform random DisCSPs where p_1=0.2*

p_2	$\#msg$ %	cpa %	back_cpa %	**fc_cpa %**	not_ok %
0.25	83,803	4.85	2.86	47.68	44.54
0.30	572,493	3.61	2.11	43.64	50.63
0.35	142,366	2.90	1.69	39.35	56.27
0.40	46,883	2.60	1.52	37.77	58.58
0.45	24,379	2.35	1.41	35.56	61.52
0.50	14,797	2.14	1.29	33.32	64.38

Table 3.2. *The percentage of messages per type exchanged by AFC to solve instances of uniform random DisCSPs where p_1=0.7*

p_v	#msg	cpa %	back_cpa %	fc_cpa %	not_ok %
0.30	76,914	23.16	23.14	49.50	4.14
0.35	119,759	24.91	24.90	47.49	2.66
0.40	209,650	23.55	23.55	47.52	5.35
0.45	104,317	19.07	19.06	57.17	4.68

Table 3.3. *The percentage of messages per type exchanged by AFC to solve instances of distributed sensor-target problem where p_c=0.4*

GridSize	#msg	cpa %	back_cpa %	fc_cpa%	not_ok %
4	39,112	2.71	1.70	50.41	44.71
6	8,376,151	2.19	1.59	49.31	46.91
8	17,911,100	2.39	1.66	53.88	42.07
10	7,855,300	2.30	1.66	52.20	43.83
12	3,653,697	1.77	1.33	57.19	39.71

Table 3.4. *The percentage of messages per type exchanged by AFC to solve instances of distributed meeting scheduling problem where k=3*

3.5. Summary

A new complete and synchronous algorithm for solving distributed CSPs is presented. This algorithm is based on the AFC and uses nogoods as justification of value removal. We called it AFC-ng. Besides its use of nogoods as justification of value removal, AFC-ng allows simultaneous backtracks going from different agents to different destinations. Thus, AFC-ng draws all the benefit it can from the asynchronism of the FC phase. The experimental results show that AFC-ng improves the AFC algorithm in terms of computational effort and number of exchanged messages.

4

Asynchronous Forward-Checking Tree (AFC-tree)

This chapter shows how to extend the nogood-based asynchronous forward-checking (AFC-ng) algorithm to the *asynchronous forward-checking tree (AFC-tree)* algorithm using a pseudo-tree arrangement of the constraint graph [WAH 13]. To achieve this goal, agents are ordered *a priori* in a pseudo-tree such that agents in different branches of the tree do not share any constraint. AFC-tree does not address the process of ordering the agents in a pseudo-tree arrangement. Therefore, the pseudo-tree ordering is built in a preprocessing step. Using this priority ordering, AFC-tree performs multiple AFC-ng processes on the paths from the root to the leaves of the pseudo-tree. The agents that are brothers are committed to concurrently finding the partial solutions of their variables. Therefore, AFC-tree takes advantage of the potential speedup of a parallel exploration in the processing of distributed problems. The good properties of the AFC-tree are described. A comparison of the AFC-tree with the AFC-ng on random distributed constraint satisfaction problems (DisCSPs) and instances from real benchmarks, sensor networks and distributed meeting scheduling, is provided.

4.1. Introduction

We have described synchronous backtracking (SBT) in Chapter 2, which is the simplest search algorithm for solving DisCSPs. Because it is a straightforward extension of the chronological algorithm for centralized CSPs, SBT performs assignments sequentially and synchronously. Thus, only the agent holding the current partial assignment (CPA) performs an assignment or backtracking [YOK 00b]. Researchers in distributed CSP area have focused a great deal on the improvement of the SBT algorithm. Thus, a variety of improvements have been proposed. Hence, Meisels and Zivan proposed the synchronous conflict-based backjumping (SCBJ) that performs backjumping instead of chronological backtracking as is done in SBT [ZIV 03].

In a subsequent study, Meisels and Zivan proposed the asynchronous forward-checking (AFC), another promising distributed search algorithm for DisCSPs [MEI 07]. The AFC algorithm is based on the forward-checking (FC) algorithm for CSPs [HAR 80]. The FC operation is performed asynchronously, whereas the search is performed synchronously. Hence, this algorithm improves on SBT by adding to them some amount of concurrency. The concurrency arises from the fact that the FC phase is processed concurrently by future agents. However, the manner in which the backtrack operation is performed is a major drawback of the AFC algorithm. The backtrack operation requires a lot of work on the part of the agents.

We presented in Chapter 3 the AFC-ng, a complete and synchronous algorithm that is based on the AFC. Besides its use of nogoods as justification of value removal, AFC-ng allows simultaneous backtracks going from different agents to different destinations. Thus, the AFC-ng enhances the asynchronism of the FC phase and attempts to avoid the drawbacks of the backtrack operation of the AFC algorithm.

In [FRE 85], Freuder and Quinn introduced the concept of pseudo-tree, an efficient structure for solving centralized CSPs. Based on a "divide and conquer" principle provided by the pseudo-tree, they performed searches in parallel. Depth-first search trees (DFS-trees) are special cases of pseudo-trees. They are used in the *Network Consistency Protocol* (NCP) proposed by Collin *et al.* [COL 91]. In NCP, agents are prioritized using a DFS-tree. Agents on the same branch of the DFS-tree act synchronously, but agents having the same parent can act concurrently. A number of other algorithms for distributed constraint optimization (DCOP) use pseudo-tree or DFS-tree orderings of the agents [MOD 03, PET 05, CHE 06, YEO 07].

In this chapter, we propose another algorithm that is based on AFC-ng and is called AFC-tree. The main feature of the AFC-tree algorithm is using different agents to search non-intersecting parts of the search space concurrently. In AFC-tree, agents are prioritized according to a pseudo-tree arrangement of the constraint graph. A preprocessing step before starting the AFC-tree algorithm is performed to convert the constraint graph into a pseudo-tree. Then, AFC-tree performs concurrent exploration on different branches (the paths from the root to the leaves) of the pseudo-tree. In other words, AFC-tree executes several AFC-ng processes, an AFC-ng process on each branch. Therefore, AFC-tree takes advantage of the potential speedup of a parallel exploration in the processing of distributed problems [FRE 85]. A solution is found when all leaf agents succeed in extending the CPA they received. Furthermore, in AFC-tree, privacy may be enhanced because communication is restricted to agents in the same branch of the pseudo-tree.

4.2. Pseudo-tree ordering

We have seen in Chapters 1 and 2 that any binary distributed constraint network (DisCSP) can be represented by a *constraint graph* $G = (X_G, E_G)$, whose vertices represent the variables and edges represent the constraints (see definition 1.2). Therefore, $X_G = \mathcal{X}$ and for each constraint $c_{ij} \in \mathcal{C}$ connecting two variables x_i, and x_j there exists an edge $\{x_i, x_j\} \in E_G$ linking vertces x_i and x_j.

Figure 4.1 shows an example of a constraint graph G of a problem involving 9 variables $\mathcal{X} = X_G = \{x_1, \ldots, x_9\}$ and 10 constraints $\mathcal{C} = \{c_{12}, c_{14}, c_{17}, c_{18}, c_{19}, c_{25}, c_{26}, c_{37}, c_{38}, c_{49}\}$. There are constraints between x_1 and x_2 (c_{12}), x_1 and x_4, etc.

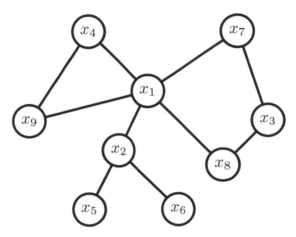

Figure 4.1. *Example of a constraint graph G*

The concept of *pseudo-tree* arrangement (see definition 1.18) of a constraint graph was first introduced by Freuder and Quinn in [FRE 85]. The purpose of this arrangement is to perform the search in parallel on independent branches of the pseudo-tree in order to improve the search in centralized constraint satisfaction problems. The aim of introducing the pseudo-tree is to boost the search by performing the search in parallel on the independent branches of the pseudo-tree. Thus, variables belonging to different branches of the pseudo-tree can be instantiated independently.

An example of a pseudo-tree arrangement T of the constraint graph G (Figure 4.1) is illustrated in Figure 4.2. Note that G and T have the same vertices ($X_G = X_T$). However, a new (dotted) edge, $\{x_1, x_3\}$, linking x_1 to x_3 is added to T where $\{x_1, x_3\} \notin E_G$. Moreover, edges $\{x_1, x_7\}$, $\{x_1, x_8\}$ and $\{x_1, x_8\}$ belonging to the constraint graph G are not part of T. They are represented in T by dashed edges to show that constrained variables must be located in the same branch of T even if there is not an edge for linking them.

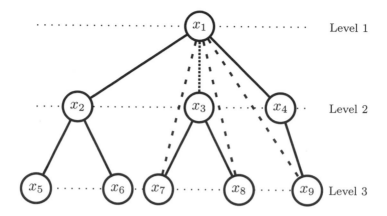

Figure 4.2. *Example of a pseudo-tree arrangement T of the constraint graph illustrated in Figure 4.1*

From a pseudo-tree arrangement of the constraint graph, we can define the following:

– A *branch* of the pseudo-tree is a path from the root to some leaf (e.g. $\{x_1, x_4, x_9\}$).

– A leaf is a vertex that has no child (e.g. x_9).

– The *children* of a vertex are its descendants connected to it through tree edges (e.g. children$(x_1) = \{x_2, x_3, x_4\}$).

– The *descendants* of a vertex x_i are vertices belonging to the subtree rooted at x_i (e.g. descendants$(x_2) = \{x_5, x_6\}$ and descendants$(x_1) = \{\mathcal{X} \setminus x_1\}$).

– The *linked descendants* of a vertex are its descendants constrained with it together with its children (e.g. linkedDescendants$(x_1) = \{x_2, x_3, x_4, x_7, x_8, x_9\}$).

– The *parent* of a vertex is the ancestor connected to it through a tree edge (e.g. parent$(x_9) = \{x_4\}$, parent$(x_3) = \{x_1\}$).

– A vertex x_i is an *ancestor* of a vertex x_j if x_i is the parent of x_j or an ancestor of the parent of x_j.

– The *ancestors* of a vertex x_i are the set of agents forming the path from the root to x_i's parent (e.g. ancestors$(x_8) = \{x_1, x_3\}$).

4.3. Distributed depth-first search tree construction

The construction of the pseudo-tree can be processed by a centralized procedure. First, a *system agent* must be elected to gather information about the constraint graph. Such system/master agent can be chosen using a leader election algorithm such as the one presented in [ABU 88]. Once all information about the constraint graph is gathered by the system agent, it can perform a centralized algorithm to build the pseudo-tree ordering (see section 1.2.2.1). A decentralized modification of the procedure for building the pseudo-tree was introduced by Chechetka and Sycara in [CHE 05]. This algorithm allows the distributed construction of pseudo-trees without needing to deliver any global information about the whole problem to a single process.

Whatever the method (centralized or distributed) for building the pseudo-tree, the obtained pseudo-tree may require the addition of some edges not belonging to the original constraint graph. In the example presented in Figure 4.2, a new edge linking x_1 to x_3 is added to the resulting pseudo-tree T. The structure of the pseudo-tree will be used for communication between agents. Thus, the added link between x_1 and x_3 will be used to exchange messages between them. However, in some distributed applications, the communication might be restricted to the neighboring agents (i.e. a message can be passed only locally between agents that share a constraint). The solution in such applications is to use a *DFS-tree*. DFS-trees are special cases of pseudo-trees where all edges belong to the original graph.

We present in algorithm 4.1 a simple distributed algorithm, called DistributedDFS algorithm, for the distributed construction of the DFS-tree. The DistributedDFS is similar to the algorithm proposed by Cheung in [CHE 83]. The DistributedDFS algorithm is a distribution of a DFS traversal of the constraint graph. Each agent maintains a set *Visited* where it stores its neighbors that have already been visited (line 2). The first step is to design the root agent using a leader election algorithm (line 1). An example of a leader election algorithm was presented by Abu-Amara in [ABU 88]. Once the root is designed, it can start the distributed construction of the DFS-tree (procedure CheckNeighborhood() call, line 3). The designed root initiates the propagation of a *token*, which is a unique message that will be circulated on the network until "visiting" all the agents of the problem.

When an agent x_i receives the *token*, it marks all its neighbors included in the received message as visited (line 6). Next, x_i checks if the *token* is sent back by a child. If it is the case, x_i sets all agents belonging to the subtree rooted at the message sender (i.e. its child) as its descendants (lines 7–8). Otherwise, the *token* is received for the first time from the parent of x_i. Thus, x_i marks the sender as its parent (line 10) and all agents contained in the *token* (i.e. the sender and its ancestors) as its ancestors (line 11). Afterward, x_i calls the procedure CheckNeighborhood() to check if it has to pass the *token* on to an unvisited neighbor or to return the *token* to its parent if all its neighbors have already been visited.

The procedure CheckNeighborhood() checks if all neighbors have already been visited (line 13). If it is the case, agent x_i sends the *token* back to its parent (line 14). The *token* contains the set $VisitedAgents$ composed by x_i and its descendants. Until this point, agent x_i knows all its ancestors, its children and its descendants. Thus, agent x_i terminates the execution of DistributedDFS (line 15). Otherwise, agent x_i chooses one of its neighbors (x_j) that has yet to be visited and designs it as a child (lines 17–18). Afterward, x_i passes the *token* to x_j where it puts the ancestors of the child x_j (i.e. ancestors(x_i) $\cup$ $\{x_i\}$) (line 19).

Algorithm 4.1. *The distributed depth-first search construction algorithm*

---

procedure distributedDFS()
01.   Select the root via a leader election algorithm ;
02. $Visited \leftarrow \emptyset$; $end \leftarrow$ **false** ;
03.   **if** (x_i *is the elected root*) **then** CheckNeighborhood() ;
04.   **while** ($\neg end$) **do**
05. $msg \leftarrow$ getMsg();
06. $Visited \leftarrow Visited \cup \{\Gamma(x_i) \cap msg.VisitedAgents)\}$;
07.   **if** ($msg.Sender \in$ children(x_i)) **then**
08.   descendants$(x_i)\leftarrow$ descendants(x_i) $\cup$ $msg.VisitedAgents$;
09.   **else**
10.   parent(x_i) $\leftarrow$ $msg.Sender$;
11.   ancestors(x_i) $\leftarrow$ $msg.VisitedAgents$;
12.   CheckNeighborhood() ;

procedure CheckNeighborhood()
13.   **if** ($\Gamma(x_i) = Visited$) **then**
14.   sendMsg : *token*(descendants(x_i) $\cup$ $\{x_i\}$) **to** parent(x_i) ;
15. $end \leftarrow$ **true** ;
16.   **else**
17.   select x_j in $\Gamma(x_i) \setminus Visited$;
18.   children(x_i) $\leftarrow$ children(x_i) $\cup$ $\{x_j\}$;
19.   sendMsg : **token**(ancestors(x_i) $\cup$ $\{x_i\}$) **to** A_j ;

For example, consider the constraint graph G presented in Figure 4.1. Figure 4.3 shows an example of a DFS-tree arrangement of the constraint graph G obtained by performing distributively the DistributedDFS algorithm. The DistributedDFS algorithm can be performed as follows. First, let x_1 be the elected root of the DFS-tree (i.e. the leader election algorithm elects the most connected agent). The root x_1 initiates the DFS-tree construction by calling procedure CheckNeighborhood() (line 3). Then, x_1 selects from its unvisited neighbors x_2 to be its child (lines 17–18). Next, x_1 passes the *token* to x_2 where it puts itself as the ancestor of the receiver (x_2) (line 19). After receiving the *token*, x_2 updates the set of its visited neighbors (line 6) by marking x_1 (the only neighbor included in the *token*) visited. Afterward, x_2 sets x_1 to be its parent and puts $\{x_1\}$ to be its set of ancestors (lines 10–11). Next, x_2 calls procedure CheckNeighborhood() (line 12). Until this point, x_2 has one visited neighbor (x_1) and two unvisited neighbors $(x_5$ and $x_6)$. For instance, let x_2 choose x_5 to be its child. Thus, x_2 sends the *token* to x_5 where it sets the DFS set to $\{x_1, x_2\}$. After receiving the *token*, x_5 marks its single neighbor x_2 as visited (line 6), sets x_2 to be its parent (line 10), sets $\{x_1, x_2\}$ to be its ancestors and sends the *token* back to x_2 where it puts itself. After receiving back the *token* from x_5, x_2 adds x_5 to its descendants and selects the last unvisited neighbor (x_6) to be its child and passes the *token* to x_6.

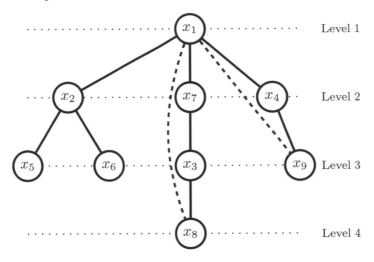

Figure 4.3. *A DFS-tree arrangement of the constraint graph in Figure 4.1*

In a similar way, x_6 returns the *token* to x_2. Then, x_2 sends back the *token* to its parent x_1 because all its neighbors have been visited. The *token* contains the descendants of x_1 ($\{x_2, x_5, x_6\}$) on the subtree rooted at x_2. After receiving the *token* back from x_2, x_1 will select an agent from its unvisited neighbors $\{x_4, x_7, x_8, x_9\}$. Hence, the subtree rooted at x_2, where each agent knows its ancestors and its descendants, is built without delivering any global information. The other subtrees, respectively, rooted at x_7 and x_4 are built in a similar manner. Thus, we obtain the DFS-tree shown in Figure 4.3.

4.4. The AFC-tree algorithm

The AFC-tree algorithm is based on AFC-ng performed on a pseudo-tree ordering of the constraint graph (built in a preprocessing step). Agents are prioritized according to the pseudo-tree ordering in which each agent has a single parent and various children. Using this priority ordering, AFC-tree performs multiple AFC-ng processes on the paths from the root to the leaves. The root initiates the search by generating a CPA, assigning its value to it and sending *cpa* messages to its linked descendants. Among all agents that receive the CPA, children perform AFC-ng on the sub-problem restricted to its ancestors (agents that are assigned in the CPA) and the set of its descendants. Therefore, instead of giving the privilege of assigning to only one agent, agents who are in disjoint subtrees may assign their variables simultaneously. AFC-tree thus takes advantage of the potential speedup of a parallel exploration in the processing of distributed problems. The degree of asynchronism is enhanced.

An execution of AFC-tree on a sample DisCSP problem is shown in Figure 4.4. At time t_1, the root x_1 sends copies of the CPA on *cpa* messages to its linked descendants. Children x_2, x_3 and x_4 assign their values simultaneously in the received CPAs and then perform concurrently the AFC-tree algorithm. Agents x_7, x_8 and x_9 only perform an FC. At time t_2, x_9 finds an empty domain and sends an *ngd* message to x_1. At the same time, other CPAs propagate down through the other paths. For instance, a CPA has propagated down from x_3 to x_7 and x_8. x_7 detects an empty domain and sends a nogood to x_3 attached on an *ngd* message. For the CPA that propagates on the path (x_1, x_2, x_6), x_6 successfully assigned its value and initiated a solution detection. The same thing will happen on the path (x_1, x_2, x_5) when x_5 (not yet instantiated) will receive the CPA from its parent x_2. When x_1 receives the *ngd* message from x_9, it initiates a new search process by sending a new copy of the CPA, which will dominate all other CPAs where x_1 is assigned its old value. This new CPA generated by x_1 can then take advantage of efforts made by the obsolete CPAs. Consider, for instance, the subtree rooted at x_2. If the value of x_2 is consistent with the value of x_1 on the new CPA, all nogoods stored on the subtree rooted at x_2 are still valid and a solution is reached on the subtree without any nogood generation.

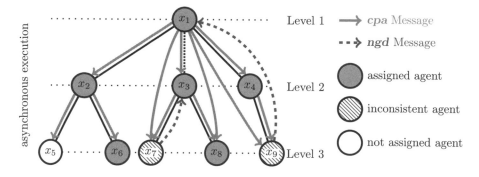

Figure 4.4. *An example of the AFC-tree execution*

In AFC-ng, a solution is reached when the last agent in the agent ordering receives the CPA and succeeds in assigning its variable. In AFC-tree, the situation is different because a CPA can reach a leaf agent without being complete. When all agents are assigned and no constraint is violated, this state is a global solution and the network has reached quiescence, meaning that no message is transmitting through it. Such a state can be detected using specialized snapshot algorithms [CHA 85], but AFC-tree uses a different mechanism that allows us to detect solutions before quiescence. AFC-tree uses an additional type of message called *accept* that informs parents of the acceptance of their CPA. Termination can be inferred earlier, and the number of messages required for termination detection can be reduced. A similar technique of solution detection was used in the Asynchronous Aggregate Search (AAS) algorithm [SIL 05].

The mechanism of solution detection is as follows: whenever a leaf node succeeds in assigning its value, it sends an *accept* message to its parent. This message contains the CPA that was received from the parent incremented by the value-assignment of the leaf node. When a non-leaf agent A_i receives *accept* messages from all its children that are all consistent with each other, all consistent with A_i's AgentView and with A_i's value, A_i builds an *accept* message being the conjunction of all received *accept* messages plus A_i's value-assignment. If A_i is the root, a solution is found, and A_i broadcasts this solution to all agents. Otherwise, A_i sends the built *accept* message to its parent.

4.4.1. *Description of the algorithm*

We present in algorithm 4.2 only the procedures that are new to or different from those of AFC-ng in algorithm 3.1. In InitAgentView(), the AgentView of A_i is initialized to the set ancestors(A_i) and t_j is set to 0 for each agent x_j in ancestors(A_i) (line 10). The new data structure storing the received *accept* messages is initialized to the empty set (line 11). In SendCPA(CPA), instead of sending copies of the CPA to all agents not yet instantiated on it, A_i sends copies of the CPA only to its linked descendants (linkedDescendants(A_i), lines 13–14). When the set linkedDescendants(A_i) is empty (i.e. A_i is a leaf), A_i calls the procedure SolutionDetection() to build and send an *accept* message. In CheckAssign(*sender*), A_i assigns its value if the CPA was received from its parent (line 16) (i.e. if *sender* is the parent of A_i).

In ProcessAccept(*msg*), when A_i receives an *accept* message from its *child* for the first time, or the CPA contained in the received *accept* message is stronger than that received before, A_i stores the content of this message (lines 17–18) and calls the SolutionDetection procedure (line 19).

In procedure SolutionDetection(), if A_i is a leaf (i.e. children(A_i) is empty, line 20), it sends an *accept* message to its parent. The *accept* message sent by A_i contains its AgentView incremented by its assignment (lines 20–21). If A_i is not a leaf, it calls function BuildAccept() to build an accept partial solution, PA (line 23). If the returned partial solution PA is not empty and A_i is the root, PA is a solution to the problem. Then, A_i broadcasts it to other agents including the system agent and sets the *end* flag to *true* (line 25). Otherwise, A_i sends an *accept* message containing PA to its parent (line 26).

In function BuildAccept, if an accept partial solution is reached, A_i generates a partial solution PA incrementing its AgentView with its assignment (line 27). Next,

A_i loops over the set of *accept* messages received from its children. If at least one *child* has never sent an *accept* message or the *accept* message is inconsistent with PA, then the partial solution has not yet been reached and the function returns empty (line 30). Otherwise, the partial solution PA is incremented by the *accept* message of *child* (line 31). Finally, the accept partial solution is returned (line 32).

Algorithm 4.2. *New lines/procedures of AFC-tree with respect to AFC-ng*

procedure AFC-tree()
01. $end \leftarrow$ **false**; $AgentView.Consistent \leftarrow$ **true**; InitAgentView() ;
02.   **if** ($A_i = IA$) **then** Assign() ;
03.   **while** ($\neg end$) **do**
04. $msg \leftarrow$ getMsg();
05.   **switch** ($msg.type$) **do**
06. cpa : ProcessCPA(msg);
07. ngd : ProcessNogood(msg);
08. stp : $end \leftarrow$ **true** ;
09. $accept$: ProcessAccept(msg);

procedure InitAgentView()
10.   **foreach** ($A_j \in$ ancestors(A_i)) **do** $AgentView[j] \leftarrow \{(x_j, empty, 0)\}$;
11.   **foreach** ($child \in$ children(A_i)) **do** $Accept[child] \leftarrow \emptyset$;

procedure SendCPA(CPA)
12.   **if** (children(A_i) $\neq \emptyset$) **then**
13.   **foreach** ($descendant \in$ linkedDescendants(A_i)) **do**
14.   sendMsg : **cpa**(CPA) **to** $descendant$;
15.   **else** SolutionDetection() ;

procedure CheckAssign($sender$)
16.   **if** (parent(A_i) $= sender$) **then** Assign() ;

procedure ProcessAccept(msg)
17.   **if** ($msg.CPA$ is stronger than $Accept[msg.Sender]$) **then**
18. $Accept[msg.Sender] \leftarrow msg.CPA$;
19.   SolutionDetection() ;

procedure SolutionDetection()
20.   **if** (children(A_i) $= \emptyset$) **then**
21.   sendMsg : **accept**($AgentView \cup \{(x_i, x_i, t_i)\}$) **to** parent($A_i$) ;
22.   **else**
23. $PA \leftarrow$ BuildAccept() ;
24.   **if** ($PA \neq \emptyset$) **then**
25.   **if** ($A_i = root$) **then** broadcastMsg : $stp(PA)$; $end \leftarrow$ **true** ;
26.   **else** sendMsg : **accept**(PA) **to** parent(A_i) ;

function BuildAccept()
27. $PA \leftarrow AgentView \cup \{(x_i, x_i, t_i)\}$;
28.   **foreach** ($child \in$ children(x_i)) **do**
29.   **if** ($Accept[child] = \emptyset \vee \neg$isConsistent($PA$, $Accept[child]$)) **then**
30.   **return** $\emptyset$;
31.   **else** $PA \leftarrow PA \cup Accept[child]$;
32.   **return** PA ;

4.5. Correctness proofs

THEOREM 4.1.– The spatial complexity of AFC-tree is polynomially bounded by $O(nd)$ per agent.

PROOF.– In AFC-tree, the size of nogoods is bounded by h ($h \leq n$), the height of the pseudo-tree where n is the total number of variables. Now, on each agent, AFC-tree only stores one nogood per removed value. Thus, the space complexity of nogoods storage is in $O(hd)$ on each agent. AFC-tree also stores its set of descendants and ancestors, which is bounded by n on each agent. Therefore, AFC-tree has a space complexity in $O(hd + n)$.

THEOREM 4.2.– AFC-tree algorithm is correct.

PROOF.– AFC-tree agents only forward CPAs. Hence, leaf agents receive only consistent CPAs. Thus, leaf agents only send *accept* message holding consistent assignments to their parent. Because a parent builds an *accept* message only when the *accept* messages received from all its children are consistent with each other and all consistent with its own value, the *accept* message it sends contains a consistent partial solution. The root broadcasts a solution only when it can build itself such an *accept* message. Therefore, the solution is correct and the AFC-tree is sound.

From lemma 3.1, we deduce that the AFC-tree agent of highest priority cannot fall into an infinite loop. By induction on the level of the pseudo-tree, no agent can fall in such a loop, which ensures the termination of an AFC-tree. AFC-tree performs multiple AFC-ng processes on the paths of the pseudo-tree from the root to the leaves. Thus, from lemma 3.2, AFC-tree inherits the property that an empty nogood cannot be inferred if the network is satisfiable (i.e. it has a solution). As AFC-tree terminates, this ensures its completeness.

4.6. Experimental evaluation

In this section, we experimentally compare AFC-tree with the AFC-ng presented previously in Chapter 3. Algorithms are evaluated on the basis of three benchmarks: uniform binary random DisCSPs, distributed sensor-target networks and distributed meeting scheduling problems (DisMSPs). All experiments were performed on the DisChoco 2.0 platform[1] [WAH 11], in which agents are simulated by Java threads that communicate only through message passing (see Chapter 8). All algorithms are tested using the same nogood selection heuristic (*HPLV*) [HIR 00].

We evaluate the performance of the algorithms by communication load [LYN 97] and computation effort. Communication load is measured by the total number of exchanged messages among agents during algorithm execution ($\#msg$), including

---

1 http://www2.lirmm.fr/coconut/dischoco/.

those of termination detection for AFC-tree. Computational effort is measured by the number of non-concurrent constraint checks ($\#nccs$) [ZIV 06b]. The metric $\#nccs$ is used in distributed constraint solving to simulate the computation time.

4.6.1. *Uniform binary random DisCSPs*

The algorithms are tested on uniform binary random DisCSPs which are characterized by $\langle n, d, p_1, p_2 \rangle$, where n is the number of agents/variables, d is the number of values in each of the domains, p_1 is the network connectivity defined as the ratio of existing binary constraints and p_2 is the constraint tightness defined as the ratio of forbidden value pairs. We solved instances of two classes of constraint graphs: sparse graphs $\langle 20, 10, 0.2, p_2 \rangle$ and dense graphs $\langle 20, 10, 0.7, p_2 \rangle$. We varied the tightness from 0.1 to 0.9 by steps of 0.05. For each pair of fixed density and tightness (p_1, p_2), we generated 25 instances, solved four times each. Then we reported average over the 100 runs.

Figures 4.5 and 4.6 present the performance of AFC-tree and AFC-ng run on the sparse instances (p_1=0.2). In terms of computational effort (Figure 4.5), we observe that at the complexity peak, AFC-tree takes advantage of the pseudo-tree arrangement to improve the speedup of AFC-ng. Concerning the communication load (Figure 4.6), AFC-tree improves on the AFC-ng algorithm. The improvement of AFC-tree over AFC-ng is approximately 30% on communication load and 35% on the number of non-concurrent constraint checks.

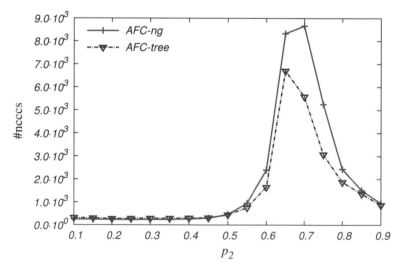

Figure 4.5. *The number of non-concurrent constraint checks ($\#nccs$) performed on sparse problems ($p_1 = 0.2$)*

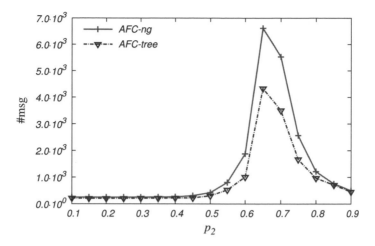

Figure 4.6. *The total number of messages sent on sparse problems ($p_1 = 0.2$)*

Figures 4.7 and 4.8 illustrate, respectively, the number of non-concurrent constraint checks ($\#nccs$) and the total number of exchanged messages performed by algorithms compared on the dense problems ($p_1 = 0.7$). On the dense graphs, AFC-tree behaves like AFC-ng with a very slight domination of AFC-ng. The AFC-tree does not benefit from the pseudo-tree arrangement, which is like a chain-tree in such graphs.

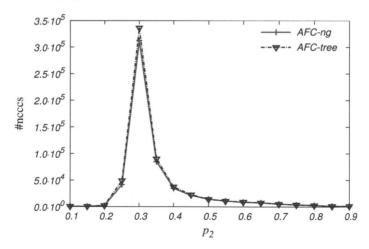

Figure 4.7. *The number of non-concurrent constraint checks ($\#nccs$) performed on the dense problems ($p_1 = 0.7$)*

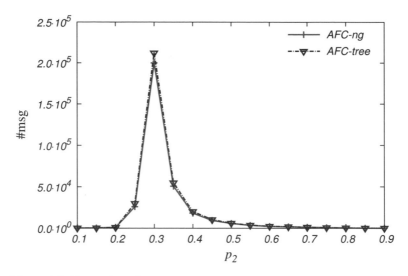

Figure 4.8. *The total number of messages sent on the dense problems ($p_1 = 0.7$)*

4.6.2. *Distributed sensor-target problems*

The *distributed sensor-target problem* (SensorDisCSP) [BÉJ 05] is a benchmark based on a real distributed problem (see section 2.1.4). It consists of n sensors that track m targets. Each target must be tracked by three sensors. Each sensor can track at most one target. A solution must satisfy visibility and compatibility constraints. The visibility constraint defines the set of sensors to which a target is visible. The compatibility constraint defines the compatibility among sensors. In our implementation of the DisCSP algorithms, the encoding of the SensorDisCSP presented in section 2.1.4 is translated into an equivalent formulation where we have three virtual agents for every real agent, each virtual agent handling a single variable.

Problems are characterized by $\langle n, m, p_c, p_v \rangle$, where n is the number of sensors, m is the number of targets, each sensor can communicate with a fraction p_c of the sensors that are in its sensing range, and each target can be tracked by a fraction p_v of the sensors having the target in their sensing range. We present results for the class $\langle 25, 5, 0.4, p_v \rangle$, where we vary p_v from 0.1 to 0.9 by steps of 0.05. Again, for each pair (p_c, p_v), we generated 25 instances, solved four times each, and averaged over the 100 runs.

We present the results obtained on the SensorDisCSP benchmark in Figures 4.9 and 4.10. Our experiments show that AFC-tree outperforms the AFC-ng algorithm when comparing the computational effort (Figure 4.9). Concerning the communication load (Figure 4.10), the ranking of algorithms is similar to that on computational effort for the instances at the complexity peak. However, it is slightly dominated by the AFC-ng on the exceptionally hard problems ($p_v = 1.5$). Hence, AFC-tree is the best on all problems except for a single point ($p_v = 1.5$), where AFC-ng shows a slight improvement.

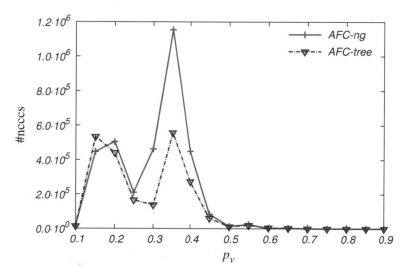

Figure 4.9. *Total number of non-concurrent constraint checks performed on instances where $p_c = 0.4$*

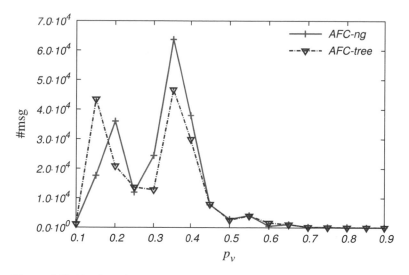

Figure 4.10. *Total number of exchanged messages on instances where $p_c = 0.4$*

4.6.3. *Distributed meeting scheduling problems*

The DisMSP is a truly distributed benchmark where agents may not desire to deliver their personal information to a centralized agent to solve the whole problem [WAL 02, MEI 04] (see section 2.1.3). The DisMSP consists of a set of n agents having a personal private calendar and a set of m meetings, each taking place in a specified location.

We encode the DisMSP in DisCSP as follows. Each DisCSP agent represents a real agent and contains k variables representing the k meetings in which the agent participates. These k meetings are selected randomly among the m meetings. The domain of each variable contains $d \times h$ slots, where a meeting can be scheduled. A slot is 1 h long, and there are h slots per day and d days. There is an equality constraint for each pair of variables corresponding to the same meeting in different agents. There is an *arrival-time* constraint between all variables/meetings belonging to the same agent. We place meetings randomly on the nodes of a uniform grid of size $g \times g$ and the traveling time between two adjacent nodes is 1 h. Thus, the traveling time between two meetings equals the Euclidean distance between nodes representing the locations where they will be held. For varying the tightness of the arrival-time constraint, we vary the size of the grid on which meetings are placed.

Problems are characterized by $\langle n, m, k, d, h, g \rangle$, where n is the number of agents, m is the number of meetings, k is the number of meetings/variables per agent, d is the number of days and h is the number of hours per day, and g is the grid size. The duration of each meeting is 1 h. In our implementation of the DisCSP algorithms, this encoding is translated into an equivalent formulation where we have k (number of meetings per agent) virtual agents for every real agent, each virtual agent handling a single variable. We present results for the class $\langle$ 20, 9, 3, 2, 10, $g \rangle$, where we vary g from 2 to 22 by steps of 2. Again, for each g, we generated 25 instances, solved four times each and averaged over the 100 runs.

In this class of meeting scheduling benchmarks, AFC-tree continues to perform well compared to AFC-ng. AFC-tree is significantly better than AFC-ng both for computational effort (Figure 4.11) and communication load (Figure 4.12). The improvement on the complexity peak approximates 45% for the number of non-concurrent constraint checks. Regarding the number of exchanged messages, this improvement approximates 30%.

4.6.4. *Discussion*

Our experiments demonstrated that AFC-tree is almost always better than or equivalent to AFC-ng both in terms of communication load and computational effort. When the graph is sparse, AFC-tree benefits from running separate search processes in disjoint problem subtrees. When agents are highly connected (dense graphs), the AFC-tree runs on a pseudo-tree having a form of a pseudo-chain and thus it imitates the AFC-ng.

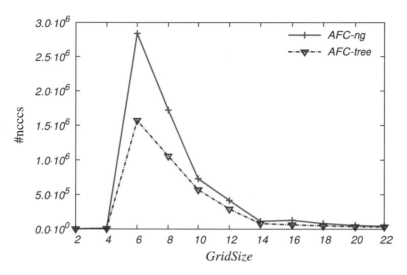

Figure 4.11. *Total number of non-concurrent constraint checks performed on meeting scheduling benchmarks where the number of meetings per agent is 3 (i.e. $k = 3$)*

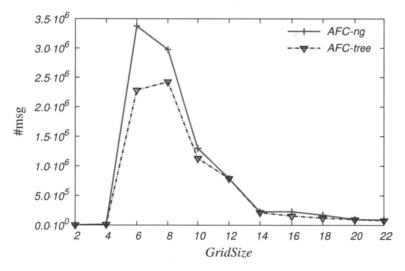

Figure 4.12. *Total number of exchanged messages on meeting scheduling benchmarks where the number of meetings per agent is 3 (i.e. $k = 3$)*

4.7. Other related works

The SBT [YOK 00b] is the naive search method for solving distributed CSPs. SBT is a decentralized extension of the chronological backtracking algorithm for centralized CSPs. Although this algorithm communicates only consistent CPAs, it does not take advantage of parallelism because the problem is solved sequentially and only the agent holding the CPAs is activated, while other agents are in an idle state. Collin *et al.* proposed the NCP, a variation of the SBT [COL 91]. NCP agents are prioritized using a DFS-tree. Despite the fact that agents on the same branch act synchronously, agents having the same parent can act concurrently. Thus, instead of giving the privilege of assigning to only one agent, as is done in SBT, an agent passes the privilege of extending the CPA or backtracking to all its children concurrently.

In interleaved asynchronous backtracking (IDIBT) [HAM 02], agents participate in multiple processes of asynchronous backtracking. Each agent keeps a separate AgentView for each search process in IDIBT. The number of search processes is fixed by the first agent in the ordering. The performance of the concurrent asynchronous backtracking [HAM 02] was tested and found to be ineffective for more than two concurrent search processes [HAM 02].

4.8. Summary

A new complete, asynchronous algorithm, which needs polynomial space, is presented. This algorithm called AFC-tree is based on the AFC-ng and is performed on a pseudo-tree arrangement of the constraint graph. AFC-tree runs simultaneous AFC-ng processes on each branch of the pseudo-tree to take advantage of the parallelism inherent in the problem. Our experiments show that AFC-tree is more robust than AFC-ng. It is particularly good when the problems are sparse because it takes advantage of the pseudo-tree ordering.

5

Maintaining Arc Consistency Asynchronously in Synchronous Distributed Search

Nogood-based asynchronous forward checking (AFC-ng), presented in Chapter 3, is an efficient and robust algorithm for solving distributed constraint satisfaction problems (DisCSPs). AFC-ng performs an asynchronous forward-checking (FC) phase during synchronous search. In this chapter, we propose two algorithms based on the same mechanism as AFC-ng [WAH 12a]. However, instead of using FC as a filtering property, they maintain the arc consistency asynchronously (MACA). The first algorithm, called MACA-del, enforces arc consistency due to an additional type of message, deletion messages. The second algorithm, called MACA-not, achieves arc consistency without any new type of message. A theoretical analysis and an experimental evaluation of the proposed approach are provided. The experiments show the good performance of MACA algorithms, particularly those of MACA-not.

5.1. Introduction

We described in Chapter 1 many backtrack search algorithms that were developed for solving constraint satisfaction problems. Typical backtrack search algorithms try to build a solution to a CSP by interleaving variable instantiation with constraint propagation. FC [HAR 80] and maintaining arc consistency (MAC) [SAB 94] are examples of such algorithms. In the 1980s, FC was considered as the most efficient search algorithm. In the mid-1990s, several studies have empirically shown that MAC is more efficient than FC on hard and large problems [BES 96, GRA 96].

Although many studies incorporated FC successfully into distributed CSPs [BRI 03, MEI 07, EZZ 09], MAC has not yet been well investigated. The only attempts to include arc consistency maintenance in distributed algorithms were done on the asynchronous backtracking (ABT) algorithm. Silaghi *et al.* introduced the distributed maintaining asynchronously consistency for ABT (DMAC-ABT), the first algorithm able to maintain arc consistency in distributed CSPs [SIL 01b]. DMAC-ABT considers consistency maintenance as a hierarchical nogood-based inference. Brito and Meseguer proposed ABT-uac and ABT-dac, two algorithms that connect ABT with arc consistency [BRI 08]. ABT-uac propagates unconditionally deleted values to enforce an amount of full arc consistency. ABT-dac propagates conditionally and unconditionally deleted values using directional arc consistency. ABT-uac shows minor improvement in communication load and ABT-dac does not fit in many instances.

In this chapter, we present two synchronous search algorithms based on the same mechanism as AFC-ng. However, instead of maintaining FC asynchronously on agents not yet instantiated, we propose to maintain arc consistency asynchronously on these future agents. We call this new scheme MACA. As in AFC-ng, only the agent holding the current partial assignment (CPA) can perform an assignment. However, unlike the AFC-ng, MACA attempts to maintain the arc consistency instead of performing only FC. The first algorithm we propose, MACA-del, enforces arc consistency due to an additional type of message, that is deletion message (*del*). Hence, whenever values are removed during a constraint propagation step, MACA-del agents notify other agents that may be affected by these removals, sending them a *del* message. *del* messages contain all removed values and the nogood justifying their removal. The second algorithm, MACA-not, achieves arc consistency without any new type of message. We achieve this by storing all deletions performed by an agent on domains of its neighboring agents and sending this information to the neighbors within the CPA message.

5.2. Maintaining arc consistency

Constraint propagation is a central feature of efficiency for solving CSPs [BES 06]. The oldest and most commonly used technique for propagating constraints is arc consistency (AC).

The maintaining arc consistency (MAC) algorithm [SAB 94] alternates exploration steps and constraint propagation steps. That is, at each step of the search, a variable assignment is followed by a filtering process that corresponds to enforcing arc consistency. For implementing MAC in a distributed CSP, each agent A_i is assumed to know all constraints in which it is involved and the agents with whom it shares a constraint (i.e. $\Gamma(x_i)$). These agents and the constraints linking them to A_i form the local constraint network of A_i, denoted by $CSP(i)$.

DEFINITION 5.1.– *The* local constraint network $CSP(i)$ *of an agent* $A_i \in \mathcal{A}$ *consists of all constraints involving* x_i *and all variables of these constraints (i.e. its neighbors).*

To allow agents to maintain arc consistency in distributed CSPs, our proposed approach consists of enforcing arc consistency on the local constraint network of each agent. Basically, each agent A_i locally stores copies of all variables in $CSP(i)$. We also assume that each agent knows the neighborhood that it has in common with its own neighbors without knowing the constraints which relate them. That is, for each of its neighbors A_k, an agent A_i knows the list of agents A_j such that there is a constraint between x_i and x_j and a constraint between x_k and x_j.

Agent A_i stores nogoods for its removed values. They are stored in $NogoodStore[x_i]$. But in addition to nogoods stored for its own values, A_i needs to store nogoods for values removed from variables x_j in $CSP(i)$. Nogoods justifying the removal of values from $D(x_j)$ are stored in $NogoodStore[x_j]$. Hence, the NogoodStore of an agent A_i is a vector of several NogoodStores, one for each variable in $CSP(i)$.

5.3. Maintaining arc consistency asynchronously

In AFC-ng, the FC phase aims to anticipate the backtrack. Nevertheless, we do not take advantage of the value removals caused by FC if it does not completely wipe out the domain of the variable. We can investigate these removals by enforcing arc consistency. This is motivated by the fact that the propagation of a value removal, for an agent A_i, may generate an empty domain for a variable in its local constraint network $CSP(i)$. We can then detect an earlier dead-end and then anticipate as soon as possible the backtrack operation.

In synchronous search algorithms for solving DisCSPs, agents sequentially assign their variables. Thus, agents perform the assignment of their variable only when they hold the CPA. We propose an algorithm in which agents assign their variables one by one following a total ordering on agents. Hence, whenever an agent succeeds in extending the CPA by assigning its variable to it, it sends the CPA to its successor to extend it. Copies of this CPA are also sent to the other agents whose assignments are not yet on the CPA in order to *maintain arc consistency asynchronously*. Therefore, when an agent receives a copy of the CPA, it maintains arc consistency in its local constraint network. To enforce arc consistency on all variables of the problem, agents communicate information about value removals produced locally with other agents. We propose two methods to achieve this. The first method, called MACA-del, uses a new type of message (*del* messages) to share this information. The second method, called MACA-not, includes the information about deletions generated locally within *cpa* messages.

5.3.1. *Enforcing AC using del messages (MACA-del)*

In MACA-del, each agent A_i maintains arc consistency on its local constraint network, $CSP(i)$, whenever a domain of a variable in $CSP(i)$ is changed. Changes can occur either on the domain of A_i or on another domain in $CSP(i)$. In MACA-del on agent A_i, only removals on $D(x_i)$ are externally shared with other agents. The propagation of the removals on $D(x_i)$ is achieved by communicating to other agents the nogoods justifying these removals. These removals and their associated nogoods are sent to neighbors via *del* messages.

The pseudo-code of MACA-del, executed by each agent A_i, is shown in algorithm 5.1. Agent A_i starts the search by calling procedure MACA-del(). In procedure MACA-del(), A_i calls function Propagate() to enforce arc consistency (line 1) in its local constraint network, that is $CSP(i)$. Next, if A_i is the initializing agent IA (the first agent in the agent ordering), it initiates the search by calling procedure Assign() (line 2). Then, a loop considers the reception and the processing of the possible message types.

When calling procedure Assign(), A_i tries to find an assignment which is consistent with its AgentView. If A_i fails to find a consistent assignment, it calls procedure Backtrack() (line 12). If A_i succeeds, it increments its counter t_i and generates a CPA from its AgentView augmented by its assignment (lines 9 and 10). Afterward, A_i calls procedure SendCPA(CPA) (line 11). If the CPA includes all agents, assignments (A_i is the lowest agent in the order, line 13), A_i reports the CPA as a solution to the problem and marks the *end* flag *true* to stop the main loop (line 13). Otherwise, A_i sends the CPA forward to all agents whose assignments are not yet on the CPA (line 14). So, the next agent on the ordering (successor) will try to extend this CPA by assigning its variable to it while other agents will maintain arc consistency asynchronously.

Whenever A_i receives a *cpa* message, procedure ProcessCPA() is called (line 6). The received message will be processed only when it holds a CPA stronger than the AgentView of A_i. If it is the case, A_i updates its AgentView (line 16) and then updates the NogoodStore of each variable in $CSP(i)$ to be compatible with the received CPA (line 17). Afterward, A_i calls function Propagate() to enforce arc consistency on $CSP(i)$ (line 18). If arc consistency wipes out a domain in $CSP(i)$ (i.e. $CSP(i)$ is not arc consistent), A_i calls procedure Backtrack() (line 18). Otherwise, A_i checks if it has to assign its variable (line 19). A_i tries to assign its variable by calling procedure Assign() only if it receives the *cpa* from its predecessor.

Algorithm 5.1. *MACA-del algorithm running by agent A_i.*

---

procedure MACA-del()
01. $end \leftarrow$ **false**; Propagate() ;
02.   **if** ($A_i = IA$) **then** Assign() ;
03.   **while** ($\neg end$) **do**
04. $msg \leftarrow$ getMsg();
05.   **switch** ($msg.type$) **do**
06. cpa : ProcessCPA(msg); ngd : ProcessNogood(msg);
07. del : ProcessDel(msg); stp : $end \leftarrow$ **true**;

procedure Assign()
08.   **if** ($D(x_i) \neq \emptyset$) **then**
09. $v_i \leftarrow$ ChooseValue() ; $t_i \leftarrow t_i$+1 ;
10.   CPA $\leftarrow \{AgentView \cup (x_i, v_i, t_i)\}$;
11.   SendCPA(CPA) ;
12.   **else** Backtrack() ;

procedure SendCPA(CPA)
13.   **if** (size(CPA) $= n$) **then** broadcastMsg : stp(CPA) ; $end \leftarrow$ **true** ;
14.   **else foreach** ($x_k \succ x_i$) **do** sendMsg : cpa(CPA) to A_k ;

procedure ProcessCPA(msg)
15.   **if** ($msg.CPA$ is stronger than the $AgentView$) **then**
16. $AgentView \leftarrow CPA$;
17.   Remove all nogoods incompatible with $AgentView$;
18.   **if** ($\neg$Propagate()) **then** Backtrack() ;
19.   **else if** ($msg.sender =$ predecessor(A_i)) **then** Assign() ;

function Propagate()
20.   **if** ($\neg$AC($CSP(i)$)) **then** **return** *false* ;
21.   **else if** ($D(x_i)$ was changed) **then**
22.   **foreach** ($x_j \in CSP(i)$) **do**
23. $nogoods \leftarrow$ get nogoods from $NogoodStore[x_i]$ that are relevant to x_j ;
24.   sendMsg : del($nogoods$) to A_j ;
25.   **return** *true* ;

procedure ProcessDel(msg)
26.   **foreach** ($ng \in msg.nogoods$ **such that** Compatible(ng, $AgentView$)) **do**
27.   add(ng, $NogoodStore[x_k]$) ;   /* A_k is the agent that sent msg */
28.   **if** ($D(x_k) = \emptyset \wedge x_i \in NogoodStore[x_k]$) **then**
29.   add(solve($NogoodStore[x_k]$), $NogoodStore[x_i]$) ; Assign() ;
30.   **else if** ($D(x_k) = \emptyset \vee \neg$Propagate()) **then** Backtrack() ;

procedure Backtrack()
31. $newNogood \leftarrow$ solve($NogoodStore[x_k]$) ;   /* x_k is a variable such that $D(x_k)=\emptyset$ */
32.   **if** ($newNogood =$ empty) **then** broadcastMsg : $stp(\emptyset)$; $end \leftarrow$ **true** ;
33.   **else**   /* Let x_j be the variable on the **rhs** ($newNogood$) */
34.   sendMsg : ngd($newNogood$) to A_j ;
35.   **foreach** ($x_l \succeq x_j$) **do** $AgentView[x_l].Value \leftarrow empty$;
36.   Remove all nogoods incompatible with $AgentView$;

procedure ProcessNogood(msg)
37.   **if** (Compatible(lhs($msg.nogood$), $AgentView$)) **then**
38.   add($msg.nogood$, $NogoodStore[x_i]$) ;   /* using to the HPLV [HIR 00] */
39.   **if** (rhs($msg.nogood$).$Value = v_i$) **then** Assign() ;
40.   **else if** ($\neg$Propagate()) **then** Backtrack() ;

When calling function Propagate(), A_i restores arc consistency on its local constraint network according to the assignments on its AgentView (line 20). In our implementation, we used *AC-2001* [BES 01c] to enforce arc consistency but any generic AC algorithm can be used. MACA-del requires storing a nogood for each removed value from the algorithm enforcing arc consistency. When two nogoods are possible for the same value, we select the best with the *highest possible lowest variable* heuristic [HIR 00]. If enforcing arc consistency on $CSP(i)$ has failed, that is a domain was wiped out, the function returns *false* (line 20). Otherwise, if the domain of x_i was changed (i.e. there are some deletions to propagate), A_i informs its constrained agents by sending them *del* messages that contain nogoods justifying these removals (lines 23–24). Finally, the function returns *true* (line 25). When sending a *del* message to a neighboring agent A_j, only nogoods in which all variables in their left-hand sides have a higher priority than A_j will be communicated to A_j. Furthermore, all nogoods having the same left-hand side are factorized in one single nogood whose right-hand side is the set of all values removed by this left-hand side.

Whenever A_i receives a *del* message, it adds to the NogoodStore of the sender, say A_k (i.e. $NogoodStore[x_k]$), all nogoods compatible with the AgentView of A_i (lines 26-27). Afterward, A_i checks if the domain of x_k is wiped out (i.e. the remaining values in $D(x_k)$ are removed by nogoods that have just been received from A_k) and x_i belongs to the NogoodStore of x_k (i.e. x_i is already assigned and its current assignment is included in at least one nogood removing a value from $D(x_k)$) (line 28). If it is the case, A_i removes its current value by storing the resolved nogood from the NogoodStore of x_k (i.e. solve($NogoodStore[x_k]$)) as justification of this removal and then calls procedure Assign() to try another value (line 29). Otherwise, when $D(x_k)$ is wiped out (x_i is not assigned) or if a dead-end occurs when trying to enforce arc consistency, A_i has to backtrack, and thus it calls procedure Backtrack() (line 30).

Each time a dead-end occurs on a domain of a variable x_k in $CSP(i)$ (including x_i), the procedure Backtrack() is called. The nogoods that generated the dead-end are resolved by computing a new nogood $newNogood$ (line 31). The $newNogood$ is the conjunction of the left-hand sides of all these nogoods stored by A_i in $NogoodStore[x_k]$. If the new nogood $newNogood$ is empty, A_i terminates execution after sending an *stp* message to all agents in the system, meaning that the problem is unsolvable (line 32). Otherwise, A_i backtracks by sending an *ngd* message to agent A_j, the owner of the variable on the right-hand side of $newNogood$ (line 34). Next, A_i updates its AgentView in order to keep only the assignments of agents that are placed before A_j in the total ordering (line 35). A_i also updates the NogoodStore of all variables in $CSP(i)$ by removing nogoods incompatible with its new AgentView (line 36).

Whenever an *ngd* message is received, A_i checks the validity of the received nogood (line 37). If the received nogood is compatible with its AgentView, A_i adds this nogood to its NogoodStore (i.e. $NogoodStore[x_i]$, line 38). Then, A_i checks if the value on the right-hand side of the received nogood equals its current value (v_i). If it is the case, A_i calls the procedure Assign() to try another value for its variable (line 39). Otherwise, A_i calls function Propagate() to restore arc consistency. When a dead-end is generated in its local constraint network, A_i calls procedure Backtrack() (line 40).

5.3.2. *Enforcing AC without additional kind of message (MACA-not)*

In the following, we show how to enforce arc consistency without additional kinds of messages. In MACA-del, global consistency maintenance is achieved by communicating to constrained agents (agents in $CSP(i)$) all values pruned from $D^0(x_i)$. This may generate many *del* messages in the network and then result in a communication bottleneck. In addition, many *del* messages may lead agents to perform more efforts to process them. In MACA-not, communicating the removals produced in $CSP(i)$ is delayed until the agent A_i wants to send a *cpa* message. When sending the *cpa* message to a lower priority agent A_k, agent A_i attaches nogoods justifying value removals from $CSP(i)$ to the *cpa* message. But it does not attach all of them because some variables are irrelevant to A_k (not connected to x_k by a constraint).

MACA-not shares with A_k all nogoods justifying deletions on variables yet to be instantiated that share a constraint with both A_i and A_k (i.e. variables in $\{CSP(i) \cap CSP(k)\}$, \vars(*CPA*)). Thus, when A_k receives the *cpa*, it also receives deletions performed in $CSP(i)$ that can lead it to more arc consistency propagation.

We present in algorithm 5.2 the pseudo-code of MACA-not algorithm. Only procedures that are new to, or different from, those of MACA-del in algorithm 5.1 are presented. Function Propagate() no longer sends *del* messages; it only maintains arc consistency on $CSP(i)$ and returns $true$ iff no domain is wiped out.

In procedure SendCPA(CPA), when sending a *cpa* message to an agent A_k, A_i attaches itself to the CPA the nogoods justifying the removal from the domains of variables in $CSP(i)$ constrained with A_k (lines 11–15, algorithm 5.2).

Whenever A_i receives a *cpa* message, procedure ProcessCPA() is called (line 6). The received message will be processed only when it holds a CPA stronger than the AgentView of A_i. If it is the case, A_i updates its AgentView (line 17) and then updates the NogoodStore to be compatible with the received CPA (line 18). Next, all nogoods contained in the received message are added to the NogoodStore (line 19). Obviously, nogoods are added to the NogoodStore referring to the variable in their right-hand side (i.e. ng is added to $NogoodStore[x_j]$ if x_j is the variable in rhs(ng)). Afterward, A_i calls function Propagate() to restore arc consistency in $CSP(i)$ (line 20). If the domain of a variable in $CSP(i)$ is wiped out, A_i calls procedure Backtrack() (line 20). Otherwise, A_i checks if it has to assign its variable (line 21). A_i tries to assign its variable by calling procedure Assign() only if it receives the *cpa* from its predecessor.

Algorithm 5.2. *New lines/procedures for MACA-not with respect to MACA-del*

---

procedure MACA-not()
01. $end \leftarrow$ **false**; Propagate();
02.   **if** ($A_i = IA$) **then** Assign() ;
03.   **while** ($\neg end$) **do**
04. $msg \leftarrow$ getMsg();
05.   **switch** ($msg.type$) **do**
06. cpa : ProcessCPA(msg);
07. ngd : ProcessNogood(msg);
08. stp : $end \leftarrow$ **true**;

procedure SendCPA(CPA)
09.   **if** (size(CPA) $= n$) **then** broadcastMsg: stp(CPA); $end \leftarrow$ **true** ;
10.   **else**
11.   **foreach** ($x_k \succ x_i$) **do**
12. $nogoods \leftarrow \emptyset$;
13.   **foreach** ($x_j \in \{CSP(i) \cap CSP(k)\}$ such that $x_j \succ x_i$) **do**
14. $nogoods \leftarrow nogoods \cup$ getNogoods(x_j) ;
15.   sendMsg: $cpa(CPA, nogoods)$ **to** A_k ;

procedure ProcessCPA(msg)
16.   **if** ($msg.CPA$ is stronger than the $AgentView$) **then**
17. $AgentView \leftarrow CPA$;
18.   Remove all nogoods incompatible with $AgentView$;
19.   **foreach** ($nogoods \in msg.nogoods$) **do** add($nogoods, NogoodStore$) ;
20.   **if** ($\neg$Propagate()) **then** Backtrack() ;
21.   **else if** ($msg.sender =$ predecessor(A_i)) **then** Assign() ;

function Propagate()
22.   **return** AC($CSP(i)$) ;

5.4. Theoretical analysis

We demonstrate that MACA is sound, complete and terminates with a polynomial space complexity.

LEMMA 5.1.– MACA is guaranteed to terminate.

PROOF.– (Sketch) The proof is close to the one given in lemma 3.1, Chapter 3. It can easily be obtained, by induction on the agent ordering, that there will be a finite number of new generated CPAs (at most d^n, where n is the number of variables and d is the maximum domain size) and that agents can never fall into an infinite loop for a given CPA.

LEMMA 5.2.– MACA cannot infer inconsistency if a solution exists.

PROOF.– Whenever a stronger *cpa* or an *ngd* message is received, MACA agents update their NogoodStores. In MACA-del, the nogoods contained in *del* are accepted only if they are compatible with AgentView (line 27, algorithm 5.1). In MACA-not, the nogoods included in the *cpa* messages are compatible with the received CPA, and they are accepted only when the CPA is stronger than AgentView (line 16, algorithm 5.2). Hence, for every CPA that may potentially lead to a solution, agents only store valid nogoods. Because all additional nogoods are generated by logical inference when a domain wipeout occurs, the empty nogood cannot be inferred if the network is satisfiable.

THEOREM 5.1.– MACA is correct.

PROOF.– The argument for soundness is close to the one given in theorem 3.2, Chapter 3. The fact that agents only forward consistent partial solution on the *cpa* messages at only one place in procedure Assign() (line 11, algorithm 5.1) implies that the agents receive only consistent assignments. A solution is found by the last agent only in procedure SendCPA(CPA) at (line 13, algorithm 5.1 and line 9, algorithm 5.2). At this point, all agents have assigned their variables, and their assignments are consistent. Thus, MACA is sound. Completeness comes from the fact that MACA is able to terminate and does not report inconsistency if a solution exists (lemmas 5.1 and 5.2).

THEOREM 5.2.– MACA is polynomial in space.

PROOF.– On each agent, MACA stores one nogood of size, at most, n per removed value in its local constraint network. The local constraint network contains at most n variables. Thus, the space complexity of MACA is in $O(n^2 d)$ on each agent where d is the maximal initial domain size.

THEOREM 5.3.– MACA messages are polynomially bounded.

PROOF.– The largest messages for MACA-del are *del* messages. In the worst case, a *del* message contains a nogood for each value. Thus, the size of *del* messages is in $O(nd)$. In MACA-not, the largest messages are *cpa* messages. The worst case is a *cpa* message containing a CPA and one nogood for each value of each variable in the local constraint network. Thus, the size of a *cpa* message is in $O(n + n^2 d) = O(n^2 d)$.

5.5. Experimental results

In this section, we experimentally compare MACA algorithms to ABT-uac, ABT-dac [BRI 08] and AFC-ng (Chapter 3). These algorithms are evaluated on uniform random binary DisCSPs. All experiments were performed on the DisChoco 2.0 platform[1] [WAH 11], in which agents were simulated by Java threads that communicate only through message passing. All algorithms were tested on the same static agents ordering (lexicographic ordering) and the same nogood selection heuristic (*HPLV*) [HIR 00]. For ABT-dac, we implemented an improved version of Silaghi's solution detection [SIL 06] and counters for tagging assignments.

---

1 http://dischoco.sourceforge.net/.

We evaluate the performance of the algorithms by communication load [LYN 97] and computation effort. Communication load is measured by the total number of exchanged messages among agents during algorithm execution ($\#msg$), including those of termination detection (system messages). Computation effort is measured by the number of non-concurrent constraint checks ($\#ncccs$) [ZIV 06b]. $\#ncccs$ is used in distributed constraint solving to simulate the computation time.

The algorithms are tested on uniform random binary DisCSPs which are characterized by $\langle n, d, p_1, p_2 \rangle$, where n is the number of agents/variables, d is the number of values in each of the domains, p_1 is the network connectivity defined as the ratio of existing binary constraints and p_2 is the constraint tightness defined as the ratio of forbidden value pairs. We solved instances of two classes of constraint networks: sparse networks $\langle 20, 10, 0.25, p_2 \rangle$ and dense networks $\langle 20, 10, 0.7, p_2 \rangle$. We varied the tightness from 0.1 to 0.9 by steps of 0.1. For each pair of fixed density and tightness (p_1, p_2), we generated 100 instances. The average over the 100 instances is reported.

First, we present the performance of the algorithms on the sparse instances, $p_1 = 0.25$ (Figures 5.1 and 5.2). Concerning the computational effort (Figure 5.1), algorithms enforcing an amount of arc consistency are better than AFC-ng, which only enforces FC. Among these algorithms, MACA-del is the fastest one. MACA-not behaves like ABT-dac, which is better than the ABT-uac.

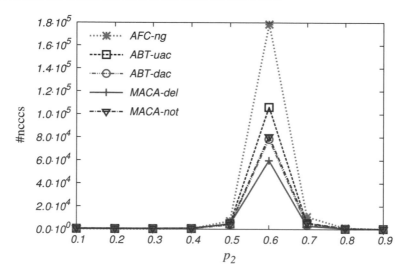

Figure 5.1. *The number of non-concurrent constraint checks ($\#ncccs$) performed for solving sparse problems ($p_1 = 0.25$)*

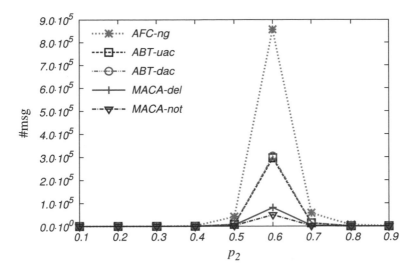

Figure 5.2. *The total number of messages sent for solving sparse problems ($p_1 = 0.25$)*

Concerning the communication load (Figure 5.2), algorithms performing an amount of arc consistency improve on AFC-ng by an even larger scale than for computational effort. ABT-uac and ABT-dac require almost the same number of exchanged messages. Among the algorithms maintaining an amount of arc consistency, the algorithms with a synchronous behavior (MACA algorithms) outperform those with an asynchronous behavior (ABT-dac and ABT-uac) by a factor of 6. It thus seems that on sparse problems, maintaining arc consistency in synchronous search algorithms provides more benefit than in asynchronous ones. MACA-not exchanges slightly fewer messages than MACA-del at the complexity peak.

In the following, we present the performance of the algorithms on the dense instances ($p_1 = 0.7$). Concerning the computational effort (Figure 5.3), the first observation is that asynchronous algorithms are less efficient than those performing assignments sequentially. Among all compared algorithms, AFC-ng is the fastest one on these dense problems. This is consistent with results on centralized CSPs where FC had a better behavior on dense problems than on sparse ones [BES 96, GRA 96]. As on sparse problems, ABT-dac outperforms ABT-uac. Contrary to sparse problems, MACA-not outperforms the MACA-del.

Concerning the communication load (Figure 5.4), on dense problems, asynchronous algorithms (ABT-uac and ABT-dac) require a large number of exchanged messages. MACA-del does not improve on AFC-ng because of a very large number of exchanged *del* messages. On these problems, MACA-not is the algorithm that requires the smallest number of messages. MACA-not improves on synchronous algorithms (AFC-ng and MACA-del) by a factor of 11 and on asynchronous algorithms (ABT-uac and ABT-dac) by a factor of 40.

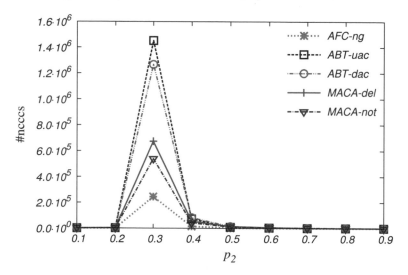

Figure 5.3. *The number of non-concurrent constraint checks (#ncccs) performed for solving dense problems ($p_1 = 0.7$)*

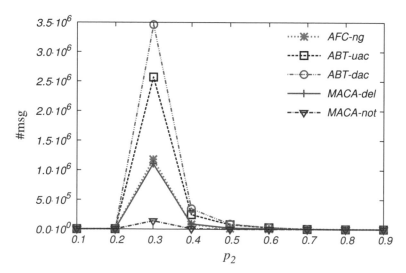

Figure 5.4. *The total number of messages sent for solving dense problems ($p_1 = 0.7$)*

5.5.1. *Discussion*

From these experiments, we can conclude that in synchronous algorithms, maintaining arc consistency is better than maintaining FC in terms of computational effort when the network is sparse, and is always better in terms of communication load. We can also conclude that maintaining arc consistency in synchronous algorithms produces much larger benefits than maintaining arc consistency in asynchronous algorithms like ABT.

5.6. Summary

We have proposed two synchronous search algorithms for solving DisCSPs. These are the first attempts to maintain arc consistency during synchronous search in DisCSPs. The first algorithm, MACA-del, enforces arc consistency due to an additional type of message, that is deletion message. The second algorithm, MACA-not, achieves arc consistency without any new type of message. Despite the synchronicity of the search, these two algorithms perform the arc consistency phase asynchronously. The experiments show that maintaining arc consistency during synchronous search produces much larger benefits than maintaining arc consistency in asynchronous algorithms like ABT. The communication load of MACA-del can be significantly lower than that of AFC-ng, the best synchronous algorithm to date. MACA-not shows even larger improvements due to its more parsimonious use of messages.

Part 3

Asynchronous Search Algorithms and Ordering Heuristics for DisCSPs

6

Corrigendum to "Min-Domain Retroactive Ordering for Asynchronous Backtracking"

The asynchronous backtracking algorithm with dynamic ordering, ABT_DO, has been proposed in [ZIV 06a]. ABT_DO allows us to change the order of agents during distributed asynchronous search. In ABT_DO, when an agent assigns a value to its variable, it can reorder lower priority agents. Retroactive heuristics, called ABT_DO-Retro, that allow more flexibility in the selection of new orders were introduced in [ZIV 09]. Unfortunately, the description of the time stamping protocol used to compare orders in ABT_DO-Retro may lead to an implementation in which ABT_DO-Retro may not terminate. In this chapter, we give an example that shows how ABT_DO-Retro can enter in an infinite loop if it uses this protocol and we propose a new correct way for comparing time stamps [MEC 12].

6.1. Introduction

Zivan and Meisels proposed the asynchronous backtracking algorithm with dynamic ordering, ABT_DO, in [ZIV 06a]. In ABT_DO, when an agent assigns a value to its variable, it can reorder lower priority agents. Each agent in ABT_DO holds a current order (i.e. a vector of agent IDs) and a vector of counters (one counter attached to each agent ID). The vector of counters attached to agent IDs forms a time stamp. Initially, all time stamp counters are set to zero, and all agents start with the same order. Each agent that proposes a new order increments its counter by one and sets counters of all lower priority agents to zero (the counters of higher priority agents are not modified). When comparing two orders, the strongest is the one with the lexicographically *larger* time stamp. In other words, the strongest order is the one for which the first different counter is larger. The most successful ordering heuristic found in [ZIV 06a] was the *nogood-triggered* heuristic in which an agent that receives a nogood moves the nogood generator to be right after it in the order.

A new type of ordering heuristics for ABT_DO is presented in [ZIV 09]. These heuristics, called retroactive heuristics (ABT_DO-Retro), enable the generator of the nogood to propose a new order in which it moves itself to a higher priority position than that of the target of the backtrack. The degree of flexibility of these heuristics depends on a parameter K. Agents that detect a dead-end are moved to a higher priority position in the order. If the length of the created nogood is larger than K, they can be moved up to the place that is right after the second to last agent in the nogood. If the length of the created nogood is smaller than or equal to K, the sending agent can be moved to a position before all the participants in the nogood and the nogood is sent and saved by all of the participants in the nogood. Because agents must store nogoods that are smaller than or equal to K, the space complexity of agents is exponential in K.

Recent attempts to implement the ABT_DO-Retro algorithm proposed in [ZIV 09] have revealed a specific detail of the algorithm that concerns its time stamping protocol. The natural understanding of the description given in [ZIV 09] of the time stamping protocol used to compare orders in ABT_DO-Retro can affect the correctness of the algorithm. In this chapter, we address this protocol by describing the undesired outcome of this protocol and propose an alternative deterministic method that ensures the outcome expected in [ZIV 09].

6.2. Background

The degree of flexibility of the retroactive heuristics mentioned above depends on a parameter K. K defines the level of flexibility of the heuristic with respect to the amount of information an agent can store in its memory. Agents that detect a dead-end move themselves to a higher priority position in the order. If the length of the nogood created is not larger than K, then the agent can move to any position it desires (even to the highest priority position) and all agents that are included in the nogood are required to add the nogood to their set of constraints and hold it until the algorithm terminates. If the size of the created nogood is larger than K, the agent that created the nogood can move up to the place that is right after the second to last agent in the nogood. Because agents must store nogoods that are smaller than or equal to K, the space complexity of agents is exponential in K.

The best retroactive heuristic introduced in [ZIV 09] is called ABT_DO-Retro-MinDom. This heuristic does not require any additional storage (i.e. $K = 0$). In this heuristic, the agent that generates a nogood is placed in the new order between the last and the second to last agents in the generated nogood. However, the generator of the nogood moves to a higher priority position than the backtracking target (the agent the nogood was sent to) only if its domain is smaller than that of the agents it passes on the way up. Otherwise, the generator of the nogood is placed right after the last agent with a smaller domain between the last and the second to last agents in the nogood.

In asynchronous backtracking algorithms with dynamic ordering, agents propose new orders asynchronously. Hence, we must enable agents to coherently decide which of the two different orders is the stronger. To this end, as it has been explained in [ZIV 06a] and recalled in [ZIV 09], each agent in ABT_DO holds a *counter vector* (one counter attached to each position in the order). The counter vector and the indexes of the agents currently in these positions form a time stamp. Initially, all counters are set to zero and all agents are aware of the initial order. Each agent that proposes a new order increments the counter attached to its position in the current order and sets to zero counters of all lower priority positions (the counters of higher priority positions are not modified). The strongest order is determined by a lexicographic comparison of counter vectors combined with the agent indexes. However, the rules for reordering agents in ABT_DO imply that the strongest order is always the one for which the first different counter is larger.

In ABT_DO-Retro, agents can be moved to a position that is higher than that of the target of the backtrack. This new feature makes it possible to generate two contradictory orders that have the same time stamp. To address this additional issue, the description given by the authors was limited to two sentences: *"The most relevant order is determined lexicographically. Ties which could not have been generated in standard ABT_DO are broken using the agents indexes"* (quoted from [ZIV 09], p. 190, theorem 1).

The natural understanding of this description is that the strongest order is the one associated with the lexicographically greater counter vector, and when the counter vectors are equal, the lexicographic order on the indexes of agents breaks the tie by preferring the one with smaller vector of indexes. We will refer to this general interpretation as method m_1. Let us illustrate method m_1 via an example. Consider two orders $\mathcal{O}_1=[A_1, A_3, A_2, A_4, A_5]$ and $\mathcal{O}_2=[A_1, A_2, A_3, A_4, A_5]$, where the counter vector associated with $\mathcal{O}_1$ equals $\mathcal{V}_1 = [2, 4, 2, 2, 0]$ and the counter vector associated with $\mathcal{O}_2$ equals $\mathcal{V}_2 = [2, 4, 2, 1, 0]$. Because in m_1 the strongest order is determined by lexicographically comparing the counter vectors, in this example, $\mathcal{O}_1$ is considered stronger than $\mathcal{O}_2$. In section 6.3, we show that method m_1 may lead ABT_DO-Retro to fall into an infinite loop when $K = 0$.

The right way to compare orders is to compare their counter vectors, one position at a time from left to right until they differ on a position (preferring the order with greater counter) or they are equal on that position but the indexes of the agents in that position differ (preferring the smaller index). We will refer to this method as m_2. Consider again the two orders $\mathcal{O}_1$ and $\mathcal{O}_2$ and associated counter vectors defined above. The counter at the first position equals 2 on both counter vectors and the index of the first agent in $\mathcal{O}_1$ (i.e. A_1) is the same as in $\mathcal{O}_2$ the counter at the second position equals 4 on both counter vectors; however, the index of the second agent in $\mathcal{O}_2$ (i.e. A_2) is smaller than the index of the second agent in $\mathcal{O}_1$ (i.e. A_3). Hence, in this case, $\mathcal{O}_2$ is considered stronger than $\mathcal{O}_1$. (Note that according to m_1, $\mathcal{O}_1$ is stronger than $\mathcal{O}_2$.) In section 6.4, we give the proof that method m_2 for comparing orders is correct.

6.3. ABT_DO-Retro may not terminate

In this section, we show that ABT_DO-Retro may not terminate when using m_1 and when $K = 0$. We illustrate this on ABT_DO-Retro-MinDom as described in [ZIV 09] as it is an example of ABT_DO-Retro where $K = 0$. Consider a DisCSP with five agents $\{A_1, A_2, A_3, A_4, A_5\}$ and domains $D(x_1)=D(x_5)=\{1,2,3,4,5\}$, $D(x_2)=D(x_3)=D(x_4)=\{6,7\}$. We assume that, initially, all agents store the same order $\mathcal{O}_1 = [A_1, A_5, A_4, A_2, A_3]$ with associated counter vector $\mathcal{V}_1 = [0,0,0,0,0]$. The constraints are:

$c_{12} : (x_1, x_2) \notin \{(1,6),(1,7)\}$;
$c_{13} : (x_1, x_3) \notin \{(2,6),(2,7)\}$;
$c_{14} : (x_1, x_4) \notin \{(1,6),(1,7)\}$;
$c_{24} : (x_2, x_4) \notin \{(6,6),(7,7)\}$;
$c_{35} : (x_3, x_5) \notin \{(7,5)\}$.

In the following, we give a possible execution of ABT_DO-Retro-MinDom (Figure 6.1).

$$\mathcal{O}_1 = [\, A_1, A_5, A_4, A_2, A_3 \,] \quad \mathcal{V}_1 = [\, 0,0,0,0,0 \,]$$
$$\mathcal{O}_2 = [\, A_4, A_1, A_5, A_2, A_3 \,] \quad \mathcal{V}_2 = [\, 1,0,0,0,0 \,]$$
$$\mathcal{O}_3 = [\, A_2, A_1, A_5, A_4, A_3 \,] \quad \mathcal{V}_3 = [\, 1,0,0,0,0 \,]$$
$$\mathcal{O}_4 = [\, A_4, A_3, A_1, A_5, A_2 \,] \quad \mathcal{V}_4 = [\, 1,1,0,0,0 \,]$$

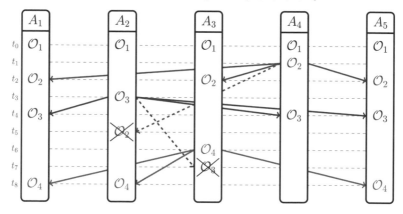

Figure 6.1. *The schema of exchanging order messages by ABT_DO-Retro*

t_0: all agents assign the first value in their domains to their variables and send *ok?* messages to their neighbors.

t_1: A_4 receives the first $ok?(x_1 = 1)$ message sent by A_1 and generates a nogood $ng_1 : \neg(x_1 = 1)$. Then, it proposes a new order $\mathcal{O}_2 = [A_4, A_1, A_5, A_2, A_3]$ with $\mathcal{V}_2 = [1,0,0,0,0]$. Afterward, it assigns the value 6 to its variable and sends $ok?(x_4 = 6)$ message to all its neighbors (including A_2).

t_2: A_3 receives $\mathcal{O}_2 = [A_4, A_1, A_5, A_2, A_3]$ and deletes $\mathcal{O}_1$ because $\mathcal{O}_2$ is stronger; A_1 receives the nogood sent by A_4, it replaces its assignment to 2 and sends an $ok?(x_1 = 2)$ message to all its neighbors.

t_3: A_2 has not yet received $\mathcal{O}_2$ and the new assignment of A_1. A_2 generates a new nogood $ng_2 : \neg(x_1 = 1)$ and proposes a new order $\mathcal{O}_3 = [A_2, A_1, A_5, A_4, A_3]$ with $V_3 = [1, 0, 0, 0, 0]$. Afterward, it assigns the value 6 to its variable and sends $ok?(x_2 = 6)$ message to all its neighbors (including A_4).

t_4: A_4 receives the new assignment of A_2 (i.e. $x_2 = 6$) and $\mathcal{O}_3 = [A_2, A_1, A_5, A_4, A_3]$. Afterward, it discards $\mathcal{O}_2$ because $\mathcal{O}_3$ is stronger; then, A_4 tries to satisfy c_{24} because A_2 has a higher priority according to $\mathcal{O}_3$. Hence, A_4 replaces its current assignment (i.e. $x_4 = 6$) by $x_4 = 7$ and sends an $ok?(x_4 = 7)$ message to all its neighbors (including A_2).

t_5: when receiving $\mathcal{O}_2$, A_2 discards it because its current order is stronger.

t_6: after receiving the new assignment of A_1 (i.e. $x_1 = 2$) and before receiving $\mathcal{O}_3 = [A_2, A_1, A_5, A_4, A_3]$, A_3 generates a nogood $ng_3 : \neg(x_1 = 2)$ and proposes a new order $\mathcal{O}_4 = [A_4, A_3, A_1, A_5, A_2]$ with $V_4 = [1, 1, 0, 0, 0]$; the order $\mathcal{O}_4$ is stronger than $\mathcal{O}_3$ according to m_1. Because in ABT_DO an agent sends the new order only to lower priority agents, A_3 will not send $\mathcal{O}_4$ to A_4 because it is a higher priority agent.

t_7: A_3 receives $\mathcal{O}_3$ and then discards it because it is obsolete.

t_8: A_2 receives $\mathcal{O}_4$, but it has not yet received the new assignment of A_4. Then, it tries to satisfy c_{24} because A_4 has a higher priority according to its current order $\mathcal{O}_4$. Hence, A_2 replaces its current assignment (i.e. $x_2 = 6$) by $x_2 = 7$ and sends an $ok?(x_2 = 7)$ message to all its neighbors (including A_4).

t_9: A_2 receives the $ok?(x_4 = 7)$ message sent by A_4 in t_4 and changes its current value (i.e. $x_2 = 7$) by $x_2 = 6$. Then, A_2 sends an $ok?(x_2 = 6)$ message to all its neighbors (including A_4). At the same time, A_4 receives $ok?(x_2 = 7)$ message sent by A_2 in t_8. A_4 changes its current value (i.e. $x_4 = 7$) by $x_4 = 6$. Then, A_4 sends an $ok?(x_4 = 6)$ message to all its neighbors (including A_2).

t_{10}: A_2 receives the $ok?(x_4 = 6)$ message sent by A_4 in t_9 and changes its current value (i.e. $x_2 = 6$) by $x_2 = 7$. Then, A_2 sends an $ok?(x_2 = 7)$ message to all its neighbors (including A_4). At the same moment, A_4 receives $ok?(x_2 = 6)$ message sent by A_2 in t_9. A_4 changes its current value (i.e. $x_4 = 6$) by $x_4 = 7$. Then, A_4 sends an $ok?(x_4 = 7)$ message to all its neighbors (including A_2).

t_{11}: we come back to the situation we were facing at time t_9, and therefore, ABT_DO-Retro-MinDom may fall into an infinite loop when using method m_1.

6.4. The right way to compare orders

Let us formally define the second method, m_2, for comparing orders in which we compare the indexes of agents as soon as the counters in a position are equal on both counter vectors associated with the orders being compared. Given any order $\mathcal{O}$, we denote by $\mathcal{O}(i)$ the index of the agent located in the ith position in $\mathcal{O}$ and by $\mathcal{V}(i)$ the counter in the ith position in the counter vector $\mathcal{V}$ associated with order $\mathcal{O}$. An order $\mathcal{O}_1$ with counter vector $\mathcal{V}_1$ is stronger than an order $\mathcal{O}_2$ with counter vector $\mathcal{V}_2$ if and only if a position $i, 1 \leq i \leq n$ exists, such that for all $1 \leq j < i$, $\mathcal{V}_1(j) = \mathcal{V}_2(j)$ and $\mathcal{O}_1(j) = \mathcal{O}_2(j)$, and $\mathcal{V}_1(i) > \mathcal{V}_2(i)$ or $\mathcal{V}_1(i) = \mathcal{V}_2(i)$ and $\mathcal{O}_1(i) < \mathcal{O}_1(i)$.

In our correctness proof for the use of m_2 in ABT_DO-Retro, we use the following notations. The initial order known by all agents is denoted by $\mathcal{O}_{init}$. Each agent, A_i, stores a current order, $\mathcal{O}_i$, with an associated counter vector, $\mathcal{V}_i$. Each counter vector $\mathcal{V}_i$ consists of n counters $\mathcal{V}_i(1), \ldots, \mathcal{V}_i(n)$ such that $\mathcal{V}_i = [\mathcal{V}_i(1), \ldots, \mathcal{V}_i(n)]$. When $\mathcal{V}_i$ is the counter vector associated with an order $\mathcal{O}_i$, we denote by $\mathcal{V}_i(k)$ the value of the kth counter in the counter vector stored by the agent A_i. We define ρ to be equal to $\max\{\mathcal{V}_i(1) \mid i \in 1..n\}$. The value of ρ evolves during the search so that it always corresponds to the value of the largest counter among all the first counters stored by agents.

Let K be the parameter defining the degree of flexibility of the retroactive heuristics (see section 6.1). Next, we show that the ABT_DO-Retro algorithm is correct when using m_2 and with $K = 0$. The proof that the algorithm is correct when $K \neq 0$ can be found in [ZIV 09].

To prove the correctness of ABT_DO-Retro, we use induction on the number of agents. For a single agent, the order is static; therefore, the correctness of standard ABT implies the correctness of ABT_DO-Retro. Assume that ABT_DO-Retro is correct for every DisCSP with $n - 1$ agents. We show in the following that ABT_DO-Retro is correct for every DisCSP with n agents. To this end, we first prove the following lemmas.

LEMMA 6.1.– Given enough time, if the value of ρ does not change, the highest priority agent in all orders stored by all agents will be the same.

PROOF.– Assume the system reaches a state σ, where the value of ρ no longer increases. Let $\mathcal{O}_i$ be the order that, when generated, caused the system to enter state σ. Inevitably, we have $\mathcal{V}_i(1) = \rho$. Assume that $\mathcal{O}_i \neq \mathcal{O}_{init}$ and let A_i be the agent that generated $\mathcal{O}_i$. The agent A_i is necessarily the highest priority agent in the new order $\mathcal{O}_i$ because the only possibility for the generator of a new order to change the position of the highest priority agent is to put itself in the first position in the new order. Thus, $\mathcal{O}_i$ is sent by A_i to all other agents because A_i must send $\mathcal{O}_i$ to all agents that have a lower priority than itself. So, after a finite time, all agents will be aware of $\mathcal{O}_i$. This is also true if $\mathcal{O}_i = \mathcal{O}_{init}$. Now, by assumption, the value of ρ no longer increases. As a result, the only way for another agent to generate an order $\mathcal{O}'$ such that the highest priority agents in $\mathcal{O}_i$ and $\mathcal{O}'$ are different (i.e. $\mathcal{O}'(1) \neq \mathcal{O}_i(1)$)

is to put itself in the first position in $\mathcal{O}'$ and to do that *before* it has received $\mathcal{O}_i$ (otherwise, $\mathcal{O}'$ would increase ρ). Therefore, the time passed from the moment the system entered state σ until a new order $\mathcal{O}'$ was generated is finite. Let $\mathcal{O}_j$ be the strongest such order (i.e. $\mathcal{O}'$) and let A_j be the agent that generated $\mathcal{O}_j$. That is, A_j is the agent with smallest index among those who generated such an order $\mathcal{O}'$. The agent A_j will send $\mathcal{O}_j$ to all other agents and $\mathcal{O}_j$ will be accepted by all other agents after a finite amount of time. Once an agent has accepted $\mathcal{O}_j$, all orders that may be generated by this agent do not reorder the highest priority agent; otherwise, ρ would increase.

LEMMA 6.2.– If the algorithm is correct for $n - 1$ agents, then it terminates for n agents.

PROOF.– If during the search ρ continues to increase, this means that some of the agents continue to send new orders in which they put themselves in the first position. Hence, the nogoods they generate when proposing the new orders are necessarily unary (i.e. they have an empty left-hand side) because in ABT_DO-Retro, when the parameter K is zero, the nogood sender cannot put itself in a higher priority position than the second last in the nogood. Suppose $ng_0 = \neg(x_i = v_i)$ is one of these nogoods sent by an agent A_j. After a finite amount of time, agent A_i, the owner of x_i, will receive ng_0. Three cases can occur. In the first case, A_i still has value v_i in its domain. So, the value v_i is pruned once and for all from $D(x_i)$ due to ng_0. In the second case, A_i has already received a nogood equivalent to ng_0 from another agent. Here, v_i no longer belongs to $D(x_i)$. When changing its value, A_i has sent an *ok?* message with its new value v'_i. If A_i and A_j were neighbors, this *ok?* message has been sent to A_j. If A_i and A_j were not neighbors when A_i changed its value to v'_i, this *ok?* message was sent by A_i to A_j after A_j requested to add a link between them at the moment it generated ng_0. Because of the assumption that messages are always delivered in a finite amount of time, we know that A_j will receive the *ok?* message containing v'_i a finite amount of time after it sent ng_0. Thus, A_j will not be able to send nogoods forever about a value v_i pruned once and for all from $D(x_i)$. In the third case, A_i already stores a nogood with a non-empty left-hand side discarding v_i. Note that although A_j moves to the highest priority position, A_i may be of lower priority, that is there can be agents with higher priority than A_i according to the current order that are not included in ng_0. Because of the standard *highest possible lowest variable involved* [HIR 00, BES 05] heuristic for selecting nogoods in ABT algorithms, we are sure that the nogood with an empty left-hand side ng_0 will replace the other existing nogood and v_i will be permanently pruned from $D(x_i)$. Thus, in all three cases, every time ρ increases, we know that an agent has moved to the first position in the order, and a value was definitively pruned a finite amount of time before or after. There is a bounded number of values in the network. Thus, ρ cannot increase forever. Now, if ρ stops increasing, then after a finite amount of time the highest priority agent in all orders stored by all agents will be the same (lemma 6.1). Because the algorithm is correct for $n-1$ agents, after each assignment of the highest priority agent, the rest of the agents will either reach an idle state,[1] generate an empty nogood indicating that there is no solution,

---

1 As proved in lemma 6.3, this indicates that a solution was found.

or generate a unary nogood, which is sent to the highest priority agent. Because the number of values in the system is finite, the third option, which is the only one that does not imply immediate termination, cannot occur forever.

LEMMA 6.3.– If the algorithm is correct for $n - 1$ agents, then it is sound for n agents.

PROOF.– Let $\mathcal{O}'$ be the strongest order generated before reaching the state of quiescence and let $\mathcal{O}$ be the strongest order generated such that $\mathcal{V}(1) = \mathcal{V}'(1)$ (and such that $\mathcal{O}$ has changed the position of the first agent – assuming $\mathcal{O} \neq \mathcal{O}_{init}$). Given the rules for reordering agents, the agent that generated $\mathcal{O}$ has necessarily put itself first because it has modified $\mathcal{V}(1)$ and thus also the position of the highest agent. So it has sent $\mathcal{O}$ to all other agents. When reaching the state of quiescence, we know that no order $\mathcal{O}_j$ with $\mathcal{O}_j(1) \neq \mathcal{O}(1)$ has been generated because this would break the assumption that $\mathcal{O}$ is the strongest order where the position of the first agent has been changed. Hence, at the state of quiescence, every agent A_i stores an order $\mathcal{O}_i$ such that $\mathcal{O}_i(1) = \mathcal{O}(1)$. (This is also true if $\mathcal{O} = \mathcal{O}_{init}$.) Let us consider the DisCSP P composed of $n - 1$ lower priority agents according to $\mathcal{O}$. As the algorithm is correct for $n - 1$ agents, the state of quiescence means that a solution was found for P. Also, because all agents in P are aware that $\mathcal{O}(1)$ is the agent with the highest priority, the state of quiescence also implies that all constraints that involve $\mathcal{O}(1)$ have been successfully tested by agents in P; otherwise, at least one agent in P would try to change its value and send an *ok?* or *ngd* message. Therefore, the state of quiescence implies that a solution was found.

LEMMA 6.4.– The algorithm is complete.

PROOF.– All nogoods are generated by logical inferences from existing constraints. Thus, an empty nogood cannot be inferred if a solution exists.

Following lemmas 6.2–6.4, we obtain the correctness of the main theorem in this chapter.

THEOREM 6.1.– The ABT_DO-Retro algorithm with $K = 0$ is correct when using the m_2 method for selecting the strongest order.

6.5. Summary

We proposed in this chapter a corrigendum of the protocol designed for establishing the priority between orders in the asynchronous backtracking algorithm with dynamic ordering using retroactive heuristics (ABT_DO-Retro). We presented an example that shows how ABT_DO-Retro can enter an infinite loop following the natural understanding of the description given by the authors of ABT_DO-Retro. We described the correct way for comparing time stamps of orders. We gave the proof that the new method for comparing orders is correct.

7

Agile Asynchronous Backtracking (Agile-ABT)

It is known from centralized constraint satisfaction problems (CSPs) that reordering variables dynamically improves the efficiency of the search procedure. Moreover, reordering in asynchronous backtracking (ABT) is required in various applications (e.g. security [SIL 01a]). All polynomial space algorithms proposed so far to improve an ABT by reordering agents during search only allow a limited amount of reordering (section 2.2.3). In this chapter, we propose Agile-ABT [BES 11], a search procedure that is able to change the ordering of agents more than previous approaches. This is done via the original notion of termination value, a vector of stamps labeling the new orders exchanged by agents during the search. In Agile-ABT, agents can reorder themselves as much as they want as long as the termination value decreases as the search progresses. Agents cooperate without any global control to reduce termination values rapidly, gaining efficiency while ensuring polynomial space complexity. We compare the performance of Agile-ABT with other algorithms, and the results show the good performance of Agile-ABT when compared with other dynamic reordering techniques.

7.1. Introduction

Several distributed algorithms for solving distributed constraint satisfaction problems (DisCSPs) have been developed, among which ABT is the central one [YOK 98, BES 05]. ABT is an asynchronous algorithm executed autonomously by each agent in the distributed problem. In ABT, the priority order of agents is static, and an agent tries to find an assignment satisfying the constraints with higher priority agents. When an agent sets a variable value, the selected value will not be changed unless an exhaustive search is performed by lower priority agents. Now, it is known from centralized CSPs that adapting the order of variables dynamically during the search drastically fastens the search procedure. Moreover, reordering in ABT is required in various applications (e.g. security [SIL 01a]).

Asynchronous weak commitment (AWC) dynamically reorders agents during search by moving the sender of a nogood higher in the order than the other agents in the nogood [YOK 95a]. But AWC requires exponential space for storing nogoods. Silaghi *et al.* tried to hybridize ABT with AWC [SIL 01c]. Abstract agents fulfill the reordering operation to guarantee a finite number of asynchronous reordering operations. In [SIL 06], the heuristic of the centralized dynamic backtracking [GIN 93] was applied to ABT. However, in both studies, the improvement obtained on ABT was minor.

Zivan and Meisels proposed another algorithm for dynamic ordering in asynchronous backtracking (ABT_DO) [ZIV 06a]. When an agent assigns a value to its variable, ABT_DO can reorder only lower priority agents. A new kind of ordering heuristics for ABT_DO is presented in [ZIV 09]. These heuristics, called retroactive heuristics ABT_DO-Retro, enable the generator of the nogood to be moved to a higher position than that of the target of the backtrack. The degree of flexibility of these heuristics is dependent on the size of the nogood storage capacity, which is predefined. Agents are limited to store nogoods that have a size smaller than or equal to a predefined size K. The space complexity of the agents is thus exponential in K. However, the best heuristic, ABT_DO-Retro-MinDom, proposed in [ZIV 09] is a heuristic that does not require this exponential storage of nogoods. In ABT_DO-Retro-MinDom, the agent that generates a nogood is placed in the new order between the last and the second to last agents in the nogood if its domain size is smaller than that of the agents it passes on the way up.

In this chapter, we propose Agile asynchronous backtracking (Agile-ABT), an asynchronous dynamic ordering algorithm that does not follow the standard restrictions in asynchronous backtracking algorithms. The order of agents appearing *before* the agent receiving a backtrack message can be changed with a great freedom while ensuring polynomial space complexity. Furthermore, that agent receiving the backtrack message, called the backtracking *target*, is not necessarily the agent with the lowest priority within the conflicting agents in the current order. The principle of Agile-ABT is based on termination values exchanged by agents during search. A termination value is a tuple of positive integers attached to an order. Each positive integer in the tuple represents the expected current domain size of the agent in that position in the order. Orders are changed by agents without any global control so that the termination value decreases lexicographically as the search progresses. Because a domain size can never be negative, termination values cannot decrease indefinitely. An agent informs the others of a new order by sending them its new order and its new termination value. When an agent compares two contradictory orders, it keeps the order associated with the smallest termination value.

7.2. Introductory material

In Agile-ABT, all agents start with the same order $\mathcal{O}$. Then, agents are allowed to change the order asynchronously. Each agent $A_i \in \mathcal{A}$ stores a unique order denoted by $\mathcal{O}_i$. $\mathcal{O}_i$ is called the current order of A_i. Agents appearing before A_i in $\mathcal{O}_i$ are the higher priority agents (predecessors) denoted by $\mathcal{O}_i^-$ and conversely the lower priority agents (successors) $\mathcal{O}_i^+$ are agents appearing after A_i.

Agents can infer inconsistent sets of assignments, called nogoods. A nogood can be represented as an implication. There are clearly many different ways of representing a given nogood as an implication. For example, $\neg[(x_i{=}v_i) \wedge (x_j{=}v_j) \wedge \cdots \wedge (x_k{=}v_k)]$ is logically equivalent to $[(x_j{=}v_j) \wedge \cdots \wedge (x_k{=}v_k)] \rightarrow (x_i \neq v_i)$. When a nogood is represented as an implication, the *left-hand side* (lhs) and the *right-hand side* (rhs) are defined from the position of $\rightarrow$. A nogood ng is *relevant* with respect to an order $\mathcal{O}_i$ if all agents in lhs(ng) appear before rhs(ng) in $\mathcal{O}_i$.

The current domain of x_i is the set of values $v_i \in D^0(x_i)$ such that $x_i \neq v_i$ does not appear in any of the rhs of the nogoods stored by A_i. Each agent keeps only one nogood per removed value. The size of the current domain of A_i is denoted by d_i (i.e. $|D(x_i)| = d_i$). The initial domain size of a variable x_i, before any value has been pruned, is denoted by d_i^0 (i.e. $d_i^0 = |D^0(x_i)|$ and $d_i = |D(x_i)|$).

Before presenting Agile-ABT, we need to introduce new notions and present some key subfunctions.

7.2.1. *Reordering details*

To allow agents to asynchronously propose new orders, they must be able to coherently decide which order to select. We propose that the priority between the different orders is based on *termination values*. Informally, if $\mathcal{O}_i = [A_1, \ldots, A_n]$ is the current order known by an agent A_i, then the tuple of domain sizes $[d_1, \ldots, d_n]$ is the termination value of $\mathcal{O}_i$ on A_i. To build termination values, agents need to know the current domain sizes of other agents. To this end, agents exchange *explanations*.

DEFINITION 7.1.– *An* explanation e_j *is an expression* lhs$(e_j) \rightarrow d_j$, *where* lhs(e_j) *is the conjunction of the left-hand sides of all nogoods stored by A_j as justifications of value removals for x_j, and d_j is the number of values not pruned by nogoods in the domain of A_j. d_j is the right-hand side of e_j,* rhs(e_j).

Each time an agent communicates its assignment to other agents (by sending them an *ok?* message, see section 7.3), it inserts its explanation in the *ok?* message for allowing other agents to build their termination value.

The variables on the lhs of an explanation e_j must precede the variable x_j in the order because the assignments of these variables have been used to determine the current domain of x_j. An explanation e_j induces ordering constraints, called *safety conditions* in [GIN 94] (see section 1.2.1.4).

DEFINITION 7.2.– *A safety condition is an assertion $x_k \prec x_j$. Given an explanation e_j, $S(e_j)$ is the set of safety conditions induced by e_j, where $S(e_j)$={$(x_k \prec x_j)$ | $x_k \in$ lhs(e_j)}.*

An explanation e_j is **relevant** to an order $\mathcal{O}$ if all variables in lhs(e_j) appear before x_j in $\mathcal{O}$. Each agent A_i stores a set of explanations $\mathcal{E}_i$ sent by other agents. During the search, $\mathcal{E}_i$ is updated to remove explanations that are no longer *valid*.

DEFINITION 7.3.– *An explanation e_j in $\mathcal{E}_i$ is valid on agent A_i if it is relevant to the current order $\mathcal{O}_i$ and lhs(e_j) is compatible with the AgentView of A_i.*

When $\mathcal{E}_i$ contains an explanation e_j associated with A_j, A_i uses this explanation to justify the size of the current domain of A_j. Otherwise, A_i assumes that the size of the current domain of A_j is equal to its initial domain size d_j^0. The termination value depends on the order and the set of explanations.

DEFINITION 7.4.– *Let $\mathcal{E}_i$ be the set of explanations stored by A_i, $\mathcal{O}$ be an order on the agents such that every explanation in $\mathcal{E}_i$ is relevant to $\mathcal{O}$, and $\mathcal{O}(k)$ be such that $A_{\mathcal{O}(k)}$ is the kth agent in $\mathcal{O}$. The termination value TV($\mathcal{E}_i, \mathcal{O}$) is the tuple $[tv^1, \ldots, tv^n]$, where $tv^k =$ rhs$(e_{\mathcal{O}(k)})$ if $e_{\mathcal{O}(k)} \in \mathcal{E}_i$, otherwise, $tv^k = d_{\mathcal{O}(k)}^0$.*

In Agile-ABT, an order $\mathcal{O}_i$ is always associated with a termination value TV_i. When comparing two orders, the **strongest** order is that associated with the lexicographically *smallest* termination value. In case of ties, we use the lexicographic order on agents IDs, the smaller being the stronger.

EXAMPLE 7.1.– Consider, for instance, two orders $\mathcal{O}_1 = [A_1, A_2, A_5, A_4, A_3]$ and $\mathcal{O}_2 = [A_1, A_2, A_4, A_5, A_3]$. If the termination value associated with $\mathcal{O}_1$ is equal to the termination value associated with $\mathcal{O}_2$, $\mathcal{O}_2$ is stronger than $\mathcal{O}_1$ because the vector $[1, 2, 4, 5, 3]$ of IDs in $\mathcal{O}_2$ is lexicographically smaller than the vector $[1, 2, 5, 4, 3]$ of IDs in $\mathcal{O}_1$.

In the following, we will show that the interest of the termination values is not limited to the role of establishing a priority between the different orders proposed by agents. We use them to provide more flexibility in the choice of the backtracking target and to speed up the search.

7.2.2. The backtracking target

When all the values of an agent A_i are ruled out by nogoods, these nogoods are resolved, producing a new nogood, *newNogood*. The *newNogood* is the conjunction of the lhs of all nogoods stored by A_i. If *newNogood* is empty, then the inconsistency is proved. Otherwise, one of the conflicting agents must change its value. In standard ABT, the backtracking target (i.e. the agent that must change its value) is the agent with the lowest priority. Agile-ABT overcomes this restriction by allowing A_i to select the backtracking target with great freedom. When a new nogood $newNogood$ is produced by resolution, the only condition to choose a variable x_k as the backtracking target (i.e. the variable to put on the rhs of $newNogood$) is to find an order $\mathcal{O}'$ such that $\text{TV}(up\_\mathcal{E}_i, \mathcal{O}')$ is lexicographically smaller than the termination value associated with the current order of A_i (i.e. $\mathcal{O}_i$). $up\_\mathcal{E}_i$ is obtained by updating $\mathcal{E}_i$ after placing x_k on the rhs $(newNogood)$.

Function UpdateExplanations takes the set of explanations stored by A_i (i.e. $\mathcal{E}_i$) as arguments, the generated nogood $newNogood$ and the variable x_k to place on the rhs of $newNogood$. UpdateExplanations removes all explanations that are no longer compatible with the AgentView of A_i after placing x_k on the rhs of $newNogood$. (The assignment of x_k will be removed from AgentView after backtracking.). Next, it updates the explanation of agent A_k stored in A_i and it returns a set of (updated) explanations $up\_\mathcal{E}_i$.

This function does not create cycles in the set of safety conditions $S(up\_\mathcal{E}_i)$ if $S(\mathcal{E}_i)$ is acyclic. Indeed, all the explanations added to or removed from $S(\mathcal{E}_i)$ to obtain $S(up\_\mathcal{E}_i)$ contain x_k. Hence, if $S(up\_\mathcal{E}_i)$ contains cycles, all these cycles should contain x_k. However, no safety condition of the form $x_k \prec x_j$ in $S(up\_\mathcal{E}_i)$ exists because all of these explanations have been removed in line 3. Thus, $S(up\_\mathcal{E}_i)$ cannot be cyclic. As we will show in section 7.3, the updates performed by A_i ensure that $S(\mathcal{E}_i)$ always remains acyclic. As a result, $S(up\_\mathcal{E}_i)$ is acyclic as well, and it can be represented by a directed acyclic graph $\overrightarrow{G} = (X_{\overrightarrow{G}}, E_{\overrightarrow{G}})$, where $X_{\overrightarrow{G}} = \mathcal{X} = \{x_1, \ldots, x_n\}$. An edge $(x_j, x_l) \in E_{\overrightarrow{G}}$ if the safety condition $(x_j \prec x_l) \in S(up\_\mathcal{E}_i)$, that is $e_l \in up\_\mathcal{E}_i$ and $x_j \in \text{lhs}(e_l)$. Any topological sort of $\overrightarrow{G}$ is an order relevant to the safety conditions induced by $up\_\mathcal{E}_i$.

Algorithm 7.1. *Function update explanations*

---

function UpdateExplanations $(\mathcal{E}_i, newNogood, x_k)$
01. $up\_\mathcal{E}_i \leftarrow \mathcal{E}_i$;
02.   SetRhs $(newNogood, x_k)$;
03.   remove each $e_j \in up\_\mathcal{E}_i$ such that $x_k \in \text{lhs}(e_j)$;
04.   **if** ($e_k \notin up\_\mathcal{E}_i$) **then**
05. $e_k \leftarrow \{\emptyset \rightarrow d_k^0\}$;
06.   add$(e_k, up\_\mathcal{E}_i)$;
07. $e_k' \leftarrow \{[\text{lhs}(e_k) \cup \text{lhs}(newNogood)] \rightarrow \text{rhs}(e_k) - 1\}$;
08.   replace e_k by e_k' ;
09.   **return** $up\_\mathcal{E}_i$;

To recap, when all values of an agent A_i are ruled out by some nogoods, they are resolved, producing a new nogood $(newNogood)$. In Agile-ABT, A_i can select the variable x_k, with great freedom, whose value is to be changed. The only restriction to place a variable x_k on the rhs $(newNogood)$ is to find an order $\mathcal{O}'$ such that TV $(up\_\mathcal{E}_i, \mathcal{O}')$ is lexicographically smaller than the termination value associated with the current order of A_i. Note that $up\_\mathcal{E}_i$ being acyclic, there are always one or more topological orders that agree with $S(up\_\mathcal{E}_i)$. In the following, we will discuss in more detail how to choose the order $\mathcal{O}'$.

7.2.3. *Decreasing termination values*

Termination of Agile-ABT is based on the fact that the termination values associated with orders selected by agents decrease as search progresses. To speed up the search, Agile-ABT is written so that agents decrease termination values whenever they can. When an agent resolves its nogoods, it checks whether it can find a new order of agents such that the associated termination value is smaller than that of the current order. If so, the agent will replace its current order and termination value by those just computed and will inform all other agents.

Assume that after resolving its nogoods, an agent A_i decides to place x_k on the rhs of the nogood $(newNogood)$ produced by the resolution and let $up_\mathcal{E}_i = $ UpdateExplanations $(\mathcal{E}_i, newNogood, x_k)$. The function ComputeOrder takes, as a parameter, the set $up\_\mathcal{E}_i$ and returns an order $\mathcal{O}$ relevant to the partial ordering induced by $up\_\mathcal{E}_i$. Let $\overrightarrow{G}$ be the acyclic directed graph associated with $up\_\mathcal{E}_i$. The function ComputeOrder works by determining, at each iteration p, the set $Roots$ of vertices that have no predecessor (line 14). As we aim at minimizing the termination value, function ComputeOrder selects the vertex x_j in $Roots$ that has the smallest domain size (line 15). This vertex is placed at the pth position. Finally, p is incremented after removing x_j and all outgoing edges from x_j from $\overrightarrow{G}$ (lines 16–17).

Algorithm 7.2. *Function compute order*

---

function ComputeOrder $(up\_\mathcal{E}_i)$

10. $\overrightarrow{G} = (X_{\overrightarrow{G}}, E_{\overrightarrow{G}})$ is the acyclic directed graph associated to $up\_\mathcal{E}_i$;

11. $p \leftarrow 1$;

12. $\mathcal{O}$ is an array of length n ;

13.   **while** ($\overrightarrow{G} \neq \emptyset$) **do**

14. $Roots \leftarrow \{x_j \in X_{\overrightarrow{G}} \mid x_j$ has no incoming edges$\}$;

15. $\mathcal{O}(p) \leftarrow x_j$ such that $d_j = \min\{d_k \mid x_k \in Roots\}$;

16.   remove x_j from $\overrightarrow{G}$;   /* with all outgoing edges from x_j */

17. $p \leftarrow p + 1$;

18.   **return** $\mathcal{O}$;

Having proposed an algorithm that determines an order with small termination value for a given backtracking target x_k, we need to know how to choose this variable to obtain an order decreasing the termination value more. The function ChooseVariableOrder iterates through all variables x_k included in the nogood, computes a new order and termination value with x_k as the target (lines 21–23), and stores the target and the associated order if it is the strongest order found so far (lines 24–28). Finally, the information corresponding to the strongest order is returned.

Algorithm 7.3. *Function choose variable ordering*

---

function ChooseVariableOrder($\mathcal{E}_i$, $newNogood$)
19. $\mathcal{O}' \leftarrow \mathcal{O}_i$; $TV' \leftarrow TV_i$; $\mathcal{E}' \leftarrow nil$; $x' \leftarrow nil$;
20.   **foreach** ($x_k \in newNogood$) **do**
21. $up\_\mathcal{E}_i \leftarrow$ UpdateExplanations($\mathcal{E}_i$, $newNogood$, x_k) ;
22. $up\_\mathcal{O} \leftarrow$ ComputeOrder($up\_\mathcal{E}_i$) ;
23. $up\_TV \leftarrow$ TV($up\_\mathcal{E}_i$, $up\_\mathcal{O}$) ;
24.   **if** (up_TV is smaller than TV') **then**
25. $x' \leftarrow x_k$;
26. $\mathcal{O}' \leftarrow up\_\mathcal{O}$;
27. $TV' \leftarrow up\_TV$;
28. $\mathcal{E}' \leftarrow up\_\mathcal{E}_i$;
29.   **return** $\langle x', \mathcal{O}', TV', \mathcal{E}' \rangle$;

7.3. The algorithm

Each agent, say A_i, keeps some amount of local information about the global search, namely an AgentView, a NogoodStore, a set of explanations ($\mathcal{E}_i$), a current order ($\mathcal{O}_i$) and a termination value (TV_i). Agile-ABT allows the following types of messages (where A_i is the sender):

ok?: The *ok?* message is sent by A_i to lower agents to ask whether a chosen value is acceptable. Besides the chosen value, the *ok?* message contains an explanation c_i, which communicates the current domain size of A_i. An *ok?* message also contains the current order $\mathcal{O}_i$ and the current termination value TV_i stored by A_i.

ngd: The *ngd* message is sent by A_i when all its values are ruled out by its NogoodStore. This message contains a nogood, as well as $\mathcal{O}_i$ and TV_i.

order: The *order* message is sent to propose a new order. This message includes the order $\mathcal{O}_i$ proposed by A_i accompanied by the termination value TV_i.

Agile-ABT (algorithms 7.4 and 7.5) is executed on every agent A_i. After initialization, each agent assigns a value and informs lower priority agents of its decision (CheckAgentView call, line 31) by sending *ok?* messages. Then, a loop considers the reception of the possible message types. If no message is transmitting through the network, the state of quiescence is detected by a specialized algorithm [CHA 85], and a global solution is announced. The solution is given by the current variables' assignments.

Algorithm 7.4. *The Agile-ABT algorithm executed by an agent A_i (part 1)*

---

procedure Agile-ABT()
30. $t_i \leftarrow 0$; $TV_i \leftarrow [\infty, \infty, \ldots, \infty]$; $end \leftarrow$ **false**; $v_i \leftarrow empty$;
31.   CheckAgentView() ;
32.   **while** ($\neg end$) **do**
33. $msg \leftarrow$ getMsg();
34.   **switch** ($msg.type$) **do**
35. $ok?$: ProcessInfo(msg); ngd : ResolveConflict(msg);
36. $order$: ProcessOrder(msg); stp : $end \leftarrow$ **true**;

procedure ProcessInfo(msg)
37.   CheckOrder($msg.Order, msg.TV$) ;
38.   UpdateAgentView($msg.Assig \cup$ lhs($msg.Exp$)) ;
39.   **if** ($msg.Exp$ is **valid**) **then** add($msg.Exp, \mathcal{E}_i$) ;
40.   CheckAgentView() ;

procedure ProcessOrder(msg)
41.   CheckOrder($msg.Order, msg.TV$) ;
42.   CheckAgentView() ;

procedure ResolveConflict(msg)
43.   CheckOrder($msg.Order, msg.TV$) ;
44.   UpdateAgentView($msg.Assig \cup$ lhs($msg.Nogood$)) ;
45.   **if** (Compatible($msg.Nogood, AgentView \cup myAssig$)) **then**
46.   **if** (Relevant($msg.Nogood, \mathcal{O}_i$)) **then**
47.   add($msg.Nogood, NogoodStore$) ;
48. $v_i \leftarrow empty$;
49.   CheckAgentView() ;
50.   **else if** (rhs($msg.Nogood$) $= v_i$) **then**
51.   sendMsg : $ok?(myAssig, e_i, \mathcal{O}_i, TV_i)$ **to** $msg.Sender$

procedure CheckOrder($\mathcal{O}', TV'$)
52.   **if** ($\mathcal{O}'$ is stronger than $\mathcal{O}_i$) **then**
53. $\mathcal{O}_i \leftarrow \mathcal{O}'$;
54. $TV_i \leftarrow TV'$;
55.   remove nogoods and explanations non relevant to $\mathcal{O}_i$;

procedure CheckAgentView()
56.   **if** (($\neg$isConsistent($v_i, AgentView$)) **then**
57. $v_i \leftarrow$ ChooseValue() ;
58.   **if** (v_i) **then**
59.   **foreach** ($x_k \succ x_i$) **do**
60.   sendMsg : $ok?(myAssig, e_i, \mathcal{O}_i, TV_i)$ **to** A_k ;
61.   **else** Backtrack() ;
62.   **else if** ($\mathcal{O}_i$ was *modified*) **then**
63.   **foreach** ($x_k \succ x_i$) **do**
64.   sendMsg : $ok?(myAssig, e_i, \mathcal{O}_i, TV_i)$ **to** A_k ;

procedure UpdateAgentView($Assignments$)
65.   **foreach** ($x_j \in Assignments$) **do**
66.   **if** ($Assignments[j].tag > AgentView[j].tag$) **then**
67. $AgentView[j] \leftarrow Assignments[j]$;
68.   **foreach** ($ng \in NogoodStore$ **such that** $\neg$Compatible(lhs(ng), $AgentView$)) **do**
69.   remove($ng, myNogoodStore$) ;
70.   **foreach** ($e_j \in \mathcal{E}_i$ **such that** $\neg$Compatible(lhs(e_j), $AgentView$)) **do**
71.   remove($e_j, \mathcal{E}_i$) ;

Algorithm 7.5. *The Agile-ABT algorithm executed by an agent A_i (part 2)*

procedure Backtrack()
72. $newNogood \leftarrow$ solve($NogoodStore$) ;
73.   **if** ($newNogood =$ empty) **then**
74. $end \leftarrow$ **true**;
75.   sendMsg: $stp(\,)$ **to** $system$ agent ;
76. $\langle x_k, \mathcal{O}', TV', \mathcal{E}' \rangle \leftarrow$ ChooseVariableOrder($\mathcal{E}_i, newNogood$) ;
77.   **if** (TV' *is* smaller than TV_i) **then**
78. $TV_i \leftarrow TV'$;
79. $\mathcal{O}_i \leftarrow \mathcal{O}'$;
80. $\mathcal{E}_i \leftarrow \mathcal{E}'$;
81.   SetRhs($newNogood, x_k$) ;
82.   sendMsg: $ngd(newNogood, \mathcal{O}_i, TV_i)$ **to** A_k ;
83.   remove e_k from $\mathcal{E}_i$;
84.   broadcastMsg: $order(\mathcal{O}_i, TV_i)$;
85.   **else**
86.   SetRhs($newNogood, x_k$) ;   /* x_k is the lower agent in $newNogood$ */
87.   sendMsg: $ngd(newNogood, \mathcal{O}_i, TV_i)$ **to** A_k ;
88.   UpdateAgentView($x_k \leftarrow unknown$) ;
89.   CheckAgentView() ;

function ChooseValue()
90.   **foreach** ($v \in D(x_i)$) **do**
91.   **if** (isConsistent($v, AgentView$)) **then return** v ;
92.   **else** store the best nogood for v ;
93.   **return** empty;

When an agent A_i receives a message (of any type), it checks if the order included in the received message is stronger than its current order $\mathcal{O}_i$ (CheckOrder call, lines 37, 41 and 43). If it is the case, A_i replaces $\mathcal{O}_i$ and TV_i by those newly received (line 52). The nogoods and explanations that are no longer relevant to $\mathcal{O}_i$ are removed to ensure that $S(\mathcal{E}_i)$ remains acyclic (line 55).

If the message is an *ok?* message, the AgentView of A_i is updated to include the new assignments (UpdateAgentView call, line 38). Besides the assignment of the sender, A_i also takes newer assignments appearing on the lhs of the explanation included in the received *ok?* message to update its AgentView. Afterwards, the nogoods and the explanations that are no longer compatible with AgentView are removed (UpdateAgentView, lines 68–71). Then, if the explanation in the received message is valid, A_i updates the set of explanations by storing the newly received explanation. Next, A_i calls the procedure CheckAgentView (line 40).

When receiving an *order* message, A_i processes the new order (CheckOrder) and calls CheckAgentView (line 42).

When A_i receives an *ngd* message, it calls CheckOrder and UpdateAgentView (lines 43 and 44). The nogood contained in the message is accepted if it is compatible with the AgentView and the assignment of x_i and relevant to the current order of A_i.

Otherwise, the nogood is discarded and an *ok?* message is sent to the sender as in ABT (lines 50 and 51). When the nogood is accepted, it is stored, acting as justification for removing the current value of A_i (line 47). A new value consistent with the AgentView is searched (CheckAgentView call, line 49).

The procedure CheckAgentView checks if the current value v_i is consistent with the AgentView. If v_i is consistent, A_i checks if $\mathcal{O}_i$ was modified (line 62). If so, A_i must send its assignment to lower priority agents through *ok?* messages. If v_i is not consistent with its AgentView, A_i tries to find a consistent value (ChooseValue call, line 57). In this process, some values of A_i may appear as inconsistent. In this case, the nogoods justifying their removal are added to the NogoodStore (line 92 of function ChooseValue()). If a new consistent value is found, an explanation e_i is built and the new assignment is notified to the lower priority agents of A_i through *ok?* messages (line 60). Otherwise, every value of A_i is forbidden by the NogoodStore and A_i has to backtrack (Backtrack call, line 61).

In procedure Backtrack(), A_i resolves its nogoods, deriving a new nogood (*newNogood*). If the *newNogood* is empty, the problem has no solution. A_i terminates execution after sending an *stp* message (lines 74–75). Otherwise, one of the agents included in *newNogood* must change its value. The function ChooseVariableOrder selects the variable to be changed (x_k) and a new order ($\mathcal{O}'$) such that the new termination value TV' is as small as possible. If TV' is smaller than that stored by A_i, the current order and the current termination value are replaced by $\mathcal{O}'$ and TV' and A_i updates its explanations from those returned by ChooseVariableOrder (lines 78–80). Then, an *ngd* message is sent to agent A_k, the owner of x_k (line 82). e_k is removed from $\mathcal{E}_i$ because A_k will probably change its explanation after receiving the nogood (line 83). Afterward, A_i sends an *order* message to all other agents (line 84). When TV' is not smaller than the current termination value, A_i cannot propose a new order and the variable to be changed (x_k) is the variable that has the lowest priority according to the current order of A_i (lines 86 and 87). Next, the assignment of x_k (the target of the backtrack) is removed from the AgentView of A_i (line 88). Finally, the search is continued by calling the procedure CheckAgentView (line 89).

7.4. Correctness and complexity

In this section, we demonstrate that Agile-ABT is sound, it is complete, it terminates, and that its space complexity is polynomially bounded.

THEOREM 7.1.– The spatial complexity of Agile-ABT is polynomial.

PROOF.– The size of nogoods, explanations, termination values and orderings is bounded by n, the total number of variables. Now, on each agent, Agile-ABT only stores one nogood per value, one explanation per agent, one termination value and one ordering. Thus, the space complexity of Agile-ABT is in $O(nd + n^2 + n + n) = O(nd + n^2)$ on each agent.

THEOREM 7.2.– The algorithm Agile-ABT is sound.

PROOF.– Let us assume that the state of quiescence is reached. The order (say $\mathcal{O}$) known by all agents is the same because when an agent proposes a new order, it sends it to all other agents. Obviously, $\mathcal{O}$ is the strongest order that has ever been calculated by agents. Also, the state of quiescence implies that every pair of constrained agents satisfies the constraint between them. To prove this, assume that some constraints exist that are not satisfied. This implies that there are at least two agents A_i and A_k that do not satisfy the constraint between them (i.e. c_{ik}). Let A_i be the agent that has the highest priority between the two agents according to $\mathcal{O}$. Let v_i be the current value of A_i when the state of quiescence is reached (i.e. v_i is the most up-to-date assignment of A_i) and let M be the last $ok?$ message sent by A_i before the state of quiescence is reached. Clearly, M contains v_i; otherwise, A_i would have sent another $ok?$ message when it chose v_i. Moreover, when M was sent, A_i already knew the order $\mathcal{O}$; otherwise A_i would have sent another $ok?$ message when it received (or generated) $\mathcal{O}$. A_i sent M to all its successors according to $\mathcal{O}$ (including A_k). The only case where A_k can forget v_i after receiving it is the case where A_k derives a nogood proving that v_i is not feasible. In this case, A_k should send a nogood message to A_i. If the nogood message is accepted by A_i, A_i must send an $ok?$ message to its successors (and therefore M is not the last one). Similarly, if the nogood message is discarded, A_i has to resend an $ok?$ message to A_k (and therefore M is not the last one). So the state of quiescence implies that A_k knows both $\mathcal{O}$ and v_i. Thus, the state of quiescence implies that the current value of A_k is consistent with v_i; otherwise, A_k would send at least one message and our quiescence assumption would be wrong.

THEOREM 7.3.– The algorithm Agile-ABT is complete.

PROOF.– All nogoods are generated by logical inferences from existing constraints. Therefore, an empty nogood cannot be inferred if a solution exists.

The proof of termination is based on lemmas 7.1 and 7.2.

LEMMA 7.1.– For any agent A_i, while a solution is not found and the inconsistency of the problem is not proved, the termination value stored by A_i decreases after a finite amount of time.

PROOF.– Let $TV_i = [tv^1, \ldots, tv^n]$ be the current termination value of A_i. Assume that A_i reaches a state where it cannot improve its termination value. If another agent succeeds in generating a termination value smaller than TV_i, lemma 7.1 holds because A_i will receive the new termination value. Now assume that Agile-ABT reaches a state σ where no agent can generate a termination value smaller than TV_i. We show that

Agile-ABT will exit σ after a finite amount of time. Let t be the time when Agile-ABT reaches the state σ. After a finite time δt, the termination value of each agent $A_{j \in \{1,...,n\}}$ will be equal to TV_i, either because A_j has generated itself a termination value equal to TV_i or because A_j has received TV_i in an order message. Let $\mathcal{O}$ be the lexicographically smallest order among the current orders of all agents at time $t + \delta t$. The termination value associated with $\mathcal{O}$ is equal to TV_i. While Agile-ABT is getting stuck in σ, no agent will be able to propose an order stronger than $\mathcal{O}$ because no agent is allowed to generate a new order with the same termination value as the one stored (algorithm 7.5, line 77). Thus, after a finite time $\delta' t$, all agents will receive $\mathcal{O}$. They will take it as their current order and Agile-ABT will behave as ABT, which is known to be complete and to terminate.

We know that $d^0_{\mathcal{O}(1)} - tv^1$ values have been removed once and for all from the domain of the variable $x_{\mathcal{O}(1)}$ (i.e. $d^0_{\mathcal{O}(1)} - tv^1$ nogoods with empty lhs have been sent to $A_{\mathcal{O}(1)}$). Otherwise, the generator of $\mathcal{O}$ could not have put $A_{\mathcal{O}(1)}$ in the first position. Thus, the domain size of $x_{\mathcal{O}(1)}$ cannot be greater than tv^1 ($d_{\mathcal{O}(1)} \leq tv^1$). After a finite amount of time, if a solution is not found and the inconsistency of the problem is not proved, a nogood – with an empty lhs – will be sent to $A_{\mathcal{O}(1)}$, which will cause it to replace its assignment and reduce its current domain size ($d'_{\mathcal{O}(1)} = d_{\mathcal{O}(1)} - 1$). The new assignment and the new current domain size of $A_{\mathcal{O}(1)}$ will be sent to the $(n-1)$ lower priority agents. After receiving this message, we are sure that any generator of a new nogood (say A_k) will improve the termination value. Indeed, when A_k resolves its nogoods, it computes a new order such that its termination value is minimal. At worst, A_k can propose a new order where $A_{\mathcal{O}(1)}$ keeps its position. Even in this case, the new termination value $TV'_k = [d'_{\mathcal{O}(1)}, \ldots]$ is lexicographically smaller than $TV_i = [tv^1, \ldots]$ because $d'_{\mathcal{O}(1)} = d_{\mathcal{O}(1)} - 1 \leq tv^1 - 1$. After a finite amount of time, all agents (including A_i) will receive TV'_k. This will cause A_i to update its termination value and exit the state σ. This completes the proof.

LEMMA 7.2.– Let $TV = [tv^1, \ldots, tv^n]$ be the termination value associated with the current order of any agent. We have $tv^j \geq 0, \forall j \in 1...n$.

PROOF.– Let A_i be the agent that generated TV. We first prove that A_i never stores an explanation with an rhs smaller than 1. An explanation e_k stored by A_i was either sent by A_k or generated when calling ChooseVariableOrder. If e_k was sent by A_k, we have rhs(e_k) ≥ 1 because the size of the current domain of any agent is always greater than or equal to 1. If e_k was computed by ChooseVariableOrder, the only case where rhs(e_k) is made smaller than the rhs of the previous explanation stored for A_k by A_i is in (line 7 of UpdateExplanations). This happens when x_k is selected to be the backtracking target (lines 21 and 28 of ChooseVariableOrder), and in such a case, the explanation e_k is removed just after sending the nogood message to A_k (algorithm 7.5, line 83, of Backtrack()). Hence, A_i never stores an explanation with an rhs equal to zero.

We now prove that it is impossible that A_i generated TV with $tv^j < 0$ for some j. From the viewpoint of A_i, tv^j is the size of the current domain of $A_{\mathcal{O}(j)}$. If A_i does not store any explanation for $A_{\mathcal{O}(j)}$ at the time it computes TV, A_i assumes that tv^j is equal to $d^0_{\mathcal{O}(j)} \geq 1$. Otherwise, tv^j is equal to $\text{rhs}(e_{\mathcal{O}(j)})$, where $e_{\mathcal{O}(j)}$ was either already stored by A_i or generated when calling $\texttt{ChooseVariableOrder}$. Now, we know that every explanation e_k stored by A_i has $\text{rhs}(e_k) \geq 1$, and we know that $\texttt{ChooseVariableOrder}$ cannot generate an explanation e'_k with $\text{rhs}(e'_k) < \text{rhs}(e_k) - 1$, where e_k was the explanation stored by A_i (line 7 of $\texttt{UpdateExplanations}$). Therefore, we are sure that TV is such that $tv^j \geq 0, \forall j \in 1...n$.

THEOREM 7.4.– The algorithm Agile-ABT terminates.

PROOF.– The termination value of any agent decreases lexicographically and does not stay infinitely unchanged (lemma 7.1). A termination value $[tv^1, \ldots, tv^n]$ cannot decrease infinitely because $\forall i \in \{1, \ldots, n\}$, we have $tv^i \geq 0$ (lemma 7.2). Hence, the theorem is proved.

7.5. Experimental results

We compared Agile-ABT to ABT, ABT_DO and ABT_DO-Retro (ABT_DO with retroactive heuristics). All experiments were performed on the DisChoco 2.0 [WAH 11] platform[1], in which agents were simulated by Java threads that communicate only through message passing. We evaluated the performance of the algorithms by communication load and computation effort. Communication load is measured by the total number of messages exchanged among agents during algorithm execution ($\#msg$), including termination detection (system messages). Computation effort is measured by an adaptation of the number of non-concurrent constraint checks (generic number of non-concurrent constraint checks $\#gncccs$ [ZIV 06b]).

For ABT, we implemented the standard version where we use counters for tagging assignments. For ABT_DO [ZIV 06a], we implemented the best version, using the *nogood-triggered* heuristic where the receiver of a nogood moves the sender to be in front of all other lower priority agents (denoted by ABT_DO-ng). For ABT_DO with retroactive heuristics [ZIV 09], we implemented the best version, in which a nogood generator moves itself to be in a higher position between the last and the second to last agents in the generated nogood[2]. However, it moves before an agent only if its current domain is smaller than the domain of that agent (denoted by ABT_DO-Retro-MinDom).

---

1 http://dischoco.sourceforge.net/.
2 There are some discrepancies between the results reported in [ZIV 09] and our version. This is due to a bug that we fixed to ensure that ABT_DO-ng and ABT_DO-Retro-MinDom actually terminate [MEC 12], see Chapter 6.

7.5.1. *Uniform binary random DisCSPs*

The algorithms are tested on uniform binary random DisCSPs characterized by $\langle n, d, p_1, p_2 \rangle$, where n is the number of agents/variables, d is the number of values per variable, p_1 is the network connectivity defined as the ratio of existing binary constraints and p_2 is the constraint tightness defined as the ratio of forbidden value pairs. We solved instances of two classes of problems: sparse problems $\langle 20, 10, 0.2, p_2 \rangle$ and dense problems $\langle 20, 10, 0.7, p_2 \rangle$. We varied the tightness p_2 from 0.1 to 0.9 by steps of 0.1. For each pair of fixed density and tightness (p_1, p_2), we generated 25 instances, solved four times each. We reported the average over the 100 runs.

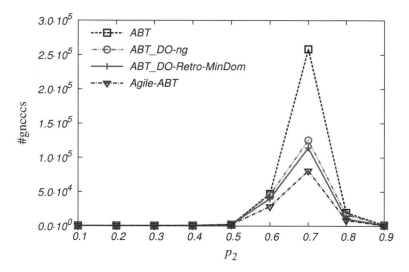

Figure 7.1. *The generic number of non-concurrent constraint checks (#gncccs) performed for solving dense problems ($p_1 = 0.2$)*

Figures 3.2 and 3.3 present the performance of the algorithms on the sparse instances (p_1=0.2). In terms of computational effort, $\#gncccs$ (Figure 3.2), ABT is the less efficient algorithm. ABT_DO-ng improves ABT by a large scale, and ABT_DO-Retro-MinDom is more efficient than ABT_DO-ng. These findings are similar to those reported in [ZIV 09]. Agile-ABT outperforms all these algorithms, suggesting that on sparse problems, the more sophisticated the algorithm is, the better it is.

Regarding the number of exchanged messages, $\#msg$ (Figure 7.2), the situation is a bit different. ABT_DO-ng and ABT_DO-Retro-MinDom require a number of messages substantially larger than ABT algorithm. Agile-ABT is the algorithm that requires the smallest number of messages. This is not only because Agile-ABT terminates faster than the other algorithms (see $\#gncccs$). Agile-ABT is more parsimonious than ABT_DO algorithms in proposing new orders. Termination values seem to focus changes on those orderings which will pay off.

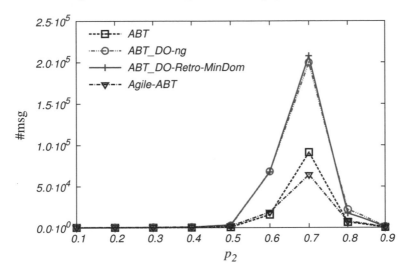

Figure 7.2. *The total number of messages sent for solving dense problems ($p_1=0.2$)*

Figures 7.3 and 7.4 illustrate the performance of the algorithms on the dense instances ($p_1=0.7$). Some differences appear compared to sparse problems. Concerning $\#gncccs$ (Figure 7.3), ABT_DO algorithms deteriorate compared to ABT. However, Agile-ABT still outperforms all these algorithms. Regarding the communication load, $\#msg$ (Figure 7.4), ABT_DO-ng and ABT_DO-Retro-MinDom show the same bad performance as in sparse problems. Agile-ABT shows similar communication load as ABT. This confirms its good behavior observed on sparse problems.

7.5.2. *Distributed sensor target problems*

The *distributed sensor-target problem* (SensorDisCSP) [BÉJ 05] is a benchmark based on a real distributed problem (see section 2.1.4). It consists of n sensors that track m targets. Each target must be tracked by three sensors. Each sensor can track at most one target. A solution must satisfy visibility and compatibility constraints. The visibility constraint defines the set of sensors to which a target is visible. The compatibility constraint defines the compatibility among sensors. In our implementation of the DisCSP algorithms, the encoding of the SensorDisCSP presented in section 2.1.4 is translated into an equivalent formulation where we have three virtual agents for every real agent, each virtual agent handling a single variable.

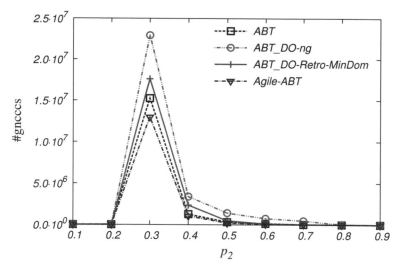

Figure 7.3. *The generic number of non-concurrent constraint checks (#gncccs) performed for solving dense problems ($p_1 = 0.7$)*

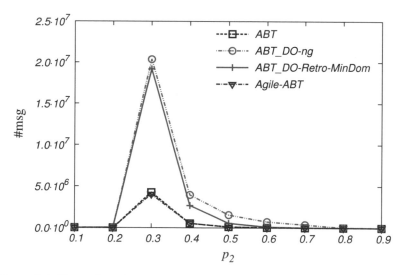

Figure 7.4. *The total number of messages sent for solving dense problems ($p_1 = 0.7$)*

Problems are characterized by $\langle n, m, p_c, p_v \rangle$, where n is the number of sensors, m is the number of targets, each sensor can communicate with a fraction p_c of the sensors that are in its sensing range, and each target can be tracked by a fraction p_v of the sensors having the target in their sensing range. We present results for the class

$\langle$ 25, 5, 0.4, $p_v \rangle$, where we vary p_v from 0.1 to 0.9 by steps of 0.1. Again, for each p_v we generated 25 instances, solved four times each and averaged over the 100 runs. The results are shown in Figures 7.5 and 7.6.

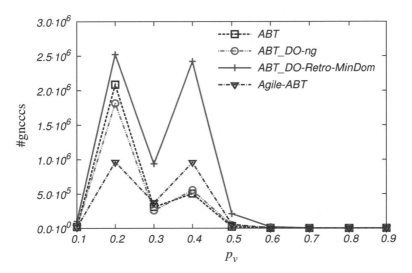

Figure 7.5. *The generic number of non-concurrent constraint checks performed on instances where* $p_c = 0.4$

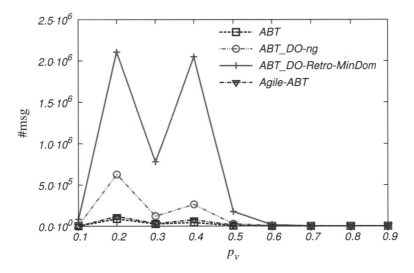

Figure 7.6. *Total number of exchanged messages on instances where* $p_c = 0.4$

When comparing the speedup of algorithms (Figure 7.5), Agile-ABT is slightly dominated by ABT and ABT_DO-ng in the interval $[0.3\ 0.5]$, while outside of this interval, Agile-ABT outperforms all the algorithms. Nonetheless, the performance of ABT and ABT_DO-ng significantly deteriorates in the interval $[0.1\ 0.3]$. Concerning the communication load (Figure 7.6), as opposed to other dynamic ordering algorithms, Agile-ABT is always better than or as good as the standard ABT.

7.5.3. Discussion

From the experiments above, we can conclude that Agile-ABT outperforms other algorithms in terms of computation effort ($\#gncccs$) while solving random DisCSP problem. On structured problems (SensorDCSP), our results suggest that Agile-ABT is more robust than other algorithms whose performance is affected by the type of problems solved. Concerning the communication load ($\#msg$), Agile-ABT is more robust than other versions of ABT with dynamic agent ordering. As opposed to them, it is always better than or as good as the standard ABT on difficult problems.

At first sight, Agile-ABT seems to need less messages than other algorithms but these messages are longer than messages sent by other algorithms. One could argue that for Agile-ABT, counting the number of exchanged messages is biased. However, counting the number of exchanged messages would be biased only if $\#msg$ was smaller than the number of *physically* exchanged messages (going out from the network card). Now, in our experiments, they are the same.

The International Organization for Standardization (ISO) has designed the Open Systems Interconnection (OSI) model to standardize networking. Transmission Control Protocol (TCP) and User Datagram Protocol (UDP) are the principal transport layer protocols using OSI model. The Internet protocols IPv4 (http://tools.ietf.org/html/rfc791) and IPv6 (http://tools.ietf.org/html/rfc2460) specify the minimum datagram size that we can send without fragmentation of a message (in one physical message). This is 568 bytes for IPv4 and 1,272 bytes for IPv6 when using either TCP or UDP (UDP is 8 bytes less than TCP, see RFC-768 – http://tools.ietf.org/html/rfc768).

Figure 7.7 shows the size of the longest message sent by each algorithm on our random and sensor problems. It is clear that Agile-ABT requires lengthy messages compared to other algorithms. However, the longest message sent is always less than 568 bytes (in the worst case, it is less than 350 bytes, see Figure 7.7b)).

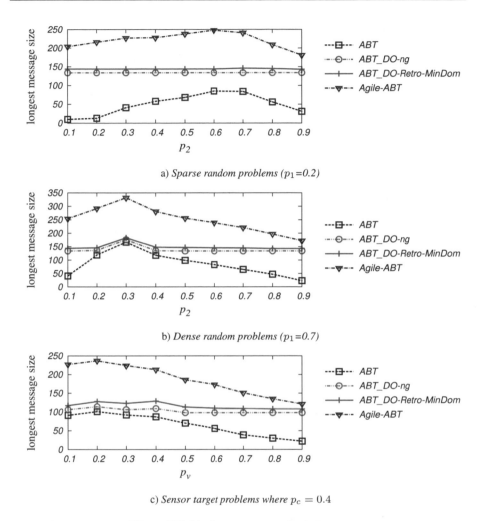

a) *Sparse random problems* ($p_1=0.2$)

b) *Dense random problems* ($p_1=0.7$)

c) *Sensor target problems where* $p_c = 0.4$

Figure 7.7. *Maximum message size in bytes*

7.6. Related works

In [GIN 94], Ginsberg and McAllester proposed partial order dynamic backtracking (PODB), a polynomial space algorithm for centralized CSP that attempted to address the rigidity of dynamic backtracking. The *generalized partial order dynamic backtracking* (GPODB), an algorithm that generalizes both PODB [GIN 94] and the dynamic backtracking (DBT) [GIN 93], was proposed in [BLI 98]. GPODB maintains a set of ordering constraints (also known as safety conditions) on the variables. These ordering constraints imply only a partial order on the variables. This provides flexibility in the reordering of variables in a nogood. Agile-ABT has some similarities with GPODB because Agile-ABT also maintains a set of safety conditions (induced by explanations). However, the set of safety conditions maintained by Agile-ABT allows more total orderings than the set of safety conditions maintained by GPODB. In addition, whenever a new nogood is generated by GPODB, the target of this nogood must be selected such that the safety conditions induced by the new nogood satisfy all existing safety conditions. On the contrary, Agile-ABT allows discarding explanations, and thus, relaxing some of the safety conditions. These two points give Agile-ABT more flexibility in choosing the backtracking target.

7.7. Summary

We have proposed Agile-ABT, an algorithm that is able to change the ordering of agents more agilely than all previous approaches. Because of the original concept of termination value, Agile-ABT is able to choose a backtracking target that is not necessarily the agent with the current lowest priority within the conflicting agents. Furthermore, the ordering of agents appearing before the backtracking target can be changed. These interesting features are unusual for an algorithm with polynomial space complexity. Our experiments confirm the significance of these features.

PART 4

DisChoco 2.0: A Platform for Distributed Constraint Reasoning

8

DisChoco 2.0

Distributed constraint reasoning is a powerful concept to model and solve naturally distributed constraint satisfaction/optimization problems. However, there are very few open source tools dedicated to solving such problems: DisChoco, DCOPolis and FRODO. A distributed constraint reasoning platform must have some important features: it should be reliable and modular in order to be easy to personalize and extend, be independent of the communication system, allow the simulation of agents on a single virtual machine, make it easy for deployment on a real distributed framework and allow agents with local complex problems. This chapter presents DisChoco 2.0, a complete redesign of the DisChoco platform that guarantees these features and that can deal both with distributed constraint satisfaction problems and with distributed constraint optimization problems (DCOP).

8.1. Introduction

Distributed constraint reasoning (DCR) is a framework for solving various problems arising in distributed artificial intelligence. In DCR, a problem is expressed as a distributed constraint network (DCN). A DCN is composed of a group of autonomous agents where each agent has control of some elements of information about the problem, that is variables and constraints. Each agent owns its local constraint network. Variables in different agents are connected by constraints. Agents try to find a local solution (locally consistent assignment) and communicate it with other agents using a DCR protocol to check its consistency against constraints with variables owned by other agents [YOK 98, YOK 00a].

A DCN offers an elegant way for modeling many everyday combinatorial problems that are distributed by nature (e.g. distributed resource allocation [PET 04], distributed meeting scheduling [WAL 02] and sensor networks [BÉJ 05]). Several algorithms for solving this kind of problem have been developed. ABT [YOK 92], ABT-Family [BES 05], AFC [MEI 07] and Nogood-based AFC-ng [WAH 12b, WAH 13] were developed to solve distributed constraint satisfaction problems (DisCSP). Asynchronous distributed constraints optimization (Adopt)

[MOD 05], asynchronous forward-bounding (AFB) [GER 06], asynchronous forward-bounding with backjumping (AFB_BJ) [GER 09] asynchronous branch-and-bound (BnB-Adopt) [YEO 08], Adopt$^+$ and BnB-Adopt$^+$ [GUT 10], and dynamic backtracking for distributed constraint optimization (DyBop) [EZZ 08a] were developed to solve DCOP.

Programming DCR algorithms is a difficult task because the programmer must explicitly juggle many very different concerns, including centralized programming, parallel programming, asynchronous and concurrent management of distributed structures and others. In addition, there are very few open source tools for solving DCR problems: DisChoco, DCOPolis [SUL 08] and FRODO [LÉA 09]. Researchers in DCR are concerned with developing new algorithms and comparing their performance with existing algorithms. Open source platforms are essential tools for integrating and testing new ideas without having the burden of reimplementing an *ad hoc* solver from scratch. For this reason, a DCR platform should have the following features:

- It should be reliable and modular, so it is easy to personalize and extend.

- It should be independent from the communication system.

- It should allow the simulation of multi-agent systems on a single machine.

- It should make it easy to implement a real distributed framework.

- It should allow the design of agents with local constraint networks.

In this chapter, we present DisChoco 2.0[1], a completely redesigned platform that guarantees the features above. It allows us to represent both DisCSPs and DCOPs, as opposed to other platforms. It is not a distributed version of the centralized solver Choco, but it implements a model to solve DCN with local complex problems (i.e. several variables per agent) by using Choco[2] as a local solver to each agent. DisChoco 2.0 is an open source Java library that aims to implement DCR algorithms from an abstract model of an agent (already implemented in DisChoco). A single implementation of a DCR algorithm can run as a simulation on a single machine, or on a network of machines that are connected via the Internet or via a wireless *ad hoc* network or even on mobile phones compatible with J2ME.

8.2. Architecture

To reduce the time of development and, therefore, the cost of the design, we choose a component approach allowing pre-developed components to be reused. This component approach is based on two principles:

- Each component is developed independently.

- An application is an assemblage of particular components.

---

1 http://dischoco.sourceforge.net/.
2 http://choco.emn.fr/.

Figure 8.1 shows the general structure of the DisChoco kernel. It shows a modular architecture with a clear separation between the modules used, which makes the platform easily maintainable and extensible.

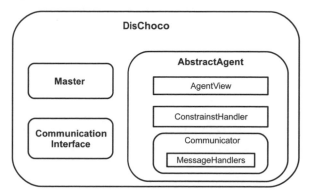

Figure 8.1. *Architecture of DisChoco kernel*

The kernel of DisChoco consists of an abstract model of an agent and several components, namely the communicator, messages handlers, constraints handler, the Agent View (AgentView), a Master who controls the global search (i.e. send messages to launch and to stop the search) and a communication interface.

8.2.1. *Communication system*

Thanks to independence between the kernel of DisChoco and the communication system that will be used (Figure 8.2), DisChoco enables both: the simulation on one machine and the full deployment on a real network. This is done independently of the type of network, which can be a traditional wired network or an *ad hoc* wireless network.

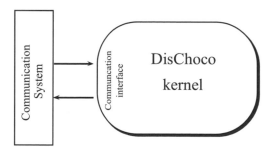

Figure 8.2. *Independence between the kernel of DisChoco and the communication system*

Instead of rewriting a new system of communication between DisChoco agents, we adopted the component approach. Thus, a communication component pre-developed can be used as a communication system if it satisfies a criterion of tolerance to failure. This allows us to use only the identifiers of agents (IDs) to achieve communication between agents. Thus when agent A_i wants to send a message to the agent A_j, it only attaches its ID (i) and the ID (j) of the recipient. It is the communication interface that will deal with mapping between the IDs and IP addresses of agents (we assume that an agent identifier is unique).

In the case of a simulation on a single Java Virtual Machine, agents are simulated by Java threads. Communication among agents is done using an Asynchronous Message Delay Simulator (MailerAMDS) [ZIV 06b, EZZ 07]. MailerAMDS is a simulator that models the asynchronous delays of messages. Then, agents IDs are sufficient for communication. In the case of a network of Java Virtual Machines, we have used Simple Agent Communication Infrastructure (SACI) [3] as communication system. The validity of this choice has not yet been validated by an in-depth analysis. Future work will be devoted to testing a set of communication systems on different types of networks.

8.2.2. *Event management*

DisChoco performs constraint propagation via events on variables and events on constraints, as in Choco. These events are generated by changes on variables, and managing them is one of the main tasks of a constraint solver. In a distributed system, there are some other events that must be exploited. These events correspond to a reception of a message, changing the state of an agent (wait, idle and stop) or to changes on the AgentView.

The AgentView of a DisChoco agent consists of external variables (copy of other agents' variables). Whenever an event occurs on one of these external variables, some external constraints can be awakened and so added to the queue of constraints that will be propagated. Using a queue of constraints to be propagated allows us to only process constraints concerned by changes on the AgentView instead of browsing the list of all constraints. To this end, the DisChoco user can use methods offered by the constraints handler (*ConstraintsHandler*).

Detecting the termination of a distributed algorithm is not a trivial task. It strongly depends on statements of agents. To make the implementation of a termination detection algorithm easy, we introduced a mechanism that generates events for changes on the statements of an agent during its execution into the DisChoco platform. A module for detecting termination is implemented under each agent as a listener of events on statements changes. When the agent state changes, the

---

3 http://www.lti.pcs.usp.br/saci/.

termination detector receives the event, recognizes the type of the new state and executes methods corresponding to termination detection.

The events corresponding to an incoming message are managed in DisChoco in a manner different from the standard method. Each agent has a Boolean object that is set to false as long as the inbox of the agent is empty. When a message has arrived at the inbox, the agent is notified by the change of this Boolean object to true. The agent can use methods available in the communicator module to dispatch the received message to its corresponding handler.

8.2.3. *Observers in layers*

DisChoco provides a Java interface (*AgentObserver*) that allows the user to track operations of a DCR algorithm during its execution. This interface defines two main functions: *whenSendMessage* and *whenReceivedMessage*. The class *AbstractAgent* provides a list of observers and functions to add one or several observers. Thus, when we want to implement an application using DisChoco, we can use *AgentObserver* to develop a specific observer. This model is shown in Figure 8.3a).

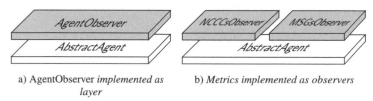

a) AgentObserver *implemented as layer*   b) *Metrics implemented as observers*

Figure 8.3. *Layer model for observers*

When developing new algorithms, an important task is to compare their performance to other existing algorithms. There are several metrics for measuring performance of DCR algorithms: non-concurrent constraint checks ($\#ncccs$ [MEI 02b]), equivalent non-concurrent constraint checks ($\#encccs$ [CHE 06]), number of exchanged messages ($\#msg$ [LYN 97]), degree of privacy loss [BRI 09], etc. DisChoco simply uses *AgentObserver* to implement these metrics as shown in Figure 8.3b). The user can enable metrics when he/she needs them or disable some or all these metrics. The user can develop his/her specific metric or methods for collecting statistics by implementing *AgentObserver*.

8.3. Using DisChoco 2.0

Figure 8.4 represents a definition of a distributed problem named *"Hello DisChoco"* using the Java code. In this problem, there are three agents $\mathcal{A} = \{A_1, A_2, A_3\}$, where each agent controls exactly one variable. The domain of

A_1 and A_2 contains two values $D_1 = D_2 = \{1, 2\}$ and that of A_3 contains one value $D_3 = \{2\}$. There are two constraints of *difference*: the first constraint is between A_1 and A_2 and the second is between A_2 and A_3. After defining our problem we can configure our solver. Thus, the problem can be solved using a specified implemented protocol (ABT, for example).

```
1   AbstractMaster master = Protocols.getMaster(Protocols.ABT);
2   DisProblem disCSP = new DisProblem("Hello DisChoco", master);
3   SimpleAgent[] agents = new SimpleAgent[3];
4   IntVar[] variables = new IntVar[3];
5   // Make agents
6   agents[0] = (SimpleAgent) disCSP.makeAgent("A1", "");
7   agents[1] = (SimpleAgent) disCSP.makeAgent("A2", "");
8   agents[2] = (SimpleAgent) disCSP.makeAgent("A3", "");
9   // Make one single variable for each agent
10  variables[0] = agents[0].makeInternalVar(new int[] {1, 2}); // x1
11  variables[1] = agents[1].makeInternalVar(new int[] {1, 2}); // x2
12  variables[2] = agents[2].makeInternalVar(new int[] {2}); // x3
13  // Make two constraints, we must to create external var on each agent
14  // But each agent must known its constraints
15  // x1!=x2
16  agents[0].neqY(agents[0].makeExternalVar(variables[1]));
17  agents[1].neqY(agents[1].makeExternalVar(variables[0]));
18  // x2!=x3
19  agents[1].neqY(agents[1].makeExternalVar(variables[2]));
20  agents[2].neqY(agents[2].makeExternalVar(variables[1]));
21  // Make a simulator to resolve the problem
22  DisCPSolver solver = new DisSolverSimulator(disCSP);
23  solver.setCentralizedAO(new LexicographicAO());
24  solver.addNCCCMetric();
25  solver.addCommunicationMetric();
26  solver.solve();
27  System.out.println("Problem : " + disCSP.getProblemName());
28  System.out.println("Solution of the problem using " + disCSP.master.getClass());
29  System.out.println("-----------------------------------------------------------");
30  System.out.println(solver.getGlobalSolution());
31  System.out.println("-----------------------------------------------------------");
32  System.out.println("Statistics :");
33  System.out.println(solver.getStatistics());
```

Figure 8.4. *Definition of a distributed problem using Java code*

For DisChoco inputs, we choose to use an XML format called *XDisCSP* derived from the famous format XCSP 2.1[4]. Figure 8.5 shows an example of representation of the problem defined above in the *XDisCSP* format. Each variable has a unique ID, which is the concatenation of the ID of its owner agent and index of the variable in the agent. This is necessary when defining constraints (scope of constraints). For constraints, we used two types of constraints: TKC for totally known constraints and PKC for partially known constraints [BRI 09]. Constraints can be defined in extension or as a Boolean function. Different types of constraints are predefined: equal to $eq(x, y)$, different from $ne(x, y)$, greater than or equal to $ge(x, y)$, greater than $gt(x, y)$, less than or equal to $le(x, y)$, less than $lt(x, y)$, etc.

---

4 http://www.cril.univ-artois.fr/ lecoutre/benchmarks.html.

```
1   <instance>
2     <presentation name="Hello DisChoco" model="Simple" maxConstraintArity="2" format="XDisCSP 1.0" />
3     <agents nbAgents="3">
4       <agent name="A1" id="1" description="Agent 1" />
5       <agent name="A2" id="2" description="Agent 2" />
6       <agent name="A3" id="3" description="Agent 3" />
7     </agents>
8     <domains nbDomains="2">
9       <domain name="D1" nbValues="2">1 2</domain>
10      <domain name="D2" nbValues="1">2</domain>
11    </domains>
12    <variables nbVariables="3">
13      <variable agent="A1" name="X1.0" id="0" domain="D1" description="Variable x_1" />
14      <variable agent="A2" name="X2.0" id="0" domain="D1" description="Variable x_2" />
15      <variable agent="A3" name="X3.0" id="0" domain="D2" description="Variable x_3" />
16    </variables>
17    <predicates nbPredicates="1">
18      <predicate name="P0">
19        <parameters>int x int y</parameters>
20        <expression>
21          <functional>ne(x,y)</functional>
22        </expression>
23      </predicate>
24    </predicates>
25    <constraints nbConstraints="2">
26      <constraint name="C1" model="TKC" arity="2" scope="X1.0 X2.0" reference="P0">
27        <parameters>X1.0 X2.0</parameters>
28      </constraint>
29      <constraint name="C2" model="TKC" arity="2" scope="X2.0 X3.0" reference="P0">
30        <parameters>X2.0 X3.0</parameters>
31      </constraint>
32    </constraints>
33  </instance>
```

Figure 8.5. *Definition of the* Hello DisChoco *problem in XDisCSP 1.0 format*

According to this format, we can model DisCSPs and DCOPs. Once a distributed constraint network problem is expressed in the *XDisCSP* format, we can solve it using one of the protocols developed on the platform. The algorithms currently implemented in DisChoco 2.0 are ABT [YOK 92, BES 05], ABT-Hyb [BRI 04], ABT-dac [BRI 08], AFC [MEI 07], AFC-ng [EZZ 09], AFC-tree [WAH 12b], DBA [YOK 95b] and DisFC [BRI 09] in the class of DisCSPs with simple agents. In the class of DisCSPs where agents have local complex problems, ABT-cf [EZZ 08b] was implemented. For DCOPs, the algorithms that are implemented in DisChoco 2.0 are Adopt [MOD 05], BnB-Adopt [YEO 08] and AFB [GER 09]. For solving a problem, we can use a simple command line:

```
1   java -cp dischoco.jar dischoco.simulation.Run protocol problem.xml
```

The graphical user interface (GUI) of DisChoco allows us to visualize the constraint graph. Hence, the user can analyze the structure of the problem to be solved. This also helps to debug the algorithms. An example of the visualization is shown in Figure 8.6.

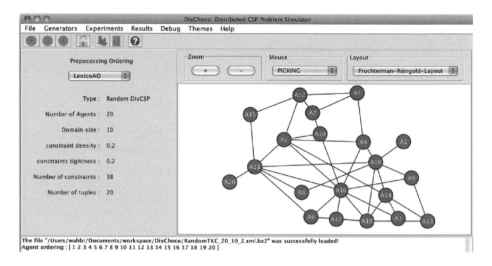

Figure 8.6. *Visualization of the structure of the distributed constraint graph*

8.4. Experimentations

In addition to its good properties (reliable and modular), DisChoco provides several other facilities, especially for performing experimentation. The first facility is in the generation of benchmark problems. DisChoco offers a library of generators for distributed constraint satisfaction/optimization problems (e.g. random binary DisCSPs using model B, random binary DisCSPs with complex local problems, distributed graph coloring, distributed meeting scheduling, sensor networks and distributed N-queens). These generators allow the user to test his/her algorithms on various types of problems ranging from purely random problems to real-world problems.

DisChoco is equipped with a GUI for manipulating all the above generators. A screenshot of the GUI of DisChoco shows various generators implemented on DisChoco (Figure 8.7). Once the instances have been generated, an XML configuration file is created to collect the instances. The generated instances are organized in a specific manner for each kind of problem generator in a directory indicated by the user. The configuration file can also contain details related to the configuration of the communicator and the list of algorithms to be compared. It will be used for launching experiments. After all these configurations have been set, the user can launch the experiments either on the GUI mode or on the command mode.

DisChoco is also equipped with a complete manager of results. The user does not have to worry about organizing and plotting results. All this is offered by DisChoco that automatically generates *gnuplot* plots of the requested measures. The user can also handle all results and compare algorithms using the GUI of DisChoco. Figure 8.8 shows an example of a plot generated from experimentations on some algorithms implemented in DisChoco.

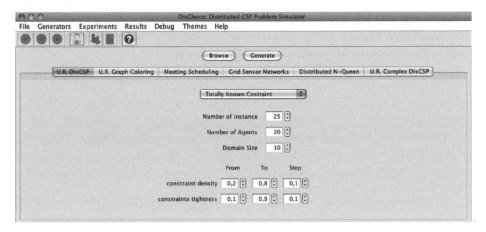

Figure 8.7. *A screenshot of the graphical user interface showing generators in DisChoco*

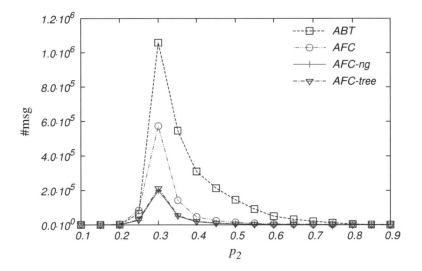

Figure 8.8. *Total number of exchanged messages on dense graph*
$$\langle n = 20,\ d = 10,\ p_1 = 0.7,\ p_2 \rangle$$

8.5. Conclusion

In this chapter, we have presented the new version 2.0 of the DisChoco platform for solving DCR problems. This version contains several interesting features: it is reliable and modular; it is easy to personalize and to extend; it is independent of the communication system; and it allows a deployment on a real distributed system as well as the simulation on a single Java Virtual Machine.

Conclusions

In this book, we addressed the distributed constraint satisfaction problem (DisCSP) framework. We proposed several complete distributed search algorithms and reordering heuristics for solving DisCSPs. We provided a complete evaluation of the efficiency of the proposed contributions against the existing approaches in literature. The experimental results show that they improve the current state of the art.

After defining the centralized constraint satisfaction problem framework (CSP) and presenting some examples of academic and real combinatorial problems that can be modeled as CSPs, we reported the main existing algorithms and heuristics used for solving centralized CSPs. Next, we formally defined the DisCSP framework. We illustrated how some instances of real-world applications in multi-agent coordination can be encoded in DisCSPs. We introduced the meeting scheduling problem in its distributed form where agents may solve the problem, due to the DisCSP, without delivering their personal information to a centralized agent. We described a real distributed resource allocation application, that is the distributed sensor network problem, and formalized it as a distributed CSP. These two problems have been used as benchmarks when comparing the algorithms proposed in this book. We have also described the state-of-the-art algorithms and heuristics for solving DisCSP.

In this book we proposed numerous algorithms for solving DisCSPs. The first contribution is the nogood-based asynchronous forward checking (AFC-ng) algorithm. AFC-ng is a nogood-based version of the asynchronous forward-checking (AFC) algorithm. AFC incorporates the idea of the forward checking into a synchronous search procedure. However, agents perform the forward checking phase asynchronously. Instead of using the shortest inconsistent partial assignments, AFC-ng uses nogoods as justifications of value removal. In the application, AFC-ng imitates the conflict-directed backjumping (CBJ) of the centralized case, whereas AFC only imitates the simple backjumping (BJ). Moreover, unlike the AFC, AFC-ng allows concurrent backtracks to be performed at the same time coming from different agents having an empty domain to different destinations. AFC-ng tries to enhance the asynchronism of the forward checking phase.

To enhance the asynchronism in the AFC-ng algorithm, we extended it to the asynchronous forward-checking tree (AFC-tree). The main feature of the AFC-tree algorithm is using different agents to search non-intersecting parts of the search space concurrently. In AFC-tree, agents are prioritized according to a pseudo-tree arrangement of the constraint graph. The pseudo-tree ordering is built in a preprocessing step. Using this priority ordering, AFC-tree performs multiple AFC-ng processes on the paths from the root to the leaves of the pseudo-tree. The agents that are brothers are committed to concurrently finding the partial solutions of their variables. Therefore, AFC-tree takes advantage of the potential speedup of a parallel exploration in the processing of distributed problems.

Because the experiments show that AFC-ng is a very efficient and robust algorithm for solving DisCSP, we proposed two new algorithms based on the same mechanism as AFC-ng to maintain arc consistency in synchronous search procedure. Thereby, instead of using forward checking as a filtering property, we maintain arc consistency asynchronously (MACA). The first algorithm proposed by us enforces arc consistency due to an additional type of message, that is the deletion message. This algorithm is called MACA-del. The second algorithm, which we called MACA-not, achieves arc consistency without any new type of message.

In the contributions mentioned above, the agents assign values to their variables in a sequential way. These contributions can be classified under the category of synchronous algorithms. The other category of algorithms for solving DisCSPs are algorithms in which the process of proposing values to the variables and exchanging these proposals is performed asynchronously between the agents. In the last category, we proposed agile asynchronous backtracking (Agile-ABT), an asynchronous dynamic ordering algorithm that is able to change the ordering of agents more agilely than all previous approaches. Because of the original concept of termination value, Agile-ABT is able to choose a backtracking target that is not necessarily the agent with the current lowest priority within the conflicting agents. Furthermore, the ordering of agents appearing before the backtracking target can be changed. These interesting features are unusual for an algorithm with polynomial space complexity.

In this book, we proposed a corrigendum of the protocol designed for establishing the priority between orders in the asynchronous backtracking algorithm with dynamic ordering using retroactive heuristics (ABT_DO-Retro). We presented an example that shows how ABT_DO-Retro can fall into an infinite loop following the natural understanding of the description given by the authors of ABT_DO-Retro. We described the correct way for comparing time stamps of orders. We finally provided the proof that the new method for comparing orders is correct.

Finally, we presented the new version of the DisChoco platform for solving distributed constraint reasoning (DCR) problems, DisChoco 2.0. This version has several interesting features: it is reliable and modular, it is easy to personalize and extend, its kernel is independent of the communication system and it allows a deployment in a real distributed system as well as a simulation on a single Java virtual machine. DisChoco 2.0 is an open-source Java library, which aims to implement distributed constraint reasoning algorithms from an abstract model of an agent (already implemented in DisChoco). A single implementation of a distributed constraint reasoning algorithm can run as a simulation on a single machine or on a network of machines. DisChoco 2.0 then offers a complete tool for the research community to evaluate algorithms' performance or to be used for solving real applications. All algorithms proposed in this book were implemented and tested using this DisChoco 2.0 platform.

Bibliography

[ABU 88] ABU-AMARA H.H., "Fault-tolerant distributed algorithm for election in complete networks", *IEEE Transactions on Computers*, vol. 37, pp. 449–453, April 1988.

[BAC 95] BACCHUS F., VAN RUN P., "Dynamic variable ordering in CSPs", in *Proceedings of the 1st International Conference on Principles and Practice of Constraint Programming, CP'95*, pp. 258–275, 1995.

[BÉJ 05] BÉJAR R., DOMSHLAK C., FERNÁNDEZ C., *et al.*, "Sensor networks and distributed CSP: communication, computation and complexity", *Artificial Intelligence*, vol. 161, pp. 117–147, 2005.

[BES 93] BESSIERE C., CORDIER M.-O., "Arc-consistency and arc-consistency again", in *Proceedings of the 11th National Conference on Artificial Intelligence, AAAI '93*, AAAI Press, pp. 108–113, 1993.

[BES 94] BESSIERE C., "Arc-consistency and arc-consistency again", *Artificial Intelligence*, vol. 65, no. 1, pp. 179–190, January 1994.

[BES 96] BESSIERE C., RÉGIN J.-C., "MAC and combined heuristics: two reasons to forsake FC (and CBJ?) on hard problems", in *Proceedings of the 2nd International Conference on Principles and Practice of Constraint Programming, CP '96*, pp. 61–75, 1996.

[BES 99] BESSIERE C., FREUDER E.C., RÉGIN J.-C., "Using constraint metaknowledge to reduce arc consistency computation", *Artificial Intelligence*, vol. 107, no. 1, pp. 125–148, January 1999.

[BES 01a] BESSIERE C., CHMEISS A., SAIS L., "Neighborhood-based variable ordering heuristics for the constraint satisfaction problem", in *Proceedings of the 7th International Conference on Principles and Practice of Constraint Programming, CP '01*, Springer-Verlag, London, UK, pp. 565–569, 2001.

[BES 01b] BESSIERE C., MAESTRE A., MESEGUER P., "Distributed dynamic backtracking", in *Proceedings of Workshop on Distributed Constraint Reasoning, IJCAI '01*, Seattle, WA, 4 August 2001.

[BES 01c] BESSIERE C., RÉGIN J.-C., "Refining the basic constraint propagation algorithm", in *Proceedings of the 17th International Joint Conference on Artificial Intelligence, IJCAI'01*, vol. 1, Morgan Kaufmann Publishers Inc., San Francisco, CA, pp. 309–315, 2001.

[BES 05] BESSIERE C., MAESTRE A., BRITO I., *et al.*, "Asynchronous backtracking without adding links: a new member in the ABT family", *Artificial Intelligence*, vol. 161, pp. 7–24, 2005.

[BES 06] BESSIERE C., "Chapter 3 constraint propagation", in FRANCESCA R., VAN BEEK P., *et al.*, Eds., *Handbook of Constraint Programming*, vol. 2, Foundations of Artificial Intelligence, Elsevier, pp. 29–83, 2006.

[BES 11] BESSIERE C., BOUYAKHF E.H., MECHQRANE Y., *et al.*, "Agile asynchronous backtracking for distributed constraint satisfaction problems", in *Proceedings of the IEEE 23rd International Conference on Tools with Artificial Intelligence, ICTAI '11*, Boca Raton, FL, pp. 777–784, November 2011.

[BIT 75] BITNER J.R., REINGOLD E.M., "Backtrack programming techniques", *Communications of the ACM*, vol. 18, pp. 651–656, November 1975.

[BLI 98] BLIEK C., "Generalizing partial order and dynamic backtracking", in *Proceedings of the 15th National/tenth Conference on Artificial Intelligence/Innovative Applications of Artificial Intelligence, AAAI '98/IAAI '98*, American Association for Artificial Intelligence, Menlo Park, CA, pp. 319–325, 1998.

[BOU 04] BOUSSEMART F., HEMERY F., LECOUTRE C., *et al.*, "Boosting systematic search by weighting constraints", in *Proceedings of the 16th Eureopean Conference on Artificial Intelligence, ECAI '04*, pp. 146–150, 2004.

[BRÉ 79] BRÉLAZ D., "New methods to color the vertices of a graph", *Communications of the ACM*, vol. 22, no. 4, pp. 251–256, April 1979.

[BRI 03] BRITO I., MESEGUER P., "Distributed forward checking", in *Proceedings of 9th International Conference on Principles and Practice of Constraint Programming, CP '03*, Ireland, pp. 801–806, 2003.

[BRI 04] BRITO I., MESEGUER P., "Synchronous, asynchronous and hybrid algorithms for DisCSP", in *Proceedings of the 5th Workshop on Distributed Constraints Reasoning*, DCR '04, Toronto, Canada, pp. 80–94, September 2004.

[BRI 08] BRITO I., MESEGUER P., "Connecting ABT with arc consistency", in *Proceedings of the 14th International Conference on Principles and Practice of Constraint Programming, CP'08*, pp. 387–401, 2008.

[BRI 09] BRITO I., MEISELS A., MESEGUER P., *et al.*, "Distributed constraint satisfaction with partially known constraints", *Constraints*, vol. 14, pp. 199–234, June 2009.

[CHA 85] CHANDY K.M., LAMPORT L., "Distributed snapshots: determining global states of distributed systems", *ACM Transactions on Computer Systems*, vol. 3, no. 1, pp. 63–75, February 1985.

[CHE 83] CHEUNG T.-Y., "Graph traversal techniques and the maximum flow problem in distributed computation", *IEEE Transactions on Software Engineering*, vol. 9, no. 4, pp. 504–512, 1983.

[CHE 05] CHECHETKA A., SYCARA K., A decentralized variable ordering method for distributed constraint optimization, Report no. CMU-RI-TR-05-18, Robotics Institute, Carnegie Mellon University, Pittsburgh, PA, May 2005.

[CHE 06] CHECHETKA A., SYCARA K., "No-commitment branch and bound search for distributed constraint optimization", in *Proceedings of the 5th International Joint Conference on Autonomous Agents and Multiagent Systems, AAMAS '06*, Hakodate, Japan, pp. 1427–1429, 2006.

[CHI 82] CHINN P.Z., CHVÁTALOVÁ J., DEWDNEY A.K., *et al.*, "The bandwidth problem for graphs and matrices-a survey", *Journal of Graph Theory*, vol. 6, no. 3, pp. 223–254, 1982.

[CHO 06] CHONG Y.L., HAMADI Y., "Distributed log-based reconciliation", in *Proceedings of the 17th European Conference on Artificial Intelligence, ECAI '06*, pp. 108–112, 2006.

[COL 91] COLLIN Z., DECHTER R., KATZ S., "On the feasibility of distributed constraint satisfaction", in *Proceedings of the International Joint Conference on Artificial Intelligence, IJCAI '91*, Morgan Kaufmann, pp. 318–324, 1991.

[DAV 62] DAVIS M., LOGEMANN G., LOVELAND D., "A machine program for theorem-proving", *Communications of the ACM*, vol. 5, pp. 394–397, July 1962.

[DEC 88] DECHTER R., PEARL J., "Network-based heuristics for constraint satisfaction problems", *Artificial Intelligence*, vol. 34, pp. 1–38, 1988.

[DEC 89] DECHTER R., MEIRI I., "Experimental evaluation of preprocessing techniques in constraint satisfaction problems", in *Proceedings of the 11th International Joint Conference on Artificial Intelligence, IJCAI '89*, vol. 1, Morgan Kaufmann Publishers Inc., San Francisco, CA, pp. 271–277, 1989.

[DEC 90] DECHTER R., "Enhancement schemes for constraint processing: backjumping, learning, and cutset decomposition", *Artificial Intelligence*, vol. 41, no. 3, pp. 273–312, January 1990.

[DEC 92] DECHTER R., *Constraint Networks (survey)*, John Wiley & Sons, Inc., New York, NY, USA, 2nd ed., vol. 1, pp. 276–285, 1992.

[DEC 02] DECHTER R., FROST D., "Backjump-based backtracking for constraint satisfaction problems", *Artificial Intelligence*, vol. 136, no. 2, pp. 147–188, April 2002.

[DEK 80] DE KLEER J., SUSSMAN G.J., "Propagation of constraints applied to circuit synthesis", *International Journal of Circuit Theory and Applications*, vol. 8, no. 2, pp. 127–144, 1980.

[EZZ 07] EZZAHIR R., BESSIERE C., BELAISSAOUI M., *et al.*, "DisChoco: a platform for distributed constraint programming", in *Proceedings of the IJCAI'07 Workshop on Distributed Constraint Reasoning*, Hyderabad, India, pp. 16–21, 8 January 2007.

[EZZ 08a] EZZAHIR R., BESSIERE C., BENELALLAM I., *et al.*, "Dynamic backtracking for distributed constraint optimization", in *Proceedings of the 18th European Conference on Artificial Intelligence, ECAI '08*, IOS Press, Amsterdam, The Netherlands, pp. 901–902, 2008.

[EZZ 08b] EZZAHIR R., BESSIERE C., BOUYAKHF E.H., *et al.*, "Asynchronous backtracking with compilation formulation for handling complex local problems", *ICGST International Journal on Artificial Intelligence and Machine Learning*, vol. 8, pp. 45–53, 2008.

[EZZ 09] EZZAHIR R., BESSIERE C., WAHBI M., *et al.*, "Asynchronous inter-level forward-checking for DisCSPs", in *Proceedings of the 15th International Conference on Principles and Practice of Constraint Programming, CP '09*, Lisbon, Portugal, pp. 304–318, 2009.

[FOX 82] FOX M.S., ALLEN B.P., STROHM G., "Job-shop scheduling: an investigation in constraint-directed reasoning", in *Proceedings of the National Conference on Artificial Intelligence, AAAI'82*, pp. 155–158, 1982.

[FRA 87] FRAYMAN F., MITTAL S., "COSSACK: a constraint-based expert system for configuration tasks", in *Knowledge-Based Expert Systems in Engineering, Planning and Design*, pp. 144–166, 1987.

[FRE 82] FREUDER E.C., "A sufficient condition for backtrack-free search", *Journal of the ACM*, vol. 29, pp. 24–32, 1982.

[FRE 85] FREUDER E.C., QUINN M.J., "Taking advantage of stable sets of variables in constraint satisfaction problems", in SRIRAM D., ADEY R.A. (eds.), *Proceedings of the International Joint Conference on Artificial Intelligence, IJCAI '85*, Los Angeles, CA, pp. 1076–1078, 1985.

[FRO 94] FROST D., DECHTER R., "In search of the best constraint satisfaction search", in *Proceedings of the 12th National Conference of Artificial Intelligence, AAAI '94*, pp. 301–306, 1994.

[FRO 95] FROST D., DECHTER R., "Look-ahead value ordering for constraint satisfaction problems", in *Proceedings of the 14th International Joint Conference on Artificial Intelligence, IJCAI '95*, vol. 1, Morgan Kaufmann Publishers Inc., San Francisco, CA, pp. 572–578, 1995.

[GAR 96] GARRIDO L., SYCARA K., "Multiagent meeting scheduling: preliminary experimental results", in *Proceedings of the 2nd International Conference on Multiagent Systems, ICMAS '96*, pp. 95–102, 1996.

[GAS 74] GASCHNIG J., "A constraint satisfaction method for inference making", in *Proceedings of the 12th Annual Allerton Conference on Circuit and System Theory*, pp. 866–874, 1974.

[GAS 78] GASCHNIG J., "Experimental case studies of backtrack vs. waltz-type vs. new algorithms for satisficing assignment problems", in *Proceedings of the 2nd Canadian Conference on Artificial Intelligence*, pp. 268–277, 1978.

[GEE 92] GEELEN P.A., "Dual viewpoint heuristics for binary constraint satisfaction problems", in *Proceedings of the 10th European Conference on Artificial Intelligence, ECAI '92*, John Wiley & Sons, Inc., New York, NY, pp. 31–35, 1992.

[GEF 87] GEFFNER H., PEARL J., "An improved constraint-propagation algorithm for diagnosis", in *Proceedings of the 10th International Joint Conference on Artificial Intelligence, IJCAI '87*, vol. 2, Morgan Kaufmann Publishers Inc., San Francisco, CA, pp. 1105–1111, 1987.

[GEN 96] GENT I.P., MACINTYRE E., PRESSER P., *et al.*, "An empirical study of dynamic variable ordering heuristics for the constraint satisfaction problem", in *Proceedings of the 2nd International Conference on Principles and Practice of Constraint Programming, CP '96*, pp. 179–193, 1996.

[GER 06] GERSHMAN A., MEISELS A., ZIVAN R., "Asynchronous forward-bounding for distributed constraints optimization," in *Proceedings of the 17th European conference on Artificial intelligence, ECAI'06*, IOS Press, Amsterdam, The Netherlands, pp. 103–107, 2006.

[GER 09] GERSHMAN A., MEISELS A., ZIVAN R., "Asynchronous forward bounding for distributed COPs", *Journal of Artificial Intelligence Research*, vol. 34, pp. 61–88, 2009.

[GIN 90] GINSBERG M.L., FRANK M., HALPIN M.P., *et al.*, "Search lessons learned from crossword puzzles", in *Proceedings of the 8th National Conference on Artificial Intelligence, AAAI '90*, vol. 1, AAAI Press, pp. 210–215, 1990.

[GIN 93] GINSBERG M.L., "Dynamic backtracking", *Journal of Artificial Intelligence Research*, vol. 1, pp. 25–46, 1993.

[GIN 94] GINSBERG M.L., MCALLESTER D.A., "GSAT and dynamic backtracking", in *Proceedings of the 4th International Conference on Principles of Knowledge Representation and Reasoning, KR'94*, Morgan Kaufmann, pp. 226–237, 1994.

[GOL 65] GOLOMB S.W., BAUMERT L.D., "Backtrack programming", *Journal of the ACM*, vol. 12, pp. 516–524, October 1965.

[GRA 96] GRANT S.A., SMITH B.M., "The phase transition behaviour of maintaining Arc consistency", in *Proceedings of the 12th European Conference on Artificial Intelligence, ECAI '96*, pp. 175–179, 1996.

[GUT 10] GUTIERREZ P., MESEGUER P., "Saving redundant messages in BnB-ADOPT", in *Proceedings of the 24th AAAI Conference on Artificial Intelligence, AAAI'10*, AAAI Press, 2010.

[HAM 98] HAMADI Y., BESSIERE C., QUINQUETON J., "Backtracking in distributed constraint networks", in *Proceedings of the 13th European Conference on Artificial Intelligence, ECAI '98*, Brighton, UK, pp. 219–223, 1998.

[HAM 02] HAMADI Y., "Interleaved backtracking in distributed constraint networks", *International Journal of Artificial Intelligence Tools*, vol. 11, pp. 167–188, 2002.

[HAR 79] HARALICK R.M., ELLIOTT G.L., "Increasing tree search efficiency for constraint satisfaction problems", in *Proceedings of the 6th International Joint Conference on Artificial Intelligence, IJCAI '79*, Morgan Kaufmann Publishers Inc., San Francisco, CA, pp. 356–364, 1979.

[HAR 80] HARALICK R.M., ELLIOTT G.L., "Increasing tree search efficiency for constraint satisfaction problems", *Artificial Intelligence*, vol. 14, no. 3, pp. 263–313, 1980.

[HIR 00] HIRAYAMA K., YOKOO M., "The effect of nogood learning in distributed constraint satisfaction", in *Proceedings of the the 20th International Conference on Distributed Computing Systems, ICDCS '00*, IEEE Computer Society, Washington, DC, pp. 169–177, 2000.

[HOR 00] HORSCH M.C., HAVENS W.S., "An empirical study of probabilistic arc consistency as a variable ordering heuristic", in *Proceedings of the 6th International Conference on Principles and Practice of Constraint Programming, CP '00*, Springer-Verlag, London, UK, pp. 525–530, 2000.

[JUN 01] JUNG H., TAMBE M., KULKARNI S., "Argumentation as distributed constraint satisfaction: applications and results", in *Proceedings of the 5th International Conference on Autonomous Agents, AGENTS '01*, pp. 324–331, 2001.

[KAS 04] KASK K., DECHTER R., GOGATE V., "Counting-based look-ahead schemes for constraint satisfaction", in *Proceedings of the 10th International Conference on Constraint Programming, CP '04*, pp. 317–331, 2004.

[LÉA 09] LÉAUTÉ T., OTTENS B., SZYMANEK R., "FRODO 2.0: An open-source framework for distributed constraint optimization", in *Proceedings of the IJCAI'09 Workshop on Distributed Constraint Reasoning*, Pasadena, CA, pp. 160–164, 2009.

[LÉA 11] LÉAUTÉ T., FALTINGS B., "Coordinating logistics operations with privacy guarantees", in *Proceedings of the 22nd International Joint Conference on Artificial Intelligence, IJCAI '11*, pp. 2482–2487, 16–22 July 2011.

[LEC 04] LECOUTRE C., BOUSSEMART F., HEMERY F., "Backjump-Based techniques versus conflict-directed heuristics", in *Proceedings of the 16th IEEE International Conference on Tools with Artificial Intelligence, ICTAI '04*, IEEE Computer Society, Washington, DC, pp. 549–557, 2004.

[LYN 97] LYNCH N.A., *Distributed Algorithms*, Morgan Kaufmann Series, 1997.

[MAC 77] MACKWORTH A., "Consistency in networks of relations", *Artificial Intelligence*, vol. 8, no. 1, pp. 99–118, 1977.

[MAC 83] MACKWORTH A.K., "On seeing things, again", in *Proceedings of the 8th International Joint Conference on Artificial Intelligence, IJCAI '83*, pp. 1187–1191, 1983.

[MAH 04] MAHESWARAN R.T., TAMBE M., BOWRING E., *et al.*, "Taking DCOP to the real world: efficient complete solutions for distributed multi-event scheduling", in *Proceedings of the International Joint Conference on Autonomous Agents and Multiagent Systems, AAMAS '04*, 2004.

[MEC 12] MECHQRANE Y., WAHBI M., BESSIERE C., *et al.*, "Corrigendum to "Min-domain retroactive ordering for asynchronous backtracking"", *Constraints*, vol. 17, pp. 348–355, 2012.

[MEI 97] MEISELS A., SHIMONY S.E., SOLOTOREVSKY G., "Bayes networks for estimating the number of solutions to a CSP", in *Proceedings of the 14th National Conference on Artificial Intelligence and 9th Conference on Innovative Applications of Artificial Intelligence, AAAI '97/IAAI '97*, AAAI Press, pp. 179–184, 1997.

[MEI 02a] MEISELS A., RAZGON I., "Distributed forward-checking with conflict-based backjumping and dynamic ordering", in *Proceedings of the CoSolv Workshop, CP,02*, Ithaca, NY, 2002.

[MEI 02b] MEISELS A., RAZGON I., KAPLANSKY E., *et al.*, "Comparing performance of distributed constraints processing algorithms", in *Proceedings of the AAMAS '02 Workshop on Distributed Constraint Reasoning*, Bologna, pp. 86–93, 2002.

[MEI 03] MEISELS A., ZIVAN R., "Asynchronous forward-checking for distributed CSPs", in ZHANG W., (ed.), *Frontiers in Artificial Intelligence and Applications*, IOS Press, 2003.

[MEI 04] MEISELS A., LAVEE O., "Using additional information in DisCSP search", in *Proceedings of the 5th Workshop on Distributed Constraints Reasoning, DCR '04*, 2004.

[MEI 07] MEISELS A., ZIVAN R., "Asynchronous forward-checking for DisCSPs", *Constraints*, vol. 12, no. 1, pp. 131–150, 2007.

[MIN 92] MINTON S., JOHNSTON M.D., PHILIPS A.B., *et al.*, "Minimizing conflicts: a heuristic repair method for constraint satisfaction and scheduling problems", *Artificial Intelligence*, vol. 58, no. 1–3, pp. 161–205, December 1992.

[MOD 03] MODI P.J., SHEN W.-M., TAMBE M., *et al.*, "An asynchronous complete method for distributed constraint optimization", in *Proceedings of the 2nd International Joint Conference on Autonomous Agents and Multiagent Systems, AAMAS '03*, pp. 161–168, 2003.

[MOD 05] MODI P.J., SHEN W.-M., TAMBE M., *et al.*, "Adopt: asynchronous distributed constraint optimization with quality guarantees", *Artificial Intelligence*, vol. 161, pp. 149–180, 2005.

[MOH 86] MOHR R., HENDERSON T.C., "Arc and path consistency revisited", *Artificial Intelligence*, vol. 28, no. 2, pp. 225–233, March 1986.

[MON 74] MONTANARI U., "Networks of constraints: fundamental properties and applications to picture processing", *Information Sciences*, vol. 7, pp. 95–132, 1974.

[NAD 83] NADEL B.A., "Consistent-labeling problems and their algorithms: expected-complexities and theory-based heuristics", *Artificial Intelligence*, vol. 21, no. 1–2, pp. 135–178, March 1983.

[NAD 90] NADEL B.A., "Some applications of the constraint satisfaction problem", in *AAAI-90 Workshop on Constraint Directed Reasoning Working Notes*, Boston, Mass., 1990.

[NAD 91] NADEL B.A., LIN J., "Automobile transmission design as a constraint satisfaction problem: modelling the kinematic level", *Artificial Intelligence for Engineering, Design, Analysis and Manufacturing*, vol. 5, pp. 137–171, 1991.

[NGU 04] NGUYEN V., SAM-HAROUD D., FALTINGS B., "Dynamic distributed backjumping", in *Proceedings of the 5th Workshop on Distributed Constraints Reasoning, DCR'04*, Toronto, 2004.

[NGU 05] NGUYEN V., SAM-HAROUD D., FALTINGS B., "Dynamic distributed backjumping", in FALTINGS B., PETCU A., FAGES F., *et al.*, (eds.), *Recent Advances in Constraints*, vol. 3419, *Lecture Notes in Computer Science*, Springer, Berlin/Heidelberg, pp. 71–85, 2005.

[PET 04] PETCU A., FALTINGS B., "A value ordering heuristic for distributed resource allocation", in *Proceedings of the Joint Annual Workshop of ERCIM/CoLogNet on Constraint Solving and Constraint Logic Programming, CSCLP '04*, pp. 86–97, February 2004.

[PET 05] PETCU A., FALTINGS B., "DPOP: A scalable method for multiagent constraint optimization", in *Proceedings of the 19th International Joint Conference on Artificial Intelligence, IJCAI'05*, San Francisco, CA, USA, Morgan Kaufmann Publishers Inc., Edinburgh, Scotland, pp. 266–271, August 2005.

[PRO 92] PROSSER P., CONWAY C., MULLER C., "A constraint maintenance system for the distributed resource allocation problem", *Intelligent Systems Engineering*, vol. 1, no. 1, pp. 76–83, October 1992.

[PRO 93] PROSSER P., "Hybrid algorithms for the constraint satisfaction problem", *Computational Intelligence*, vol. 9, pp. 268–299, 1993.

[PUR 83] PURDOM JR. P.W., "Search rearrangement backtracking and polynomial average time", *Artificial Intelligence*, vol. 21, no. 1–2, pp. 117–133, March 1983.

[SAB 94] SABIN D., FREUDER E., "Contradicting conventional wisdom in constraint satisfaction", in *Proceedings of the 2nd International Workshop on Principles and Practice of Constraint Programming, PPCP'94*, vol. 874, pp. 10–20, 1994.

[SEN 95] SEN S., DURFEE E.H., "Unsupervised surrogate agents and search bias change in flexible distributed scheduling", in *Proceedings of the 1st International Conference on MultiAgent Systems, ICMAS '95*, pp. 336–343, 1995.

[SIL 01a] SILAGHI M.-C., SAM-HAROUD D., CALISTI M., *et al.*, "Generalized english auctions by relaxation in dynamic distributed CSPs with private constraints", in *Proceedings of the IJCAI'01 Workshop on Distributed Constraint Reasoning, DCR '11*, pp. 45–54, 2001.

[SIL 01b] SILAGHI M.-C., SAM-HAROUD D., FALTINGS B., "Consistency maintenance for ABT", in *Proceedings of the 7th International Conference on Principles and Practice of Constraint Programming, CP '01*, Paphos, Cyprus, pp. 271–285, 2001.

[SIL 01c] SILAGHI M.-C., SAM-HAROUD D., FALTINGS B., Hybridizing ABT and AWC into a polynomial space, complete protocol with reordering, Technical Report Number LIA-REPORT-2001-008, Ecole Polytechnique Federale de Lausanne (EPFL), Switzerland, 2001.

[SIL 01d] SILAGHI M.-C., SAM-HAROUD D., FALTINGS B., "Polynomial space and complete multiply asynchronous search with abstractions", in *Proceedings of the IJCAI'2001 Workshop on Distributed Constraint Reasoning, DCR '11*, pp. 17–32, 2001.

[SIL 05] SILAGHI M.-C., FALTINGS B., "Asynchronous aggregation and consistency in distributed constraint satisfaction", *Artificial Intelligence*, vol. 161, pp. 25–53, 2005.

[SIL 06] SILAGHI M.-C., "Generalized dynamic ordering for asynchronous backtracking on DisCSPs", in *Proceedings of the AAMAS'06 Workshop on Distributed Constraint Reasoning, DCR'06*, 2006.

[SMI 98] SMITH B.M., GRANT S.A., "Trying harder to fail first", in *Proceedings of the 13th European Conference on Artificial Intelligence, ECAI '98*, pp. 249–253, 1998.

[SMI 99] SMITH B.M., "The Brélaz heuristic and optimal static orderings", in *Proceedings of the 5th International Conference on Principles and Practice of Constraint Programming, CP '99*, Springer-Verlag, London, UK, pp. 405–418, 1999.

[STA 77] STALLMAN R.M., SUSSMAN G.J., "Forward reasoning and dependency-directed backtracking in a system for computer-aided circuit analysis", *Artificial Intelligence*, vol. 9, no. 2, pp. 135–196, 1977.

[STE 81] STEFIK M., "Planning with constraints (MOLGEN: part 1)", *Artificial Intelligence*, vol. 16, no. 2, pp. 111–139, 1981.

[SUL 08] SULTANIK E.A., LASS R.N., REGLI W.C., "DCOPolis: a framework for simulating and deploying distributed constraint reasoning algorithms", in *Proceedings of the 7th International Joint Conference on Autonomous Agents and Multiagent Systems, AAMAS '08*, Estoril, Portugal, pp. 1667–1668, 2008.

[VAN 92] VAN HENTENRYCK P., DEVILLE Y., TENG C.-M., "A generic arc-consistency algorithm and its specializations", *Artificial Intelligence*, vol. 57, no. 2–3, pp. 291–321, October 1992.

[VER 99] VERNOOY M., HAVENS W.S., "An examination of probabilistic value-ordering heuristics", in *Proceedings of the 12th Australian Joint Conference on Artificial Intelligence: Advanced Topics in Artificial Intelligence, AI '99*, Springer-Verlag, London, UK, pp. 340–352, 1999.

[WAH 11] WAHBI M., EZZAHIR R., BESSIERE C., *et al.*, "DisChoco 2: a platform for distributed constraint reasoning", *Proceedings of the IJCAI '11 Workshop on Distributed Constraint Reasoning, DCR '11*, Barcelona, Catalonia, Spain, pp. 112–121, 2011.

[WAH 12a] WAHBI M., EZZAHIR R., BESSIERE C., *et al.*, "Maintaining arc consistency asynchronously in synchronous distributed search", in *Proceedings of the IEEE 24th International Conference on Tools with Artificial Intelligence, ICTAI '12*, Athens, Greece, pp. 33–40, November 2012.

[WAH 12b] WAHBI M., EZZAHIR R., BESSIERE C., *et al.*, Nogood-based asynchronous forward-checking algorithms, Technical Report Number RR-12013, LIRMM, Montpellier, France, April 2012.

[WAH 13] WAHBI M., EZZAHIR R., BESSIERE C., *et al.*, "Nogood-based asynchronous forward-checking algorithms", *Constraints*, 2013, vol. 18, no. 3, pp. 404–433, Springer US, 2013.

[WAL 02] WALLACE R.J., FREUDER E.C., "Constraint-based multi-agent meeting scheduling: effects of agent heterogeneity on performance and privacy loss", in *Proceeding of the 3rd Workshop on Distributed Constrait Reasoning, DCR '02*, pp. 176–182, 2002.

[YEO 07] YEOH W., FELNER A., KOEING S., "BnB-ADOPT: an asynchronous branch-and-bound DCOP algorithm", in *Proceedings of the International Workshop on Distributed Constraint Reasoning, DCR'07*, 2007.

[YEO 08] YEOH W., FELNER A., KOENIG S., "BnB-ADOPT: an asynchronous branch-and-bound DCOP algorithm", in *Proceedings of the 7th International Joint Conference on Autonomous Agents and Multiagent Systems, AAMAS '08*, Estoril, Portugal, pp. 591–598, 2008.

[YOK 92] YOKOO M., DURFEE E.H., ISHIDA T., *et al.*, "Distributed constraint satisfaction for formalizing distributed problem solving", in *Proceedings of the 12th IEEE International Conference on Distributed Computing Systems*, pp. 614–621, 1992.

[YOK 95a] YOKOO M., "Asynchronous weak-commitment search for solving distributed constraint satisfaction problems", in *Proceedings of the 1st International Conference on Principles and Practice of Constraint Programming, CP'95*, pp. 88–102, 1995.

[YOK 95b] YOKOO M., HIRAYAMA K., "Distributed breakout algorithm for solving distributed constraint satisfaction problems", in LESSER V., (eds.), *Proceedings of the First International Conference on Multi–Agent Systems*, MIT Press, 1995.

[YOK 98] YOKOO M., DURFEE E.H., ISHIDA T., *et al.*, "The distributed constraint satisfaction problem: formalization and algorithms", *IEEE Transactions on Knowledge and Data Engineering*, vol. 10, pp. 673–685, September 1998.

[YOK 00a] YOKOO M., "Algorithms for distributed constraint satisfaction problems: a review", *Autonomous Agents and Multi-Agent Systems*, vol. 3, no. 2, pp. 185–207, 2000.

[YOK 00b] YOKOO M., *Distributed Constraint Satisfaction: Foundations of Cooperation in Multi-Agent Systems*, Springer-Verlag, London, UK, 2000.

[ZAB 90] ZABIH R., "Some applications of graph bandwidth to constraint satisfaction problems", in *Proceedings of the 8th National Conference on Artificial Intelligence*, vol. 1, AAAI Press, pp. 46–51, 1990.

[ZIV 03] ZIVAN R., MEISELS A., "Synchronous vs asynchronous search on DisCSPs", in *Proceedings of the 1st European Workshop on Multi-Agent Systems, EUMAS '03*, 2003.

[ZIV 06a] ZIVAN R., MEISELS A., "Dynamic ordering for asynchronous backtracking on DisCSPs", *Constraints*, vol. 11, no. 2–3, pp. 179–197, 2006.

[ZIV 06b] ZIVAN R., MEISELS A., "Message delay and DisCSP search algorithms", *Annals of Mathematics and Artificial Intelligence*, vol. 46, no. 4, pp. 415–439, 2006.

[ZIV 09] ZIVAN R., ZAZONE M., MEISELS A., "Min-domain retroactive ordering for asynchronous backtracking", *Constraints*, vol. 14, no. 2, pp. 177–198, 2009.

Index